THE ADVENTURES OF THE MOUNTAIN MEN

THE ADVENTURES OF THE
MOUNTAIN MEN

True Tales of Hunting, Trapping, Fighting, Adventure, and Survival

Edited and Introduced by
STEPHEN BRENNAN

Skyhorse Publishing

Skyhorse Publishing books may be purchased in bulk at special discounts for sales promotion, corporate gifts, fund-raising, or educational purposes. Special editions can also be created to specifications. For details, contact the Special Sales Department, Skyhorse Publishing, 307 West 36th Street, 11th Floor, New York, NY 10018 or info@skyhorsepublishing.com.

Skyhorse® and Skyhorse Publishing® are registered trademarks of Skyhorse Publishing, Inc.®, a Delaware corporation.

Visit our website at www.skyhorsepublishing.com.

10 9

Library of Congress Cataloging-in-Publication Data is available on file.

ISBN: 978-1-5107-1904-0
eBook ISBN: 978-1-5107-1909-5

Printed in the United States of America

CONTENTS

Appendix

INTRODUCTION

"And the devil, taking him up into a high mountain, showed unto him all the kingdoms of the world in a moment of time."

Luke 4:5

"Bring me men to match my mountains,
Bring me men to match my plains,
Men with empires in their purpose,
And new eras in their brains."

Sam Walter Foss
"The Coming American"

It is one thing to wander out upon the plains or to tramp the sea side, and you may trod the glens and dales, or trek the rolling hills, and there encounter so many adventures that you finish up flushed with pleasure, well pleased with your life's sojourn among your fellow flatlanders. But going up into the mountains is a very different thing altogether. And though we recognize the mountains as wild places of mystery and of power, of danger and of extremes, their allure has always been undeniable.

Mountains figure greatly in many of the foundational stories of our culture. Where does Moses go to receive God's laws? Why, to the mountaintop. When Abraham is given to understand that God requires he sacrifice his son, Isaac, where must the deed be done? When Noah's Ark finally does come to rest on dry land, it is on a mountain. When Jesus himself is tempted by Satan, where does this take place? And then at last, when Jesus most clearly explains his New Covenant to those that have ears to hear, it is in his Sermon on the Mount.

We do well to recognize that mountains are also a place of refuge for all manner of escapees, loners, hermits, holy men, felons, psychopaths, and dreamers. Because to be a man of the mountains, then or now, is to not only live a life of independence and adventure, but also to partake of a state of mind. Given all this, it is little wonder then that the mountain man continues to have such a hold on our imaginations.

In American history, the classic or golden era of the mountain man lasted roughly for a generation: from 1810, when Americans began to get themselves organized to take advantage of the natural resources the Louisiana Purchase had made available—particularly the abundant and portable beaver pelt—until about 1840 when that animal had been largely trapped out. But even after the last great meet-up, the final rendezvous, something of that way of life persisted. The demand for beaver may have been obviated by the recent availability of silk for headwear, but still the mountains beckoned, as they had always beckoned. There were minerals and other resources to be had—gold in them thar hills. With the conclusion of the Mexican–American War and the 1846 Oregon Treaty with the British, the United States had extended itself all the way to the Pacific coast. There followed various military expeditions of exploration, and the establishment of the great trails west. Now the trappers of earlier days found work as army scouts, hunters for mining concerns (and later for railroads), and as guides for the several great wagon train migrations.

The whole literature of the mountain men is immense, and well beyond the scope of this book, but even so, this anthology offers a sampling of some of the best of the stories, journals, and texts. W. F. Wagner's *The Trappers* offers as colorful and concise an overview of the whole of his saga as any enthusiast might desire, just as John C. Neihardt's *Jed Smith and the Ashley-Henry Men* is a story of exploration, adventure, and a partnership, out of which a determined cadre of businessmen/survivalists made a life and sought their fortunes in a wild and difficult world. With Bradbury's Coulter's *Run*, Meek's *The Merry Mountain Men*, Zenas Leonard's *Adventures*, and *Trouble in the Family* by James P. Beckworth, we glimpse the mountain man as outlandish iconoclast, outsider, braggart, clown, and God's very own fool. With the excerpts by Washington Irving from his *Adventures of Captain Bonneville* and from the *Journals of Lewis and Clark*, we apprehend the mountain man as mapmaker, explorer, and soldier. With Francis Parkman Jr.'s *A Mountain Hunt* we have the mountain man and his signal way of life as rendered by, essentially, an Eastern tourist, scion of the house of one of Boston's oldest clans. Implicit in Parkman's telling is the intense attraction of our wild man and his extreme, extraordinary way of life, even to a scion of privilege, one of Boston's bluest Brahmin families. With Grenville M. Dodge's biographical monogram on Jim Bridger we see the opposite of the man from the mountains as half-crazed wild man. Here is Bridger, tamed, honest, trustworthy, a businessman, a pillar of the community. Finally, we have Fredric Bade's rendering of John Muir's meditations on the first of his Rocky Mountain adventures. With Muir the mountain man has come full circle. He most definitely fits the type of self-sufficient loner that we've come to recognize as one foundational trait of the mountaineer's character, but his aim has changed. It is really because of Muir's lifelong work as a naturalist and environmentalist that we now have come to regard the great western mountains as something not so much to be despoiled and plundered as to be protected and enjoyed. Just as a matter of personal privilege, I'll admit that my favorite of these texts are those having to do with the minutiae, the how-to of the mountain trapper and his way of life.

The illustrations in this book are largely contemporaneous with the mountain men and their times here portrayed. The aim is to afford the reader an opportunity to get some understanding of the popular view of this ordinary, extraordinary, romantic, comical, independent, very American type.

—Stephen Brennan

CHAPTER 1

THE TRAPPERS

By W. F. Wagner

The evolution of the trapper may be traced far back to the old French régime when the *coureurs des bois,* rangers of the woods, or the peddlers of the wilderness, held sway; these were, however, more traders than trappers, and purchased the pelts from the Indians for trifles, and frequently accompanied them on their hunting excursions. They were as profligate as their successors, and their occupation passed away with the passing of the French control of Canada and with the establishment of the interior trading-posts by the merchants of Canada, who later formed companies and conducted the business in a more systematic manner. From these interior trading-posts traders and trappers were sent out to trade with the Indians and trap in their territory at the same time. The trading gradually fell into the hands of the trading-posts; the trapper meanwhile pursued his vocation, and it became his recognized and established business, and he remained an important factor in the fur-trade down to the time of its decline and ultimate death.

While Mr. Hunt was at Mackinaw engaging men for the Astoria venture, there arrived at this place some of these characters, and his description of them is so accurate that I take the liberty of giving it here:

A chance party of "Northwesters" appeared at Mackinaw from the rendezvous at Fort William. These held themselves up as the chivalry of the fur-trade. They were men of iron; proof against cold weather, hard fare, and perils of all kinds. Some would wear the Northwest button, and a formidable dirk, and assume something of a military air. They generally wore feathers in their hats, and affected the "brave." "Je suis un homme du nord!" "I am a man of the north"— one of these swelling fellows would exclaim, sticking his arms akimbo and ruffling by the Southwesters, whom he regarded with great contempt, as men softened by mild climates and the luxurious fare of bread and bacon, and whom he stigmatized with the inglorious name of pork-eaters. The superiority assumed by these vainglorious swaggerers was, in general, tacitly accepted. Indeed, some of them had acquired great notoriety for deeds of hardihood and courage; for the fur-trade had its heroes, whose names resounded throughout the wilderness.

The influence and part played by the trapper and free trapper in the development of our great West, has had up to this time but little consideration from either the government or the people. We have given entirely too much credit to "pathfinders" whose paths were as well known to the above as is the city street to the pedestrian. It is true, however, they gave to the world a more complete description, and placed these secret ways of the mountains in a more correct geographical position, than the uneducated trapper was able to do.

There was not a stream or rivulet from the border of Mexico to the frozen regions of the North, but what was as familiar to these mountain rangers and lonesome wanderers, as the most traveled highway in our rural districts. The incentive was neither geographical knowledge, nor the honor won by making new discoveries for the use and benefit of mankind in general, but a mercenary motive—the commercial value of the harmless and inoffensive little beaver. The trappers followed the course of the various streams looking for beaver signs, and had no interest whatever in any other particular. Every stream had a certain gold value if it contained this industrious little animal, and so they followed them from their source to their mouth with this one object in view. For their own comfort and convenience they observed certain land-marks and the general topography of the country, in order that they might rove from one place to another with the least labor and inconvenience. In this manner they came to have a thorough and comprehensive knowledge of the geography and topography of the great West, and were in truth the only pathfinders; but they have been robbed even of this honor to a great extent.

The life of the solitary trapper in the mountains seems unendurable to one who is fond of social intercourse or of seeing now and then one of his fellow-beings. This habit of seclusion seemed to grow on some of the men and they really loved the life on that account, with all its hardships, privations, and dangers, The free trappers formed the aristocratic class of the fur-trade, and were the most interesting people in the mountains. They were bound to no fur company, were free to go where and when they pleased. It was the height of the ordinary trapper's ambition to attain such a position. They were men of bold and adventurous spirit, for none other would have had the courage to follow so dangerous an occupation. They were liable to have too much of this spirit of bravado, and frequently did extremely foolhardy things, nor could their leaders always control them in these excesses. They were exceedingly vain of their personal appearance, and extravagantly fond of ornament for both themselves and their steeds, as well as their Indian wives. Indeed, they rivaled the proud Indian himself in the manner in which they bedecked themselves with these useless and cheap ornaments. They were utterly improvident, extremely fond of gambling and all games of chance, as well as all sorts of trials of skill, such as horsemanship and marksmanship; of course, the necessary wager to make it interesting was never wanting. As a general rule, the greater part of the proceeds of their labor was squandered at the first rendezvous or trading-post which they reached, and it was of great importance to the trader to be the first to reach such a rendezvous, thus securing the greater part of this most profitable trade.

Very little is known of their lonely vigils and wanderings, with a companion or two, in the defiles of the mountains, and of the dangers and privations they have had to endure. How frequently their bones have been left to bleach on the arid plains, as the result of Indian hatred and hostility, without the rites of burial—their names, unhonored and unsung, will never be known. Certain tribes were the uncompromising enemies of the trappers, and when they had the misfortune to meet, they waged a relentless war, until one or the sometimes party left the country or was exterminated. It is true, the returns were sometimes enormous, and had they exercised ordinary economy, even for one season, they could have retired from the dangers and privations of the mountains with a competence; but had they done so, it is altogether likely that they would sooner or later have again fallen victims to its allurements.

It is at the rendezvous and fort that the free trapper is seen in his true character. Here is usually spent the whole of his year's hard earnings in gambling, drinking, and finery. He wishes to establish the reputation of being a hale fellow, and he seldom fails so long as his money and credit last. Then he again returns to his lonely wanderings in the mountains, a sadder but not a wiser man, as the following year the same scene is enacted—provided he is so fortunate as to escape his treacherous enemies the Indians. The scenes presented at the mountain rendezvous in the early days must have been indeed wonderful, where hundreds of such characters were congregated; no pen however clever can do them full justice. The loss of life from other than natural causes from the years 1820 to 1840 cannot be estimated and will never be fully known. At each rendezvous many former hale fellows were missing, never again to appear on this gay scene; their comrades recounted the manner of their death if known—their good traits were loyally lauded and their bad ones left untold—but the living did not take warning from these examples. Such was their life, hardships, dangers, and privations, also their pleasures—they lived only in the present, with little or no regard for the future. Irving gives the following extremely good description of them:

The influx of this wandering trade has had its effects on the habits of the mountain tribes. They have found the trapping of the beaver their most profitable species of hunting; and the traffic with the white man has opened to them sources of luxury of which they previously had no idea. The introduction of firearms has rendered them more successful hunters, but at the same time more formidable foes; some of them, incorrigibly savage and warlike in their nature, have found the expeditions of the fur traders grand objects of profitable adventure. To waylay and harass a band of trappers with their packhorses when embarrassed in the rugged defiles of the mountains, has become as favorite an exploit with the Indians as the plunder of a caravan to the Arab of the desert. The Crows and Blackfeet, who were such terrors in the path of the early adventurers to Astoria, still continue their predatory habits, but seem to have brought them to greater system. They know the routes and resorts of the trappers; where to waylay them on their journeys; where to find them in the hunting seasons, and where to hover about them in winter-quarters.

The life of a trapper, therefore, is a perpetual state militant, and he must sleep with his weapons in his hands.

A new order of trappers and traders, also, have grown out of this system of things. In the old times of the great North-west Company, when the trade in furs was pursued chiefly about the lakes and rivers, the expeditions were carried on in batteaux and canoes, The voyageurs or boatmen were the rank and file in the service of the trader, and even the hardy "men of the north," those great rufflers and game birds, were fain to be paddled from point to point of their migrations.

A totally different class has now sprung up—"the Mountaineers," the traders and trappers that scale the vast mountain chains, and pursue their hazardous vocations amidst their wild recesses. They move from place to place on horseback. The equestrian exercises, therefore, in which they are engaged, the nature of the countries they traverse, the vast plains and mountains, pure exhilarating in atmospheric qualities, seem to make them physically and mentally a more lively and mercurial race than the fur traders and trappers of former days, the self-vaunting "men of the north," A man who bestrides a horse, must be essentially different from a man who cowers in a canoe. We find them, accordingly, hardy, little, vigorous, and active; extravagant in word, and thought, and deed; heedless of hard-ship; daring of danger; prodigal of the present, and thoughtless of the future.

A difference is to be perceived even between these mountain hunters and those of the lower regions along the waters of the Missouri. The latter, generally French Creoles, live comfortably in cabins or log-huts, well sheltered from the inclemencies of the seasons. They are within the reach of frequent supplies from the settlements; their life is comparatively free from danger, and from most of the vicissitudes of the upper wilderness. The consequence is that they are less hardy, self-dependent and game-spirited than the mountaineer. If the latter by chance comes among them on his way to and from the settlements, he is like the game-cock among the common roosters of the poultry-yard. Accustomised to live in tents, or to bivouac in the open air, he dispises the comforts and is impatient of the confinement of the log-house. If his meal is not ready in season, he takes his rifle, hies to the forest or prairie, shoots his own game, lights his fire, and cooks his repast. With his horse and his rifle, he is independent of the world, and spurns at all its restraints. The very superintendents at the lower posts will not put him to mess with the common men, the hirelings of the establishment, but treat him as something superior.

There is, perhaps, no class of men on the face of the earth, says Captain Bonneville, who lead a life of more continued exertion, peril, and excitement, and who are more enamored of their occupations, than the free trappers of the West. No toil, no danger, no privation can turn the trapper from his pursuit. His passionate excitement at times resembles a mania. In vain may the most vigilant and cruel savages beset his path; in vain may rocks, and precipices, and wintry torrents oppose his progress; let but a single track of a beaver meet his eye and he forgets all dangers and defies all difficulties. At times, he may be seen with his traps on his shoulder, buffeting his way across rapid streams, amidst floating blocks of ice; at other times, he is to be found with his traps swung on his back clambering the most rugged mountains, scaling or descending the most frightful precipices, searching, by routes inaccessible to the horse, and never before trodden by white man, for springs and lakes unknown to his comrades, and where he may meet with his favorite game. Such is the mountaineer, the hardy trapper of the West; and such, as we have slightly sketched it, is the wild Robin Hood kind of life, with all its strange and motley populace, now existing in full vigor among the Rocky Mountains.

Many of these men were in the mountains because of the fascination of this mountain life, and were as loyally devoted to it as any individual is to his vocation. Many who were there, as well as many of the recruits, were men whose past would not bear too close inspection. They frequently went to the mountains to escape an outraged law, and remained not because of their love for the wilderness, but through fear that justice would be meted out to them should they return to the States. This was always a dangerous and undesirable element.

Another class of recruits, and by far the most numerous, was that represented by Leonard—being composed of young men or boys of an adventurous disposition. The alluring stories of the mountains and the great fortunes to be made in the trade, as illustrated by the very few on whom dame fortune had smiled, were the inducements held out to the inexperienced candidates for the mountains; the failures were, however, not mentioned and the trials, hard-ships, dangers, and loss of life were scarcely taken into consideration. A great majority of these young men soon learned from that wonderful teacher—experience—that it was as difficult to accumulatc fortunes in the mountains as elsewhere, and infinitely more dangerous. Such was the school of hardship and privation from which many good men graduated, and later became settlers and men of prominence in the rapidly developing great West.

Many of these men, particularly those in the employ of the British companies, and not only the trappers but the officers of the company as well, contracted marriages with Indian women and for this reason did not wish to return to civilization and their former homes. They therefore remained in the West and their families developed with the rapid growth of this new country, and in this manner some of the leading families have a trace of aboriginal blood in their veins, of which they are justly proud.

Such was the school which graduated the scout and guide of later days. It was they who conducted the scientific expeditions sent out by the government, the surveying as well as exploring parties; it was they who guided the first emigrants by the overland routes to Oregon and California; and they who ferreted out in their peregrinations in the mountains the passage-ways, for none of the above expeditions would have ventured into this *terra incognita* without one of these old trappers as guide. Even the army, while in pursuit of hostile Indians, had its corps of experienced scouts and guides, which was largely made up of these mountain-men. For this kind of service they were well fitted, as they were inured to hard-ships and dangers. The decline of the fur-trade practically left them stranded, and in looking about for employment they were glad to accept such positions; nevertheless, their services have never been properly appreciated.

The most renowned of all the fur companies was that known as the Hudson Bay Company, the real founder of which was a Frenchman by the name of Groseilliers. He established a post at the southern end of Hudson Bay, under English patronage, and his success here led to the organization of the company known as "The Governor and company of adventurers of England trading into Hudson Bay," but more commonly known as the Hudson Bay Company. Their charter is dated May 2, 1670. The privileges granted under this charter were the most comprehensive that could be imagined. They were the absolute proprietors of an immense area. They had supreme jurisdiction in both civil and military affairs. They had the power to make laws to govern the same, and to wage war against the natives if to their interest to do so. It was in fact a sovereignty in itself. They were not however without their troubles in these early days. The French claimed part of the territory covered by their charter, and the posts located therein became a prey to French expeditions, which in some instances became extremely rich prizes. The company never failed to look after their own interests when the treaties were being made after the various wars between England and France, until finally the French and Indian War terminated French dominion in Canada. This war was largely due to the English invading French territory, and mostly by this company in establishing trading-posts. Nothing of any moment appeared on their horizon to cause any disquietude until 1787, when the various companies in Canada and numerous Scotch merchants of Montreal—the latter being the ruling element—formed the Northwest Fur Company.

They immediately took the field in a most aggressive manner and in many instances invaded the charter rights of the older company. To this company as partner belonged the celebrated Sir Alexander MacKenzie, who made extensive explorations in the Northwest, and was the first to cross the continent above the Spanish possessions, which he did in 1793, and shortly thereafter returned to England and wrote an account of the same, for which he received the honor of knighthood.

In the meantime the rivalry between these two companies went beyond all bounds. The old company, who had heretofore almost wholly depended on the Indian trade, was, in order to meet the competition of the new company, now compelled to send out trading and trapping parties, who frequently met those of the other, and fierce encounters took place. At this juncture, in 1811 Lord Selkirk received a grant of land, on which to establish a colony, on the United States border near Lake Winnipeg in the Red River valley. This was done in order to injure the Northwest Company, at least they so construed it. The greatest sufferers were the poor colonists, whose desperate struggles are very ably written by an old Astorian fur-trader, Alexander Ross, who settled here with his family (his wife being an Indian) as did many others with the same domestic relations. This settlement became quite an asylum for returning traders with Indian families. This Northwest Fur Company is the company which succeeded Astor in his venture at the mouth of the Columbia.

The crisis was reached in their affairs about 1816, when the Northwest Company and the Hudson Bay Company in conjunction with the colonists, resorted to actual war, and many lives were lost on both sides. England could no longer ignore or evade the issue, the parties were brought into court and a long-drawn litigation ensued in which an immense amount of money was spent by both companies. It had the beneficial effect of bringing them to their senses; and, what had long been pointed out by far-sighted individuals as the best solution of the controversy—the amalgamation of the two companies—took place in 1821. The Northwest Company went out of existence and the Hudson Bay Company was the name adopted by the new organization which acquired all the rights and privileges of the older company, with some slight exceptions, its territory being thereby somewhat increased. The trials of the Red River settler were now at an end and this colony began to flourish, being well established and well governed. This merger, however, prevented the promotion and threw out of employment many of the old servants of both companies. Alexander Ross in particular describes how he was affected by it. The condition of the engagés was not much changed as they all found employment in the new company. Many of the clerks and minor officers were not given places, and those that were had to be contented with positions much below those they formerly occupied. Many under these circumstances became dissatisfied, and sought occupation elsewhere; many found employment with the American companies, and became some of their best representatives. With the Hudson Bay Company, merit—and merit alone—was, and could be, the only road to advancement, this being one of the secrets of their success. No influence, however great, had any weight, if the applicant did not possess the necessary qualifications.

They discontinued the sale of alcoholic stimulants to the Indians, and only used it where competition compelled them to resort to this measure to hold their own with rival traders. We shall see how this operated against them when in contact with our American companies. It was undoubtedly the most perfectly organized monopoly then in existence, or which had ever existed. They also took measures to protect the fur-bearing animals, to prevent their becoming extinct. They were perfectly just in their dealings with the Indians; each article had a certain fixed value, which the Indians soon came to recognize and respect, and as a result there was much less bickering than usually occurred with other companies. While they at times had trouble, it is true, with the natives, the latter knew that they would surely be called to account for their misdeeds, when justice would be meted out to them, however long it might take. They never ignored a transgression of their law, which the Indians soon came to respect and in this manner they were kept under almost complete control. We here see the hardy Scot at his best, as the bone and sinew of this powerful company was of that nationality. They, and not the English, carried it forward; invading new territories, and overcoming all obstacles, they brought all their native shrewdness into play to pacify the Indian and make him a source of revenue, whereby the coffers of the company were filled.

The name of Mackenzie or McKensie, is one of which the fur-trading annals of America may justly be proud. They were indeed wonderful men: Alexander, who was the first to cross the continent as already stated; and Donald, who became dissatisfied with the Northwest Company, and joined in the Astor venture on the Pacific. If we may believe Alexander Ross, the latter was the greatest of all the Northwest Company's traders. The amount of furs he collected seems almost beyond belief. After the downfall of the Astor enterprise, he became a partner in the Northwest Company, and was the means of establishing Fort Nez Percés, near the forks of the Columbia. His object was to be near the Snake River country, believing it one of the most prolific in furs on the continent, and if the above authority is to be relied upon, he certainly made good his belief. The amount of furs collected in this locality between 1814 and 1825 can scarcely be realized, and the region covered will probably never be known. They trapped in the Snake River valley, and possibly the headwaters of the Missouri, as well as in Utah, Colorado, and Nevada. Ross describes it as the country beyond the Blue Mountains. He understood the Indian character thoroughly, and frequently avoided conflicts by using methods now in vogue by our politicians; if the men were surly, he would make friends with the women and children, and thus bring about a friendly feeling. He later became governor of the Red River settlement, and died and is buried in New York State.

Kenneth MacKenzie was scarcely less prominent than the above. He was one of the victims of the consolidation of 1821, after which he joined the Columbia and later Astor's American Fur Company, and was the first to establish himself permanently among the Blackfeet; he was in charge of the Upper Missouri, and was known as "King of the Upper Missouri Outfit." He was as prominent in the American Fur Company as the other two were in the British companies; but against the orders of the government, he started a distillery on the Upper Missouri, and in this manner his usefulness came to an end.

It is to be sincerely hoped that some day the seal of secrecy will be removed from the records of this monopoly—the Hudson Bay Company—that the world may learn more of the true history of the early fur-trading days.

The stirring times of the American Revolution in the east gave little opportunity to the people for commercial pursuits, and the fur-trade in particular. Soon after the close of this struggle John Jacob Astor appeared upon the scene, and before many years had elapsed, he was considered not only one of the leading merchants but fur-trader as well. The story of his career is very ably written by many authorities; we shall have much to say of his connection with the Missouri River trade.

Captain Cook, after his famous voyage of 1776-80, during which he discovered the Sandwich Islands, visited the northwest coast of America. His report was so flattering as to the fur-trade, that many, particularly the merchants of Boston, at once made preparations to visit this coast. As a rule these ventures proved extremely profitable, and up to the time of the War of 1812 almost three times as many American vessels, or "Boston ships" as they were called, visited this coast as those of all other nations combined; many were English, and they were known to the natives as "King George ships." After a trading trip on this coast, when they had collected a cargo of furs, they would sail for China and exchange them for goods suitable for the American market, mostly nankeens. China was, and always has been, the best market for the finest furs.

Previous to the purchase of Louisiana, and while this country was under Spanish rule, numerous companies and individuals were engaged in the trade along the Missouri and its tributaries, although very few ventured to the Upper Missouri. The most prominent of these companies was Maxent, Laclede and Company, which after the death of Laclede was succeeded by others.

After the purchase of Louisiana, Lewis and Clark found, on their celebrated journey, the omnipresent Scot, the representative of the Northwest Fur Company, already on the Upper Missouri. In the report of this expedition particular stress was laid upon the fact that the country along their route was especially adapted to the establishment of a chain of trading-posts which could be extended to the Pacific. Astor at once saw the advantage of such an under-taking from a commercial standpoint, and it was from this report of Lewis and Clark that he conceived the idea which he endeavored to carry out a few years later, by organizing the Pacific Fur Company, a complete history of which is to be found in Irving's *Astoria*.

About this period there was in St. Louis a trader who was second to none in the fur-trading annals of America, and, strange as it may appear, this gentle-man was a Spaniard by birth, who for energy and enterprise was not surpassed by the hardy Scot of the north. This interesting individual was Manuel Lisa. He was upright, honest, a man of sterling worth, a competent judge of men and character, and undoubtedly the best equipped man in every way engaged in the trade on the Missouri at this time. He was a past-master in the thoroughness of his knowledge of Indian character, and fully acquainted with the Indian trade of the Missouri of that day. Irving, in his *Astoria*, does not give him this reputation, but Mr. Hunt, being also engaged in the trade, was inclined to interpret many of Lisa's acts as hostile to the Astor enterprise, in which he was greatly mistaken or misinformed: Lisa's reported hostilities were only conjectu-red, with no foundation whatever. For fully twenty years previous to this time, he had been engaged in the Indian trade on the Missouri, and saw as well as did Lewis and Clark, the proportions to which the fur-trade might be develo-ped. He then formed a company in order to secure a share of this trade. In the spring of 1807, he took into his employ the celebrated John Colter, who had been with Lewis and Clark, and whose thrilling adventure with the Blackfeet is graphically related in Irving's *Astoria*. Lisa met this interesting character on the Missouri River on his return to St. Louis, and by liberal inducements prevailed upon him to turn back and guide him to the upper country. Colter was then for the third time returning from the wilderness, and again turned his face toward the sources of the Missouri. He had not been in St. Louis for some years. Lisa returned the following year (probably August), having had many adventures, but evidently quite successful, and became the organizer and leading partner in the St. Louis Missouri Fur Company. With indomitable energy he continued his trading excursions up and down the Missouri, in season and out of season, never tiring or flagging, until the year 1820 when he died. His children by his regular marriage all died without issue, but he left some progeny by an Indian wife of the Omaha tribe. His estate was much involved at the time of his death. He is buried in St. Louis.

When Lewis and Clark reached the Mandan villages, on their return from the Pacific in 1806, they persuaded one of the leading Mandan chiefs—named Shahaka, or Gros Blanc, Big White—to accompany them to St. Louis and Washington with a view of making a visit to President Jefferson, one of the express stipulations being that he should be safely escorted back to his nation. Accordingly, the following summer an expedition was organized for this purpose. The chief's party consisted of himself and an interpreter, René Jesseaume—each with his wife and child. Their escort consisted of two non-commissioned officers and eleven privates under the command of Ensign Nathaniel Pryor, who had been a member of the Lewis and Clark expedition. They started on their way back from St. Louis in May 1807, and with them a number of other parties set out for the upper country. All went well until they reached the rascally Aricaras, where, it is said, Lisa, who preceded the parties (Pryor's and Pierre Chouteau's parties having traveled together), gained passage through their territory by some underhand method, which charge is not well sustained. The latter had an extremely fierce battle with these Indians, and as a result when practically at the chief's door-step, only three days' march after their tedious journey, Ensign Pryor was compelled to retreat with his charge the entire distance to St. Louis. Thus ended the first attempt to return Big White.

The following year Governor Lewis on the part of the government made a contract with the members of the Missouri Fur Company for the return of the Mandan. The company agreed to engage one hundred and twenty-five men, of whom forty should be "Americans and expert rifle-men," under the command of Pierre Chouteau. The compensation for this service was to be seven thousand dollars, one-half to be paid on starting. In this manner it was that Big White was returned to his home, and not as stated in Coyner's *Lost Trappers*. It is altogether likely that Edward Rose was one of this party of expert riflemen. About this time occurred a decline in the value of furs, although expeditions left St. Louis regularly for purposes of trade on the Missouri. It was also about this time (1810) that Mr. Hunt made his appearance in St. Louis with his company, on his way to Astoria.

The Missouri River trade for the next ten years, owing largely to the decline in furs and the war with England, did not attain the magnitude which might have been expected from the earlier bright prospects. It must be remembered that this was long before the days of steamboats on the Missouri and the only means of transportation was by keelboats. A rope was attached and the boat pulled by fifteen or twenty men, and where this was not feasible poles were used. At this work the Canadian voyageurs were extremely valuable.

In the year 1822, Jones and Immel sent a fine cargo of furs down to St. Louis from the upper river, but in the following year met with a disaster at the hands of the Blackfeet, in which both the leaders and five men were killed, and by which they lost about fifteen thousand dollars' worth of property.

We now come to consider the Rocky Mountain Fur Company and the American Fur Company, Western department—the former very important in the Rocky Mountain trade, the latter in that of the Missouri River.

The American Fur Company had, previous to this time (1822), been doing business on the borders of the Great Lakes, on the American side, having succeeded in having certain laws enacted whereby English companies were not allowed to trade in American territory. This part of their territory became known as the Northern department, and the Missouri River trade became known as the Western department. Thus after the lapse of nearly ten years since the failure of the Pacific Fur Company, Astor was again established in this fur-trading center of the West. The new department was supplied with men, many of whom had been with Astor in the unprofitable venture on the Pacific. Ramsey Crooks and Russell Famham were two leaders. About 1827 they absorbed the Columbia Fur Company and from this company secured some of their leading men—the most prominent one being Kenneth Mac-Kenzie. The posts and territory secured from this company were on the Upper Missouri, and the name "Upper Missouri Outfit" ("U. M. O.") was given to it, and the employees of the old company were mostly retained. In this manner the American Fur Company became established on the Upper Missouri, with Kenneth MacKenzie as director. He became known as the "King of the Upper Missouri Outfit." This is the MacKenzie referred to by Leonard. The first permanent post established by them was Fort Union about two hundred miles above the mouth of the Yellowstone, in the year 1829, and later others were established. In the year 1831, MacKenzie concluded a treaty of peace with the Blackfeet, the greatest enemies to the whites on the Missouri, and thus became firmly established in their country. Following is a copy of the treaty:

> On the vigil of St. Andrew in the year 1831, the powerful and distinguished nation of the Blackfeet, Plegan, and Blood Indians by their ambassadors appeared at Fort Union near the spot where

the Yellowstone River unites its current with the Missouri, and in the council chamber of the Governor, Kenneth McKensie, and the principal chief of the Assiniboine nation, the Man-that-Holds-the-Knife, attended by his chiefs of council, le Bechu, le Borgne, the Sparrow, the Bear's Arm, La Terre qui Tremble, and l'Enfant de Medecin, when, conforming to all ancient customs and ceremonies, and observing the due mystical signs enjoined by the great medicine lodges, a treaty of peace and friendship was entered into by the said high contracting parties, and is testified by their hands and seals hereunto annexed, hereafter and forever to live as brethren of one large, united, and happy family; and may the great spirit who watcheth over us all approve our conduct and teach us to love one another.

Done, executed, ratified, and confirmed at Fort Union on the day and year, first herein written, in the presence of Jas. Archdale Hamilton.

Let us go back to the time when MacKenzie was a member of the Columbia Fur Company. At this time, as we shall see when we take up the Rocky Mountain Fur Company, General Ashley had returned from the third of his remarkably successful expeditions from beyond the Rocky Mountains. He caused much speculation in the fur-mart of St. Louis. MacKenzie looked with jealous eye on this prolific fur-bearing territory, being anxious to enter it and share its immense profits—which he eventually did, but realized very little.

An epoch in the Missouri River trade was the advent of the steamboat, replacing the faithful old keelboats, which were relegated to oblivion very much in the same manner as is the canal-boat at the present time. The first boat was built in Louisville and was named the "Yellowstone." Guided by Captain B. Young, she left St. Louis, April 16, 1831, on her maiden trip, which she made with but little difficulty. She supplied the Upper Missouri posts. In this manner the American Fur Company, a thoroughly organized company with unlimited capital, continued trading on the Missouri for many years, with no competition to cause them any alarm.

The only real rival of this company was the Rocky Mountain Fur Company, whose organization was imperfect and capital very limited, although their men, who were masters at the business, conducted affairs in the mountains with much energy. They were pushed to the wall, as we shall see, largely through the efforts of the American Fur Company, although the latter lost a great deal of money in accomplishing it. The American Fur Company carried on trade largely along the Missouri River and its tributaries. This territory the Rocky Mountain Fur Company recognized as theirs, and seldom invaded it, probably for the very good reason that its financial resources did not warrant it. The former company was not slow in invading the rich and sacred precincts of the Rocky Mountain Company, and by dogging its footsteps and hindering its trapping and trading, eventually brought about its downfall. They, however, suffered much before it was accomplished, in which one can almost see the master-hand of an Astor.

The origin of the Rocky Mountain Fur Company dates from an advertisement in the *Missouri Republican* of March 20, 1822, in which Major Andrew Henry—an old hand at the business, who had been on the Upper Missouri at the time Mr. Hunt and party crossed to the Pacific in 1811—and William H. Ashley advertised for one hundred young men to trap and trade on the Upper Missouri. The first license to trade was granted to Ashley April 11, 1822. The desired number of young men was easily obtained. They were to be absent about three years, under the command of the veteran Andrew Henry. After much loss of property and other misfortunes they finally established a post at the mouth of the Yellowstone. He had trouble with the Blackfeet and lost a number of men. In the meantime Ashley had advertised for another hundred men, and started out on his disastrous expedition of 1823. Jedediah S. Smith was a member of this party—in fact Smith, Sublette, and Jackson were all with Ashley at this time and later succeeded him in the business. Of all the expeditions up the Missouri previous to this time, Mr. Hunt and his party were about the only ones to escape the fickle and treacherous Aricaras.

The following year, they made quite a successful hunt in the Green River valley, and a party under Etienne Prevost very probably crossed the mountains by the South Pass. No doubt, they were the first whites to pass through this defile, which, later, was largely used by emigrants on their western journeys to Oregon and California. The Oregon Trail passed through it. Being well adapted to the use of wagons, it is one of the easiest passages through the Rocky Mountains within the confines of the United States.

At this period, Andrew Henry drops from the annals of the fur-trade, 1824-25, and we hear nothing more of him in this connection.

General Ashley decided to abandon the Missouri River trade; the discoveries of Henry, Smith, and Prevost convinced him of the fact that beaver were far more plentiful beyond the mountains in the neighborhood of the Great Salt Lake. Another weighty reason for this change was that at this time the Missouri Fur Company was extremely active in the trade of the Upper Missouri, and that many others were engaged in it, while the strong American Fur Company was preparing to enter it also. Probably Ashley thought this amount of competition might prove ruinous to his limited means.

At this point we must give Ashley credit for a departure from the old and time-honored methods then in vogue with the older companies; instead of forts he established the rendezvous, which was a meeting-place at some suitable point in the mountains where the trappers and friendly Indians would congregate, usually about July, as at this time furs were not taken. Here they exchanged their furs for needed supplies for the coming year, after which they returned to their lonely haunts and continued trapping until another year rolled by. Then they again made their appearance and usually squandered the greater part of their year's earnings, only to return again to the wilderness. Thus an entirely new order of things was established, and the rendezvous became an extremely unique and important feature of the mountain trade. Ashley also abandoned that great highway of the fur-trade, the Missouri River, and continued overland along the river Platte to the mountains, in the summer of 1824, and probably spent the following winter in the Green River valley. Here he met with some adventures in endeavoring to navigate the Green River the following spring. Shortly after these events, he met Prevost and his party, and continued westward to the Salt Lake valley. Prevost while traversing this territory had an encounter with the Snake Indians (a very unusual occurrence, as they were and always had been very friendly—this is probably the only instance of hostility on their part) in which he lost many men.

Ashley explored the country south of Salt Lake as far as Sevier Lake, which he named after himself. They then turned north to reach the annual rendezvous in the Upper Green River valley, and it was probably at Cache valley that he met the Hudson Bay trader, Peter Skene Ogden, with a large party, and furs estimated at from $70,000 to $200,000. Ashley came into possession of these furs, for practically nothing: some say that he found them in cache and robbed it, others say that he bought them to relieve Ogden's necessities. There seems to be a cloud over the whole transaction, and no one has ever been able to get at the facts in the affair. As a result it has caused much speculation, and as the Hudson Bay Company has never given any explanation, we are left entirely in the dark.

It was, however, the turning-point in Ashley's financial career. He had up to this time been deeply involved in debt and in this manner was enabled to pay off his indebtedness and lay the foundation for a substantial fortune. From the Green River rendezvous he returned to St. Louis with the furs, through the South Pass by way of the Bighorn to the Yellowstone, thence to and down the Missouri River. The old fort which they had established some two years previous they found in ruins. Fortune still smiled upon Ashley. Arriving at the Missouri, he had the good fortune to fall in with General Atkinson, who offered him and his outfit a safe convoy to Council Bluffs, thus making the journey to St. Louis of little danger or risk.

The rendezvous of 1826 was to be at Cache valley, where no doubt Ashley hoped to meet another Ogden. He set out for this point in March, 1826, having been married since his return. This journey was up the North Platte and Sweetwater and through the South Pass. It was on this journey that he took with him his celebrated wheeled cannon—a six-pounder—to Utah Lake, where he installed it at his trading-post. In July of this year, while at the rendezvous, he sold out his interest in the mountain trade to Jedediah S. Smith, David E. Jackson, and William L. Sublette—a worthy trio indeed, the leaders and best men under Ashley. From this time forward, they traded under the name of the Rocky Mountain Fur Company. They had an agreement with General Ashley whereby he was to supply them with goods. From the rendezvous he at once returned to St. Louis, taking with him the result of the year's hunt: one hundred and twenty-three packs of beaver-skins. General Ashley never again returned to the mountains, but, having political ambition, was later elected to Congress.

The following year Smith, Sublette, and Jackson sent down one hundred and thirty packs of beaver and were able to liquidate all their indebtedness to General Ashley. The phenomenal success of Ashley set the whole fur-trade in a flurry, and the great American Fur Company began to reach out as we have indicated. Up to this time Ashley had carried from the mountains in three or four years $250,000 worth of furs—a fabulous amount for those days. Many adventurers went to the mountains to seek a fortune, and it was probably some of these stories that influenced Leonard to engage in the trade. We elsewhere give the adventures of Jedediah S. Smith while he was a member of this company. The other two partners carried on a very successful trade in the mountains.

In the spring of 1830, the company made a departure from the old custom of using pack animals, by conveying their supplies to the mountains in wagons. This is the first instance of the use of wagons in this connection although they had long been in use on the Santa Fé trail. They followed what was later known as the Oregon trail to the rendezvous on Wind River.

At the rendezvous of this year, another change took place. The partners, following the example of Ashley, sold out their interest to their leading men— Thomas Fitzpatrick, Milton G. Sublette (brother of William), Henry Fraeb, J. B. Gervais, and James Bridger, the celebrated guide of later years. This transfer occurred August 4, 1830, and the firm continued the use of the name Rocky Mountain Fur Company. The three partners returned to St. Louis at once with an extremely valuable cargo of furs: one hundred and ninety packs of beaver.

After the breaking up of the Wind River rendezvous, in August 1830, Fitzpatrick, Sublette, and Bridger with two hundred men moved north along the Bighorn, crossed the Yellowstone, to the neighborhood of the Great Falls of the Missouri, then to the three forks, and up the Jefferson branch to the divide. They were extremely successful and a large amount of furs was taken, the party being too strong for the treacherous Blackfeet to attack. Having crossed the divide and reached Ogden's Hole, they fell in with the Hudson Bay Company trader of that name, and Fitzpatrick, following the example of Ashley, proceeded at once to relieve him of his furs. The Hudson Bay people allowed no liquor to be used in their trade—very much to their credit—but the throats of their trappers were dry—enough at any rate to overcome their scruples. The Rocky Mountain Fur Company was fortunately well supplied with this article, and Ogden, the Hudson Bay trader, was perfectly helpless, placed as he was in the hands of the unscrupulous Fitzpatrick. The result was that the latter secured the furs of all the Hudson Bay Company trappers, the product of one whole year's hard labor, at a very small cost to the Rocky Mountain Fur Company. A great deal of mystery surrounds Ashley's transaction, and we are therefore unable to say which of the two made the better bargain, he or his unscrupulous successor. It is, however, nothing to the credit of either, and is in striking contrast to the treatment accorded Jedediah S. Smith of the same company some few years previous by the Hudson Bay Company.

After this discreditable transaction at Ogden's Hole, Fitzpatrick and his party returned eastward to Powder River valley, where they arrived before the cold weather set in. In the spring of 1831, they set out for the Blackfoot country but had not proceeded far before their horses were stolen by the Crows. After some effort they recaptured their own and at the same time secured many of the horses belonging to these Indians. Shortly after this affair, Fitzpatrick with only one companion started for St. Louis, reaching Council Bluffs April 19. It must be remembered that it was just about this time that Leonard departed from St. Louis for the mountains. When the former reached St. Louis he was prevailed upon to accompany Smith, Sublette, and Jackson to Santa Fé, they having entered the Santa Fé trade, and thence to return with the outfit to the rendezvous. It was on this expedition that Jedediah S. Smith was killed on the Cimarron desert by the Comanches. Fitzpatrick, on arriving at Santa Fé, continued north along the eastern base of the mountains, and reached the North Platte near the mouth of the Laramie, late in the year. Leonard, however, says that "Fitzpatrick arrived at the mouth of the Laramie about September 1 on his way to St. Louis." Fitzpatrick was met near the Platte by Fraeb and conducted to the Powder River valley, where the five partners were gathered together to spend the winter. This is not in accord with Leonard's statement. They expected to spend a quiet winter, in which they were disappointed, as here appeared for the first time the representatives of the American Fur Company, from the Upper Missouri, presumably under orders from Kenneth MacKenzie. They now for the first time began to feel the pressure of this powerful rival, of thorough organization and unlimited means, which eventually drove them from the mountains and out of business. They at this time wished to share in the profits of the mountain trade. The men in charge of the party who were thus invading the territory of the Rocky Mountain Company were Vanderburgh, Drips, and Fontenelle, whose policy it was to follow the trappers of the above company and learn the best trapping-grounds. It was not a very honorable procedure to say the least, but such were the methods of the mountains and these companies. The Rocky Mountain Company, as we have seen, did not draw the lines very closely in this respect themselves. The object of the American Fur Company now became apparent when the two rival companies were camped side by side. Fitzpatrick and his associates quietly stole out of the country and traveled very rapidly for about four hundred miles west to the forks of the Snake River, having previously fixed the next rendezvous at Pierre's Hole, while they spent the winter with the Nez Percés and Flatheads. However, the peace, serenity, and prosperity of the Rocky Mountain Fur Company were forever at an end. During all this while, according to Leonard, Fitzpatrick was in St. Louis.

Fitzpatrick and party made their spring hunt along the course of the Snake, Salt, and John Day rivers, and then into Bear River valley, where, much to their disgust, they again met Vanderburgh and Drips, who were evidently trying to find them. They resolved to seek other trapping-grounds at once, which they did, and returned to the assemblage of trappers and Indians, at the summer rendezvous of 1832, at Pierre's Hole. It must be remembered that during this period Leonard was in the mountains about the Laramie River.

Here again the representatives of the American Fur Company made their appearance, to the infinite vexation of the Rocky Mountain Company, but their presence at this time was a far more serious matter. The time had about arrived for the trappers and Indians to assemble, and should the American Fur Company be the first to receive their supplies, they would reap the harvest that had heretofore fallen to the Rocky Mountain Fur Company. This was a serious consideration and it was of the utmost importance that their convoy of merchandise should arrive first. William L. Sublette had the contract to bring out this year's supplies. In this dilemma it was decided that Fitzpatrick should go to meet him and hurry him forward with the goods. Fitzpatrick set out with his usual promptness, and made remarkable time; he was an extremely active man, and fortunately met Sublette with the supplies on the Platte below the mouth of the Laramie River, about four hundred miles from the rendezvous. On their way back, June 13, Fitzpatrick hired a party of men at the Laramie River belonging to the firm of Gant and Blackwell, who had experienced a most unsuccessful campaign at trapping during the previous winter. This was the party to which Leonard belonged, although the timing does not quite agree with that of Leonard. We find in this statement that Fitzpatrick was at the mouth of the Laramie River previous to January 1, 1832, and again on June 13 of this year; the question arises, did Leonard see him both times?

When the party arrived at the Sweetwater, Fitzpatrick went on ahead to carry the news of Sublette's approach, and met with the adventure as related by Leonard. William L. Sublette with the supplies reached the rendezvous at Pierre's Hole July 8. Further on we shall relate the incidents which occurred at this the most celebrated rendezvous of the mountains.

From the rendezvous at Pierre's Hole Leonard went with a number of others to trap on the Humboldt or Mary's River. The rendezvous having broken up July 17, we will again follow the Rocky Mountain Company, simply to show what rivalry and intense feeling of hatred existed against the American Fur Company and its methods.

Fitzpatrick and Bridger went to the trapping-ground on the Jefferson fork of the Missouri, and here they had the mortification of learning that Vanderburgh and Drips were again on their trail. They now offered to compromise by dividing the territory, but the offer was declined. The tactics of the American Fur Company were beginning to show results, and Fitzpatrick and Bridger with all their knowledge and shrewdness could not shake them off, and the trapping season was thus slipping away. Becoming thoroughly exasperated and out of patience, they resolved to lure their opponents to follow in order to teach them a lesson. They now plunged into the forbidden land of the Blackfeet, and lured and encouraged their rivals from point to point, until they were attacked by these Indians and Vanderburgh, one of the leaders, was killed. This was the object which Fitzpatrick and Bridger had in view when they went to this neighborhood, knowing that the others would not be as well prepared and on their guard as they, and probably only regretted that the destruction was not more complete. The party of Fitzpatrick and Bridger barely escaped, and Bridger was severely wounded in the shoulder—an arrowhead remaining in his body for nearly two years, when it was removed by the celebrated missionary physician Doctor Whitman, in the mountains, while on his way to Oregon. After this affair, which shows the intense feeling that existed and the extremes to which both parties would go in matters of trade, the Rocky Mountain Fur Company wintered in the valley of the Snake River, and in the following spring made their usual hunt, and all were gathered together again at the head of Green River, which was the rendezvous for the year 1833.

We here find again side by side the two rival companies, also Captain Bonneville and his company, the energetic Yankee—Nathaniel J. Wyeth—an officer of the English army, Captain Stuart, Robert Campbell, with party and outfit fresh from St. Louis, besides a large number of Indians of various tribes, who visited the rendezvous.

The trade had by this time fallen off very much and the Rocky Mountain Fur Company sent from this rendezvous to St. Louis but fifty-five packs of beaver.

The numerous bands of trappers now departed for their fall hunt. Fitzpatrick accompanied the various parties who were returning to St. Louis by way of the Missouri, as far as the Bighorn, where they parted. He was now in the Crow land where he went to seek permission to trap the coming season, but before he could make his request known, they had robbed him of everything he possessed. Fitzpatrick charged the American Fur Company with being the instigators of this affair, but he was simply being repaid at his own game, and was in no wise to be pitied. It was during this period that Leonard was absent from the mountains with Walker on his California expedition.

The trade was now becoming completely demoralized, and the Rocky Mountain Company was in very much the same condition when they met in Green River valley in 1834. Here a dissolution of the company was agreed upon—Henry Fraeb selling out his interest for forty head of horses, forty beaver traps, eight guns, and $1,000 in merchandise; Gervais doing the same for twenty horses, thirty traps, and $500 in merchandise. This low price of the shares of the company shows that they were not considered of much value. Fitzpatrick, Sublette, and Bridger, who remained, formed a new company trading in their individual names, and assumed the obligations of the old company. Thus, with the summer rendezvous of 1834, at Green River, we have to record the death of the once mighty Rocky Mountain Fur Company.

Fitzpatrick, Sublette, and Bridger bought the post built by William L. Sublette and Robert Campbell in 1834 on the Laramie, the following year, and entered the service of the company which had caused their downfall—the American Fur Company. From this time forward this powerful organization had a monopoly on the trade, and the history of the trade is simply a history of this company. The romance, however, connected with the fur-trade had departed. Besides the leading companies mentioned, there were quite a number of individual traders in the mountains previous to 1835, namely, William L. Sublette, Robert Campbell, J. O. Pattic, Mr. Pilcher, Charles and William Bent, Ceran St. Vrain, and Mr. Gant and Mr. Blackwell.

The introduction by the whites of vices and diseases among the Indians and particularly the latter, undermined and sapped the vitality of the natives, making them today a mere shadow of their former selves, and a hopelessly degenerate race. No estimate can be made of the destructiveness of these agencies, no reliable statistics being available, but that they were exceedingly great, there can be no question. We have alluded to the destructiveness of the wars among the various Indian tribes and between the tribes and the whites—in many instances the loss of life was fearful. With them war meant death—no mercy was asked or given—prisoners, with few exceptions, were taken only with a view to torture. Yet these wars were a mere bagatelle when compared with the loss of life as a result of the vices and diseases introduced by the white people.

The use of alcoholic stimulants to which the Indians soon became slaves, as well as venereal diseases which became universal, undermined the naturally strong constitutions of the natives and tainted and weakened the constitutions of their offspring as well. The far-reaching, deteriorating influence of these conditions can only be imagined. As will be seen by studying the early history and the fur-trading and trapping era of the great West, the trappers and traders—many of them men of low moral standard—were largely responsible for this condition of affairs.

The one disease which, more than any other, is responsible for the depopulation of the Indians, is the smallpox. Whether this disease was prevalent among the Indians previous to the coming of the whites is a question that has not been definitely settled. The destructiveness of this disease among the natives is almost beyond conception—it was fatal beyond anything known to the whites, and the Indians dreaded it as they did no other enemy.

Even among the whites the epidemics of a century or two ago were more dreaded by them than almost any other disease, and in the early colonial days of this country some of the epidemics were frightful. Either the contagion or the epidemics are growing less severe, or the disease is being modified by passing through generation after generation; or vaccination may be modifying the course of the disease; at any rate, epidemics are less frequent and less severe, and the death-rate is far below what it formerly was. At the present time we know more about, and can better manage, this dreadful scourge of former years.

The Indians were absolutely ignorant of the nature of the disease, as much as a child, and their mode of living, particularly in the winter season, had a tendency to produce fatal results; it is rather remarkable that any of them recovered during ordinary epidemics, under the treatment they received.

The armamentarium of the Indian for the treatment of all diseases and ailments is the sweat-house in one form or another, and this is usually followed by a cold plunge even in the northern latitudes, in winter, and particularly along the Missouri, where some of the most dreadful epidemics raged. This is their infallible and universal remedy. If we, who know something of the nature of this disease should take a patient and place him in a sweat-house until he is in a dripping perspiration, then subject him to a cold plunge, and place him in a tepee where the temperature cannot be regulated—how many of our small-pox patients would recover, and what would be the mortality? If any should escape, they would be extremely fortunate, and the mortality would no doubt be almost as high as among the Indians.

These conditions contributed to a great extent to the high death-rate among the natives, whose constitutions were in many instances also being undermined by vices and constitutional diseases of another character. Many of the fur companies resorted to vaccination of the Indians.

Previous to 1800 there had been epidemics of the disease along the Missouri and elsewhere but not of sufficient severity to be particularly noted in the meager records of that time. The first alarming and fatal epidemic of which we have a more complete account, which made great inroads into some of the tribes, extending as far west as the Pacific, was that in the year 1800, and subsequently minor ones from time to time, until the dreadful scourge and epidemic of 1837, which surpassed anything ever known or heard of in the annals of the Missouri. This terrible pestilence was confined mostly to the Indians of the Upper Missouri, but spread from tribe to tribe, carrying death, destruction, and terror in its path; fire and the sword had no terrors as compared to it; it seemed to outdo itself, and to mock and glory in its very destructiveness. The poor Indian was struck with terror, and implored, begged, and entreated his deity and the whites, that the scourge might cease—so deadly was it that many thought it something else than the smallpox—a punishment brought on by the displeasure of the Great Spirit. The suffering, terror, and helplessness of the Indian seemed to dull his intellect and he was as one dumb, facing the fell monster without courage to resist. We have graphic accounts of it written by eye-witnesses. According to Larpenteur this scourge was introduced by the whites, having been brought in by the steamboat "St. Peters," of the American Fur Company, which arrived at Fort Union on the 24th of June 1837. Some writers say there was but one case on board, but it is quite certain there were more. The American Fur Company was criminally negligent in this affair, for, knowing the contagious nature of this disease, it should not under any circumstances have allowed the boat to ascend the river and come in contact with the Indians. The situation was, however, a rather difficult one to deal with. The Indians expected the boat, knowing that it contained goods for their benefit, and had it failed to arrive it would have been difficult to explain, and would have been interpreted as an attempt to rob them. On the other hand it was impossible for the boat to return and another to come up, for by this time the river would have fallen and been too low for steamboat navigation; and, again, it can hardly be attributed to selfish motives, for the company would no doubt have been the heaviest loser by the introduction of such a disease. The vessel should have stopped and been unloaded, thoroughly fumigated and cleansed, also the cargo, and those suffering from the disease cared for on shore; then only should it have proceeded or the goods been shipped in some other manner. The officers of the boat, it is certain, never realized the gravity of the situation until it was too late—not thinking for an instant that they were carrying one of the most dreadful scourges that ever befell the Indians or any people. The company's officers tried to avert the danger of infection by endeavoring to keep the Indians away from the boat; the latter, thinking this was merely a ruse to cheat them, could not be restrained, knowing that the boat contained goods for them. It was in vain to expostulate, implore, and explain; they were deaf to all entreaty. When the boat arrived at Fort Clark a Mandan chief stole a blanket from a man upon the boat who was suffering from the disease. Mr. Chardon, then in charge of the fort, made every effort to at once gain possession of this blanket, promising pardon for the theft, and new blankets in place of the infected one, all, however, to no purpose. He endeavored to keep the Indians away by sending them warning, using every inducement and argument in his power—explaining, entreating, and warning—but in vain; for in a short while the whole village was seen coming down the river, and pitched their tents near the fort.

In reading the early history of these fur-trading days, we have frequently had reason to admire the Mandans who were uniformly friendly to the whites, and in fact they were rather the favorites with the early traders; there is not so far as we know an unfriendly act towards the whites recorded against them; they, however, suddenly drop from the face of the earth, and out of sight and existence, from among the Missouri River tribes, but we have here the explanation.

Smallpox appeared among them about June 15, 1837, and continued apparently until it had found a victim in the very last one of them. It raged with a fatality and virulence never before known. Death was almost instantaneous. The victim was seized with an excruciating pain in the back and head, frequently with a chill, and in a few hours was dead. The body immediately turned black and swelled to thrice its natural size. Such was the fatality of the epidemic, that nearly every one who was attacked by it died.

The Indians soon found that the warnings of the whites were true, and realized the character of the calamity that was upon them. It produced a most profound effect upon their feelings. Some were for taking summary vengeance upon the whites, but before they could carry out their purpose the scourge and the hand of death were upon them. Some who saw it felt that the Great Spirit had stricken them for attempting to injure their friends, the whites. They would then supplicate the latter to defend them, imploring their forgiveness for not having listened to them in the first instance; but the whites were now quite as powerless as they to stay the hand of death. The disease spread with frightful rapidity, and found victims daily by the hundreds; it became impossible to bury them, none had the inclination or the courage, they were thrown in piles over a cliff, and as a result, in addition to all the above horrors, a sickening stench pervaded the atmosphere for miles around. In the presence of this disaster, without the power to stay or avert it, the Indians became desperate. Many resorted to self-destruction, by shooting, stabbing, or drowning. One chief, before he was stricken, but feeling that he would shortly become a victim, commanded his wife to dig his grave. Sorrowfully she performed the duty, and when the work was done, the warrior threw himself into it and at the same time stabbed himself to death. The tragedy was however not over—the broken-hearted squaw went back to her lodge and child, where, before another sun had passed, a more terrible fate overtook them in the dread disease. Two young men just stricken with the disease conferred with each other as to the best way to end their existence, and having agreed as to details, fearlessly carried it into execution. Every day was crowded with the most pathetic, sorrowful, and soul-stirring incidents to these most unfortunate of God's mortals, as the dread pestilence daily carried off victim after victim. Tenderness and passion, love and hatred, were at last blunted and blurred in the presence of this awful calamity. At last the Indians sought, by wandering singly and alone in the prairie and avoiding each other, to overcome the disease.

In this manner the great and powerful tribe of the Mandans was literally sacrificed by the almost criminal carelessness of the American Fur Company. The Mandans at the time of the visit of Lewis and Clark numbered about 1,500 or 2,000 souls, though probably somewhat less at this time; after the ravages of this disease, only about thirty persons—mostly old men and boys—were left of this once powerful tribe. "No language can picture," says one writer, "the scene of desolation which the country presents. In whatever direction we go we see nothing but melancholy wrecks of human life. The tents are still standing on every hill, but no rising smoke announces the presence of human beings, and no sounds, but the croaking of the raven and the howling of the wolf, interrupt the fearful silence."

Of all the tribes the Mandans suffered the most, and as we have seen came near actual extermination. A band of Aricaras were encamped near the afflicted Mandans and for some unknown reason escaped the disease until after it had wrought such fearful havoc with the latter. This fact made the Mandans suspicious, who at once thought the whites and Aricaras were in league to cause their destruction. The disease, however, soon broke out among the latter and very nearly exterminated them as well. It also made great inroads into the Minnetarees.

The introduction of smallpox at Fort Union would seem to have been as certain as any sequence of cause and effect, but no adequate measures were taken to prevent it. Besides the infected cargo which had to be unloaded, one of the passengers, Jacob Halsey, well known on the river as clerk and partner of the Upper Missouri Outfit, was already sick when he arrived, but nevertheless took up his residence at the fort. Halsey had been vaccinated and the disease was not malignant in his case, although it was a severe shock to a constitution naturally not strong, and further weakened by habitual dissipation. As Halsey's was the only case, it was thought that the spread of the disease could be circumvented. But Mr. E. T. Denig, another well-known clerk of the company, had it, though not fatally, and then a squaw was carried off with it. The only Indians at the post at the time were some thirty squaws, and now as the spread of the infection was hopelessly certain, "prompt measures were adopted," in the language of Larpenteur, "to prevent an epidemic." These measures were none other than the vaccination of all the squaws with the smallpox virus itself, there being no regular vaccine matter at the fort. The poor squaws knew no better and meekly submitted to the operation. "Their systems" were "prepared according to Dr. Thomas' Medical Book" and they were vaccinated from Halsey himself. This course was adopted, Larpenteur assures us, with cynical coolness, "with a view to have it all over and everything all cleaned up before any Indians should come in, on their fall trade, which commenced early in September." Such is the astonishing confession of one of the American Fur Company's servants, and such was the desperate length to which the traders would go when the interests of their business could be promoted. Thirty squaws, imprisoned within the palisades, were deliberately sacrificed to one of the most loathsome pests in nature, in order "to have it all over and everything cleaned up" before the company's trade should be injured.

But this heroic purpose utterly miscarried. Larpenteur says that the mistake made was in not vaccinating from a person of sound physical constitution, which Halsey did not have, as if a disease which was at that moment raging further down the river with unprecedented power could be much intensified by being communicated from an unsound constitution! The result of this culpable oversight was, in the terse and unsentimental language of Larpenteur, that "the operation proved fatal to most of our patients." It seems never to have occurred to him that he and his abettors were red-handed violators of the Sixth Commandment. He goes on to say: "About fifteen days afterward there was such a stench in the fort that it could be smelt at a distance of 300 yards. It was awful—the scene in the fort, where some went crazy, and others were half eaten up by maggots before they died." This was during the hottest part of summer.

As if fate were bent on making the worst of a bad situation, the Indians began coming in to trade while the epidemic was at its height. Halsey says that the fort was absolutely closed to them and they were entreated to keep away, but that probably the "air was infected" with the disease "for half a mile without the pickets." Larpenteur says that they did open the door to a celebrated chief," but on showing him a little boy who had not recovered, and whose face was still one solid scab, by holding him over the pickets, the Indians finally concluded to leave." Whatever the facts, the fearful truth is that the pestilence got abroad. It first spread among the Assiniboines, who were the Indians that had come to the fort, and it raged among them until winter. Halsey, who left Union in October, says that at that time it was "raging with the greatest destructiveness imaginable—at least ten out of twelve die with it."

At Fort Union in these trying times one John Brazeau, a familiar name in those days on the upper rivers, was undertaker, and seemed to take a fiendish satisfaction in his new occupation. "How many?" Larpenteur would ask him of a morning now and then. "Only three, sir, but according to appearances at the hospital I think I shall have a full load tomorrow or next day." These two worthies missed their opportunity in life by coming upon the stage at the wrong time and place. They would have found a more congenial atmosphere among the gruesome scenes around the French guillotines of Ninety-Three.

In spite of the destructive ravages of the disease among the Assiniboines they still came in to trade, and the business did not fall off as much as had been expected. Larpenteur says that when the Indians were asked how it was, under the circumstances, that "there were so many robes brought in, they would say laughingly that they expected to die soon and wanted to have a frolic till the end came."

The pestilence reached the Blackfeet through another most culpable act of negligence on the part of the company's officers. An Indian of that nation was permitted to get on the "St. Peters" at the mouth of the Little Missouri and then to go to his people before it was known whether he had taken the disease or not. The Crow post, Van Buren, was also infected, most likely through other acts of negligence. The disease ran its usual course there, but the Crows were at the time on Wind River, and escaped until later in the fall. But before the end of the year all the tribes of the Missouri valley above the Sioux had been stricken and the extent of the calamity was well-nigh appalling.

The Assiniboines were for declaring open war against the whites, to whom they rightfully, to a certain extent, attributed the visitation of the terrible pestilence; but they did not carry this threat into execution. The hostile Blackfeet, however, were completely humbled, some of them were about to begin a war on the whites when the scourge attacked them, which they interpreted as a judgment of Providence, for thus attempting to destroy their friends. The tribes as a rule accepted it in a philosophical manner, and did not attempt to retaliate on the whites, probably through fear of a still worse affliction.

It is next to impossible to ascertain the exact number of deaths during this memorable epidemic. Audubon, upon the authority of Mitchell, estimates it, among all tribes, at 150,000, a figure entirely too high. Another estimate was 60,000, also far too high. Chittenden places it at about 15,000, which, in view of all the circumstances and conditions, is probably very nearly correct. The tribes mostly affected were the Blackfeet, Crows, Assiniboines, Mandans, Minnetarees, and Aricaras.

The mortality of this epidemic has scarcely a parallel in the history of plagues, and fully justifies the quotation from the work of Maximilian: "The destroying angel has visited the unfortunate sons of the wilderness with terrors never before known, and has converted the extensive hunting-grounds, as well as the peaceful settlements of these tribes, into desolate and boundless cemeteries."

Chapter 2

JOURNAL OF A VOYAGE TO THE ROCKY MOUNTAINS

By François Antoine Larocque

At my arrival at Rivière Fort de la Bosse I prepared for going on a voyage of discovery to the Rocky Mountains and set off on the 2nd June with two men having each of us two horses, one of which was laden with goods to facilitate an intercourse with the Indians we might happen to see on our road. Mr. Charles McKenzie and Mr. Lassana set out with me to go & pass the summer at the Missouri, and having to pursue the same road we Kept Company as far as the B.B. village.

 Mr. McKenzie with the other men set off about at two in the afternoon, but I having [been] so very busy that I had not as yet been able to write my letters to my friends remained and wrote letters and settled some little business of my own. After sunset we supped & bidding farewell to Mr. Chabelly & Henry & to all the people, departed, every one being affected at our departure thinking it more than probable that I should not return with my men, and I confess I left the fort with a heavy heart but riding at a good rate I soon got chearful again, and thought of nothing but the [means] of ensuring success to my undertaking.

At 10 at night I arrived at the River aux Prunes where I found the people encamped asleep.

MONDAY 3rd.

I set of early in the morning and stopped at 12 to refresh our horses, and encamped at night at River la Sorie, where we had not been two hours encamped when three, and after many other Assiniboins rushed in upon us, a few endeavouring to take our horses, but seeing our guns and running to them we made them depart. They ran afterwards to our fire and seeing us well armed and by our looks that we would well defend ourselves and our property they remained quiet. There were 40 tents of them not 10 acres from us without that we had perceived them. I gave 1 fm. tobacco to their Chief to make his young men smoke & engage them to remain peaceable. Some of them offered to accompany us to the Missouri, but upon being told that we would like it well they spoke no more of it.

Thinking it however not prudent to pass the night so close to them we saddled our horses and departed although they did all in their power of engaging us to sleep at those tents. One of them conducted us to a good fording place of River la Sourie which we crossed striking in the plain. We walked all night to come out of their reach for they are worst cunning horse thieves that ever I said or heard of. A little before day light we stopped and took a nap.

TUESDAY 4th.

We proceeded on our journey early in the morning having very fine weather all day, and at night encamped on the banks of the River la Sourie at a place called Green River for its having no wood on its side for about 30 miles. We saw no other animals but four cabois of which we killed two.

WEDNESDAY 5th.

We followed the Green River till eleven o'clock when we arrived at the woods, where being an appearance of rainy weather we encamped. There was no Buffalo in sight. At 12 it began to rain and continued hard and uninterruptedly until next morning. Here we saw plenty of wild fowls, Ducks, Bustards, Geese, Swans, &c., and killed a number of them.

THURSDAY 6th.

There being an appearance of fine weather, we set off and walked about three miles, when the weather being cloudy we stopped to encamp, but before we could make a hut for our goods the rain began again, and fell amazingly hard so that in a few hours every hollows or valley in the plains were full of water, and every brook or creek was swollen to rivers. There were plenty of Buffaloes and the rain ceasing in the evening we killed a very fat young bull and a fat Elk deer. At night the rain began again and continued without intermission until morning.

FRIDAY 7th.

The weather continued cloudy, but the sun appearing now and then we hoped for fair weather but as yesterday it began to rain at 12, at two we found some wood on some sandy hills in the plains where we stopped to cook our goods, being completely trenched [drenched]. There being no water on the sand hills, we raised a Bark of Elm tree and pulling one end in a Kettle, the other end a little higher, all the water that fell on the Bark ran into the kettle and we had presently a sufficient quantity; we also made a tent with bark and passed the night comfortably enough.

SATURDAY 8th.

We set off to go to a hill called Grosse Butte to dry our things, and water our horses, but their being none here, arrived there two hours and a half where we stopped for the remainder of the day & night. The Grosse Butte is a high hill which is seen at 20 miles off on either side. At its foot on the north side is a Lake of about 8 miles in circumference in which there are middle sized pikes. Between the Lake and the hill there is some wood chiefly Elm; all around are many lakes, which by the late rain communicated with each other. From the top of the off in the turtle mountain was soon being due North, River la Sourie likewise was off in N.N.E. and south and south west, being seen on all sides of the hill excepted west.

SUNDAY 9th.

We set off early in the morning, in a course S.S.W. and at 1 o'clock in the afternoon we arrived on the Bank of the River la Sourie. The water being amazing high we made a raft to cross our things over the River and the horses swam over. We saddled immediately and encamped in a Coulé about three miles from the River.

MONDAY 10th.

Leaving this we went and slept in the Mandan plain, saw plenty of buffaloes all along, but did not dare to fire at them, being on the enemies lands is Sioux. It rained a little in the night.

TUESDAY 11th.

At 8 in the morning I saw the banks of the Missouri, at 12 arrived at the River Bourbeuse, when we unsaddled our horses where we unloaded our horses and crossed the property on our shoulders there being not more than 2 feet of water, but we sunk up to our middle in mud, the horses bemired themselves in crossing and it was with difficulty we got them over the bank beings bogs as also the bed of the river. We intended to get the villages today but being overtaken by a Shower of rain we encamped in a coulé at the Serpent lodge, being a winter village of the B. Belly's at the Elbow of the River, where I passed part of last winter. Being unwilling to untie my things before the Indians of the village as I was necessarily be put to some expense I took here a small equipment of different article for present expense, as the sight of my goods would perhaps cause the B.B. to refuse our passage to the Rocky Mountains.

WEDNESDAY 12th.

I arrived at 9 o'clock in the morning on the banks of the Missouri, fired a few shots to inform the Indians of our being there and in a few hours many came over with Canoes to cross us and our things.

Lafrance proceeded to the Mandans but I and my men with Mr. McKenzie crossed here at the B. Belly's & entered into drift lodges, gave my men each a small equipment of Knives Tobacco and ammunition to give the landlords.

THURSDAY, 13th.

Three Assiniboines arrived in the evening. 4 Canadians from the Illinois, who are hunting Beaver in these parts, came to see me. I gave each of them 6 inches of [Brazil] Tobacco which pleased them very much as they had for several months not smoked any but Indian Tobacco.

FRIDAY 14th.

The Indians here are exceedingly troublesome to sell their horses to us, the price that we usually pay them for a horse can purchase two from the Rocky

Mountain Indians who are expected daily, & they would wish us to have more goods when those Indians arrive, so as to have the whole trade themselves. I told them that the purpose of our coming was not to purchase horses either from them or the Rocky Mountains, that we came for Skins and Robes and that for that purpose one of us was to pass the summer with them and one at the Mandans; that I and two men were sent by the white people's Chief to smoke a pipe of peace & amity with the Rocky Mountain Indians and to accompany them to their lands to examine them and see if there were Beavers as is reported & to engage them to hunt it, that we would not purchase a horse from none, therefore that their best plan would be to dress Buffalo Robes, so as to have ammunition to trade with the Rocky Mountain Indians.

They pretend to be in fear of the surrounding nations, that is Assineboines, Sioux, Cheyennes & Ricaras, so as to have an excuse for not trading their guns with the Rocky Mountain Indians, and likewise to prevent us. Some of those Rocky Mountain Indians have been here already and are gone back, but more are expected, with whom I intend to go.

SATURDAY 15th.

I was sent for by one of the Chiefs who asked me what I intended to do with the pipe stem I had brought. Upon my telling him that it was for the Rocky Mountain Indians he made a long harangue to dissuade me from going there, saying that I would be obliged to winter there on account of the length of the way, that the Cheyennes and Ricaras were enemies and constantly on the Road, and that it was probable we should be killed by them. He gave the worst character possible to the Rocky Mountain Indians, saying they were thieves and liar, of which he gave an example that is of a Canadian of the name of Menard, who had lived here about 40 years and a few years ago set off to go to the Rocky Mountains to trade horses and Beavers. These Indians did all in their power to prevent him, but seeing him absolutely bent upon going they let him go. He arrived at the Rocky Mountain Indians tents, where he was well treated, & got 9 horses and 2 female slaves, besides a quantity of Beaver. He left the lodge very well pleased, but were followed by some young men who in the night stole 7 horses. A few nights after, his 2 Slaves deserted with the other horses and other young men coming took from him everything he had even to his knife. He came crying to the B. B. Village almost dead having but his robe to make shoes (with flint stone) which he tied about his feet with cords, which so pained the B.B. that they killed some of the Roche Mountain for revenge. He told me many other stories, to all which I answered that my Chief had sent me to go, and that I would or die.

There is seven nights that 5 young men are gone to meet the Rocky Mountain Indians, they are expected daily & the Rocky Mountain Indians with them.

SUNDAY 16th.

This Evening the Indian women danced the scalp of a Blackfoot Indian which they killed the last spring. The Canadians from below said they had killed some white men at the same time, that they had seen cloths such as Corduroy jackets and trousers, collars, shirts, part of Linen Tents, Cashmere waist coats, and many other things belonging to the whites. The Borgne the Great Chief of this village told me that war party had fired upon and killed people who were going down a very large River, in skin canoes, but that they could not tell whether they were Crees or Sauteux or whites. I spoke to old Cerina Grappe the father of the Chief of that party, and to the Chief himself, and they proved by the fire, Earth and Heaven that they were not whites. They made a plan of the Country through which they passed, and in my opinion it is some where [about] the Sas Ratchewini or its branches. They showed me part of what they plundered but I saw nothing that could prove them to have killed Whites except the quantity of gun powder he had, for it was no less than half a Keg and at least 200 balls. Their plunder was parted among all the warriors and their relations. Among the articles that the Cerina Grappe showed me there was a Coat made of the skin of a young horse wrought with porcupine quills and human hair, 2 skunk skins garnished with red stroud and blue beads which those Indians generally wear round their ankles, one musket by Ketland one gun by Barnett, and lastly one scalp which was evidently that of an Indian. But I really believe they have killed some white people about Fort Des Prairies for they brought more goods than ever I saw in the possession of Indians at one time.

MONDAY 17th.

I went down to the Mandan Village on horse back and purchased a saddle there for which I paid 30 lbs ammunition desired Lafrance to get some provision made for my voyage as there is no corn where I live. I returned home to my lodge. In the evening having settled some business with a man of the name of Jusseaux who was indebted to the Company.

TUESDAY 18th.

The son of the White Wolf fell from his horse and bruised his leg terribly, the flesh was taken clean of the bone from the ankle, round the leg to the calf. The Indian doctor was sent for who began his cure by blowing and singing while the child suffered quietly. Thunder storm.

WEDNESDAY 19th.

There being another sick person in my Lodge and there being rather too much fuss about medicines, conjuring & singing I went & lived in another lodge where I had placed one of my men before. Went to see the Borgne our Chief and being desirous that he should stand by me in case of need I made him a present of ¾ lb. Tobacco, one knife and 50 Rounds of ammunition at which he was well pleased—he is the greatest Chief in this place, but does not talk against our going to the Rocky Mountains as the other Chiefs do. Thunder and rain at night.

THURSDAY 20th.

I was again teased by some of the Chiefs to purchase horses and was told the Big Bellys had two hearts and that they not know whether they would allow me to go to the Rocky Mountains, and in the course of a long harangue they made use of all their art to induce me not to go representing the journey as dangerous to the last degree and that the Rocky Mountain would not come, for they were afraid of the Ricaras & Assiniboines to all which I could make no answer but by signs, as there was no one present that could speak to them properly. One of my men of the name of Souci spoke the Sioux language but there was no one there that understood that language. About [noon] two of the young B.B. that had been sent to meet the Rocky Mountains arrived, they left the Rocky Mountain Indians in the morning and they will be here in 3 or 4 days. Upon the receipt of those news, the Chief pretended to have received information that the Crils & Assiniboines were assembled to come and war upon them (which is false) and harangues were made to the people to keep their guns and ammunitions and not to trade them with the Rocky Mountain Indians, &c. All this I believe a scheme to prevent me from going, for as yet they do not like to tell me so exactly, but are for ever saying that they have two hearts which means that they are undetermined in what manner to act.

FRIDAY 21st.

I went to see the Borgne enquired of him what he and the Big Bellys thought of our going to the Rocky Mountains and whether they have a mind to prevent us. He answered to my wish, that the Rocky Mountains were good people, that they had plenty of Beaver on their hands, and that his adopted son, one of the Chiefs of the Rocky Mountains & the greater would take care of us, for that he would strongly recommend to him to put the white people in his heart and watch over them. I told him that the B.B. had no reason to be displeased for that one of us remains with them who has plenty of ammunition, Knives, tobacco, Hatchets and other articles, where with to supply their wants, whenever they would be disposed to trade. He said it was true that none would molest us. He is the only Chief that speaks so, but as he has the most authority of any I hope by his means we will pass. A certain method to get the road clear would be to assemble the Chiefs, make them a present of Tobacco and ammunition, make them smoke & speak to them what occasion I may have for them in future. I like not to do it only when I see that I cannot otherwise for assembling a Council and haranguing without a present is no better than speaking to a heap of stones. Besides I am apprehensive that paying as it were for our first going to these nations will give a footing to the B. Bellys which they will endeavor to improve every time we should go there if a trading interest takes place. So we pass this time without making them any present at all, I believe it will be done away for ever. If the Borgne retains that authority he formerly had he alone will be able to clear the Road for us and he appears to be sincerely our friend.

SATURDAY 22nd.

In the beginning I went to an Indian's tent whose two sons had been in that party that defeated the White on the Saskatchion, he gave me a full account and more like truth than any other. He says there were four Linen tents and four leather on the sides of the River where there were Skin Canoes; they fired upon the largest leather tent and Killed three men, two of whom were Indians, the other they believe to be a White man but not certain. They brought one scalp & if it is that which they showed me, it is an Indian. There was plenty of tents in all kinds besides goods. What they could not take with them, they broke and threw in the River.

SUNDAY 23rd.

Three men and one woman arrived from the Rocky Mountains about noon, the other are near hand and would have arrived today but for rain which fell in the evening.

In the evening I went to see the Brother of the Borgne, where I found two Rocky Mountain Indians, one of whom was the Chief of whom the Borgne had spoken with me. I smoked with them for some time when the Borgne told them that I was going with them and spoke very much in our favor. They appeared to be very well pleased.

MONDAY 24th.

Lafrance, with the other white people from below who reside at the Mandans, came to see the people which were arrived from the Rocky Mountains, who were prevented from coming by appearance of bad weather. It thundered the whole day but it did not rain. I gave a small knife to my Land Lady.

TUESDAY 25th.

About one in the afternoon the Rocky Mountain Indians arrived, they encamped at a little distance from the village with the warriors, to the number of 645, passed through the village on horseback with their shields & other war-like implements, they proceeded to the little village, Souliers, and then to the Mandans and returned.

There did not remain 20 persons in the village, men women and children all went to the newly arrived camp carrying a quantity of Corn raw and cooked which they traded for Leggings, Robes and dried meat. There are 20 lodges of the snake Indians & about 40 men. The other bands are more numerous.

This morning the Borgne sent for me, he showed me the Rocky Mountain Chief of the Ererokas, and told him before me that I was going with him & to take good care of us & he spoke very much in our favor telling me that the B. Bellys were undetermined whether they would allow us to go or not, but that we would go if we liked it for that he would clear the road before us if necessary. I gave to two of the Ererokas each 6 [feet] of tobacco and 20 Rounds of ammunitions.

WEDNESDAY 26th.

The Mandans, Souliers, little village people & the people of the Village, went on horse back and arrived to perform the same ceremonies round the Rocky

Mountain Camp, as the Rocky Mountains did yesterday here, they were about 500, but a great many Warriors are absent being gone to war.

THURSDAY 27th.
Assembled the chiefs of the different Bands of the Rocky Mountains and made them a present of

2 Large Axes
2 Small Axes
8 Ivory Combs
10 Wampum Shells
8 fire steels and Flint
6 Masses B.C. Beads
4 f. Tobacco
8 Cock feathers
16 large Knives
12 Small do
2 lbs. Vermillion
8 doz. Rings
4 papers co'd Glasses
4 Doz. Awls
11/ lb. Blue Beads
2 Doz. do
1000 balls & powder

Made them smoke in a stem which I told them was that of the Chief of the White people who was desirous of making them his Children & Brethren, that he knew they were pitiful and had no arms to defend themselves from their enemies, but that they should cease to be pitiful as soon as they would make themselves brave hunters. That I and two men were going with them to see their lands and that we took with us some articles to supply their present want. That our Chief sent them those goods that lay before them, to make them listen to what we were now telling them, that he expected they would treat all white people as their Brethren for that we were in peace and friendship with the Red skinned people and did not go about to get a scalp, that probably they would see White people on their lands from another quarter but that they were our brethren and of course we expected they would not hurt them, that a few years ago they pillaged and ill treated a white man who went to trade with them, that we would see how they would treat us and if they have behaved well towards us and kill Beavers, Otters & Bears they would have white people on the lands in a few years, who would winter with them and supply them with all their wants & &. I told them many other things which I thought was necessary and closed the Harangue by making them smoke the Medicin Pipe. They thanked [me] and make a present of 6 robes, one Tiger skin, 4 shirts, 2 women Cotillons 2 dressed Elk skins, 3 saddles and 13 pair leggings. I clothed the Chief of the Ererokas at the same time and gave him a flag and a Wampam Belt and told them that our Chief did not expect that we would pass many different nations and therefore had sent but one Chief Clothing, but that in the course of the summer we would fix upon a spot most convenient for them all where we would build & trade with them, if we saw that they wished to encourage the white people to go on their lands by being good hunters and that then all their Chiefs who would behave well would get a Coat.

The ceremony of adopting Children was going on at the same time, but I was so very busy that I could not attend, but about the middle of the ceremony, and therefore can give but an imperfect account of it from my own observation, but as the two people were present I will give an account of it in another place.

FRIDAY 28th.
I preferred to go off in the evening to the lodge of the Ereroka Chief in order to be ready with them in the morning but he and the other Chiefs were called to a farewell Council in the Borges Lodge so that I did not Stir.

SATURDAY 29th.
Saddled our horses and left the B. Belly village. We remained about half an hour in the Rocky Mountain Camp where they threw down their tents and all set off. We marched along the Knife River for about eight miles when we stopped and encamped. The Borgne and many other B. Belly's came and slept with us.

SUNDAY 30th.
We followed a south course for about 4 mile and stopped to dine and resumed a S.S.W. course and encamped for night, Knife River in Sight when no hills intervened, about 6 miles on our right. A thunderstorm in the evening.

JULY 1ST, MONDAY.

We set [out] at 8 o'clock in the morning and encamped at 12 having followed a South West course; we crossed three small creeks running North and N. East into the Knife River. It began to rain as soon as the lodges were pitched and continued so all day. The Indians hunted and Killed a few Bulls. I gave the people of my lodge a few articles, as Beads, Knives.

TUESDAY 2nd.

We set out at 9 o'clock followed a south Course and encamped at 2 after noon. It thundered very much the whole of the afternoon and at sun set there fell such a shower of hail as I never saw before, some of the hail stones being as large as hen eggs and the rest as a Yolk; they fell with amazing violence and broke down several tents. The wind during the storm was West; it breezed to the North and continued during the whole night.

WEDNESDAY 3rd.

We continued our journey for about 4 hours, through a very hilly country and encamped at the foot of a very high Hill on the top of which I ascended, but could see at no considerable distance, another range of hills surrounding this on all sides. I lost my spy glass in coming down the hill and could not find it again. Our course was south.

THURSDAY 4th.

We stopped after a south course for the night on the side of a small hill at a Creek which empties in the Missouri above the Panis village about 5 leagues distant from our last encampment having crossed another a little before emptying in the Missurri about one mile below the Mandans. The Scouts reported that Buffaloes were at hand.

FRIDAY 5th.

We discovered a thief last night in the act of stealing a gun from under our loads thinking we were asleep. The Chief sent two young men to sleep behind the lodge and guard our property. After three hours and a half march in a southerly direction we espied Buffaloes, and stopped all. The Chief harangued and the young men set out to hunt after which we marched on for about a league and a half and encamped. There was no Creek or River here for water only a few ponds of stagnant water which by reason of so many dogs and horses bathing in them was not drinkable being as thick as mud.

SATURDAY 6th.
A Big Belly found my spy glass and returned it to me, we set of at 8. At 11 the scouts reported that they had seen enemies. We all stopped, the men armed themselves and mounting their fleetest horses went in pursuit. They returned in a few hours, as what the scouts had taken for enemies were a party of their own people who were gone hunting and not been seen. We proceeded and encamped at one on the side of a small River running West and emptying in the lesser Missouri. It blew a hurricane in the evening. Course south about four leagues.

SUNDAY 7th.
At ten o'clock we rose the Camp and at 3 we saw Buffaloes. Harangues were made to the Young Men to go and hunt while a party of these latter who are a guard of soldiers paraded before the body of the people preventing any one from setting off till all the huntsmen were gone; after which we set off again and encamped at the foot of a hill, which we had in sight since the day before yesterday. Course S. West about 18 miles.

MONDAY 8th.
Before we rose the camp a general muster of all the guns in the Camp was taken and the number found to be 204 exclusive of ours. Our huntsmen had brought in a plenty of Buffaloes. We marched this day by a south Course about 7 miles.

TUESDAY 9th.
From the Big Belly village to the place I lost my spy glass the country was very hilly, from that to this place it was much more upon a level though not entirely so. The plains produce plenty of fine grass. In the course of this days journey we passed between two big hills on the top of which as far as the eye could discern Buffalo were seen in amazing number, we camped on the side of a small Creek running West into the lesser Missouri. The Indian hunted and killed many Buffaloes. Course South S. West & S.W. 9 miles. It blew a hurricane at night without rain. Many lodges were thrown down although well tied and picketed.

WEDNESDAY 10th.

We remained the greatest part of the day at this place to dry the meat and bury a woman that died here, and set off at 4 in the afternoon and pitched the tents by a small creek running west after having pursued our road S.W. by West for 5 miles. The Country was hilly but producing plenty of grass and numberless flowers of different Kinds.

THURSDAY 11th.

We passed through a range of hills of about 3 miles broad, on the top of every one was a heap of stones appearing as if burnt, part of the rocks had fallen down the hills. Leaving those hills we had a pretty level plain till we reach a small brook running N. West where we encamped, the lesser Missouri in Sight at about 4 miles on our right, by a course south west, we had advanced about 12 miles. On our way we saw a few Rattle Snakes but none of them very large; they are the first I saw in the Indian countries and none are to be found more northwards.

FRDAY 12th.

This day we passed through a pleasant plain and pitched the tents by a small brook 5 miles S.W. of our last encampment.

SATURDAY 13th.

We set off at 9 through hilly and barren Country, in crossing two small Creeks, and arrived at 12 on the bank of lesser Missouri. We crossed it and encamped on its border about 2 miles higher. The River is here about 3/4 of an acre in breadth from bank to bank but there is very little water running, the bed appearing dry in many places and is of sand and gravel. A few lizards scattered thinly along its banks. The rugged and barren aspect of the hills which are composed of Whitish Clay looking like rocks at a distance. The ground on which we stood was covered with a prickly heap of . . . so very thick that one does not know where to set ones feet, no grass at all. The whole forms a prospect far from pleasing. Our Course was for 12 miles S.S.W. A few days ago a child being sick I gave him a few drops of Turlington balsam which eased him immediately of his cholic. This cure gave me such a reputation of being a great physician that I am plagued to cure every distemper in the camp. A man came today to me desiring me to act the man mid wife to his wife.

SUNDAY 14th.

We remained the whole day here the Indians being busy with drying meat. I went a little distance up the River and saw a little Beaver work.

MONDAY 15th.

We crossed the river at three different times in the Course of this days journey when it happened to intersect the line of our course which was S.S.W. and encamped on its borders about 14 miles higher up. It had the same appearance in every respect as when we arrived at it. The Indians Killed a few Beavers of which I got two dressed by my men to show them how to do it.

TUESDAY 16th.

We remained here the whole day. The Indians tried to dance the Bull dance in imitation of the B. Belly's but did it very ill.

WEDNESDAY 17th.

It rained in the morning, at 11 before noon the weather clearing up, we set off following the river in a Course S.S. West about 9 miles. The bed and Banks in many places were solid Rock; there is very little water running. There is a few trees in the decline of the hill here.

THURSDAY 18th.

I went hunting with the Chief while the camp flitted, we killed one cow and returned to the river at 3 in the after noon where we found the people encamped 15 miles S.W. of our last encampment. The banks and bed of the river are rocks; the plains are a continual series of high rocky hills whose sides and tops are partly covered with the red pine and other wood such as poplar, Elm, Ash, and a kind of Maple.

FRIDAY 19th.

We stopped at an hour before sun set and encamped 5 miles higher up the river.

SATURDAY 20th.

Some one being sick we did not stir. Here the point of the River was pretty large and well stocked with wood, viz. Liard, Ash and a kind of shrub resembling the prickly Ash which bears a fruit of the size of a small pea, red and of a sourish taste but not disagreeable.

SUNDAY 21st.

The Camp rose at 8 in the morning and proceeded along the River for about 15 miles in a S.S. Westerly direction; the banks and bed of the river are of soil but muddy. I saw a beaver lying dead on the banks, here the river is fordable, without wetting ones feet in stepping over upon loose large stones, as we trotted almost the whole of this day's journey the unusual jolting of the Packages on the horses back occasioned the breaking of my thermometer. From this place we left the lesser Missouri on our left, its Course above this appears to be South to north, and stopping in the plains we encamped at one in the after noon on the side of a little river running into the lesser Missouri our course S.W. The Banks of L.M. [Lesser Missouri] in sight. We crossed two small Creeks in which there was no running water but many deep ponds in which there are Beavers. We saw this day plenty of Buffaloes.

We remained at this place 2 days. I have been very sick since some time, and so weak that it was difficult I could keep my saddle, the Indians on that occasion did not flit. I traded a few Beavers.

THURSDAY 25th.

We set off this morning at 10 following the little Creek on which we were encamped for 4 miles by a S.W. course and encamped. Wind S. E.

FRIDAY 26th.

We passed through a Range of hills whose tops and sides are covered with pine, and at the foot are many small creeks well wooded with Ash and Maple, there are plenty of different kinds of mint here which emit a very odoriferant smell. We crossed three small Creeks running north and N.W. into the Powder River whose banks we had in sight from the top of those hills. The wind was N.W. & very strong, a hurricane blew at night. The course we have pursued on a very barren soil for 22 Miles was West.

SATURDAY 27th.

We arrived at noon at the Powder River after 6 hours ride by course West by South for about 20 miles. The Powder River is here about 3/4 of an acre in breadth, its waters middling deep, but it appears to have risen lately as a quantity of leaves and wood was drifting on it. The points of the river are large with plenty of full grown trees, but no underwood, so that on our arrival we perceived diverse herds of Elk Deer through the woods. There are Beaver dams all along the river. Three of these animals have been felled by our Indians.

When we arrived here the plains on the western side of the river were covered with Buffaloes and the bottoms full of Elk and jumping deer & Bears which last are mostly yellow and very fierce. It is amazing how very barren the ground is between this and the lesser Missouri, nothing can hardly be seen but those *Corne de Raquettes*. Our horses were nearly starved. There is grass in the woods but none in the plains which by the by might with more propriety be called hills, for though there is very little wood it is impossible to find a level spot of one or two miles in extent except close to the River. The current in that river is very strong and the water so muddy as to be hardly drinkable. The Indians say it is always so, and that is the reason they call it Powder River, from the quantity of drifting fine sand set in motion by the coast wind which blinds people and dirties the water. There are very large sand shoals along the river for several acres breadth and length, the bed of the river is likewise sand, and its Course North East.

SUNDAY 28th.
We remained here the whole day to let the horses feed, the women were busily employed in dressing and drying the skins of those animals that were Killed Yesterday. I traded 3 Beavers and one Bear skin.

MONDAY 29th.
We rose the Camp late in the evening and pitched the tents about 4 miles higher up the river having followed for that short space a course S. W.

TUESDAY 30th.
Early this morning we set out; the body of the people followed the river for about 17 miles S.W. while I with the Chief and a few others went hunting. We wounded Cabrio, Buffalo, and the large horned animal, but did not Kill any, which made the Chief say that some one had thrown bad medicine on our guns and that if he could Know him he would surely die.

The Country is very hilly about the river, but it does not appear to be so much so towards the North. About two miles above the encampment a range of high hills begins on the west side of the River, and Continues North for about 20 miles, when it appears to finish. The Tongue River is close on the other side of it. There is a parting ridge between the two Rivers.

I ascended some very high hills on the side of which I found plenty of shells of the Comu amonys Species by some called snake shell, likewise a kind of shining stone lying bare at the surface of the ground having to all appearance been left there by the rain water washing away the surrounding earth, they are of different size and form, of a Clear water Color and reflect with as much force as a looking glass of its size. It is certainly those stones that have given the name of shining to that Mountain. The hills are high, rugged and barren mostly Rocks with beds of loose red gravel on their tops or near it which being washed down by the rain water give the hills a reddish appearance. On many hills a heap of calomid stone among which some time I find pumice stone.

When we left the encampment this morning we were stopped by a party of their soldiers who would not allow us to proceed, as they intended to have a general hunt, for fear that we should rise the Buffaloes, but upon promise being made by the Chief whom I accompanied that he would not hunt in the way of the Camp, and partly on my account we were suffered to go on. We were however under the necessity of gliding away unperceived to prevent Jealousy.

WEDNESDAY 31st.
We set out at 7 in the morning and proceeded up the River in a Southern course for about 13 miles and encamped about mid day; the weather being very warm and the wind from the south. I traded a few Beaver skins.

THURSDAY AUGUST 1st.
Rain and thunder storm prevented our stirring this day. The water rose about 6 inches in the river and is as thick as mud. The current very swift.

FRIDAY 2nd.
Last night some children playing at some distance from the Camp on the river, were fired at. The Camp was alarmed and watchers were set for the night but nothing appeared. It rained hard during most part of the night. We rose the Camp at one in the afternoon following the river for about 9 miles in a south

course. The hills of the River are at a less distance from one another than they were here to for, The bottoms or points of the river are not so large nor so well wooded and the grass entirely eat up by the Buffaloes and Elk.

SATURDAY 3rd.

We set out at sun rise and encamped at one in the afternoon having pursued a South Course with fare weather and a south east wind. We followed the River as usually; its bends are very short not exceeding two miles and many not one. The face of the Country indicates our approach to the large Mountains and to the heads of the River. A few jumping deer or chevreuils were Killed today. It has been very Cold these few nights.

SUNDAY 4th.

We did not rise the Camp till late in the evening. In the morning we ascended the hills of the River and saw the Rocky Mountains not at a very great distance with Spy Glass, its cliffs and hollows could be easily observed with the wood interspersed among the Rocks. We removed our camp about 4 miles higher up the River having pursued a S.E. Course.

MONDAY 5th.

We had a thick fog in the morning, the night was so Cold that one Blanket could not Keep us warm enough to sleep, so that I purchased two Buffalo Robes. About midday however it is generally very warm. We set off at 7 and continued our way for about 12 miles by a south course along the River and with a north West wind. We arrived at the forks of the Pine River which are assunder for about one mile, and encamped. The water in this River is clear and good issuing from the Mountains at a short distance from this, and is very cold, while that of the Powder River was so muddy that the Indians were under the necessity of making [holes] in the Beach and drink the water that gathered in them. We left this last mentioned river on our left where we went up the Pine River which is between 20 & 30 yards in breadth and runs over rocks. There is a rapid at every point and very little wood along its banks.

TUESDAY 6th.

We rose the Camp at 7 and proceeded upwards along the Pine River in a S. Western direction for 12 miles, having the Rocky Mountains ahead and in sight all day. The weather was foggy with a N.W. wind. An Indian shot another mans wife in the breast and wounded her dangerously. Jealousy was the occasion thereof. The Indian after inquire when I intend to depart. They appear to wish me to be off. I have 23 Beaver skins which they think a great deal, and more than we have occasion for. They thought that upon seeing the Rocky Mountains we would immediately depart as they cannot imagine what I intend to see in them. It is hard to make them understand by signs only, especially in this case for they do not want to understand.

WEDNESDAY 7th.
We set off at 6 and pitched the tents at 9 miles higher up the River having followed a South course. The Indians hunted and killed many Buffaloes and one cow came and took refuge among the horses where she were killed. At 5 in the evening we again flitted and encamped 5 miles higher up having pursued the same course as in the morning with a head wind.

THURSDAY 8th.
We marched 24 miles in a south West course along the Pine River. Many small Branches fall in it at a little distance from one another. A man and horse were wounded by a Bear but not dangerously. There is much fruit here about and many Bears. Wind S.E. We are here encamped at the foot of the mountain.

FRIDAY 9th.
The people went out hunting and returned with many skins to be dressed for tents. The weather is Cloudy and the wind south. Rapids succeed each other in the River here very fast and the current between is very swift running on a bed of Rocks.

SATURDAY 10th.
Some Indians arrived from hunting and brought 9 Beavers which I traded for Beads. Weather the same as yesterday.

SUNDAY 11th.
They are undetermined in what course to proceed from this place they have sent a party of young men along the Mountains Westerly and are to wait here

until they return. They often enquire with anxious expectation of our departure when I intend to leave them and to day they were more troublesome than usual. What I have seen of their lands hitherto has not given me the satisfaction I look for in Beavers. I told them that I would remain with them 20 or 30 days more. That I wished very much to see the River aux Roches Jaunes and the place they usually inhabit, otherwise that I would be unable to return and bring them their wants. They saw it was true, but to remove the objection of my not knowing their lands a few of them assembled and draughted on a dressed skin I believe a very good map of their Country and they showed me the place where at different season they were to be found. The only reason I think they have in wishing my departure, is their haste to get what goods I still have. Besides we not a little embarrass the people in whose tent we live. They pretend to be fond of us, treat us well and say they will shed tears when we leave them.

MONDAY 12th.

In the evening the young men that had been sent to reconnoiter returned and reported that there was plenty of Buffaloes & fruit on the Tongue and Smallhorn River, that they had seen a lately left encampment of their people who had not been at the Missouri (about 9 lodges) that they were gone across the Mountains that they had seen no appearance of their being enemies on that side. A Council ensued, and harangues were made to raise the Camp in the morning and proceed along to the River aux Roches Jaunes.

TUESDAY 13th.

We set off at half after 8 in the morning following a West Course along the Mountain, through Creeks and hills such as I never saw before, it being impossible to climb these hills with Loaded Horses we were obliged to go round them about the middle of their height from whence we were in imminent danger of rolling down being so steep that one side of the horses load rubbed against the side of the hill. One false step of the horse would certainly have been fatal to himself and rider. The wind was S. E. in the morning and north W. in the evening and the weather sultry. We encamped at 12 on the banks of a small branch of the Tongue River, whose water was very clear and cold as Ice. The people Killed two Bears to day. I traded a few Bears. I saw a few crows today which are the only birds I have seen since I left the Missouri except a few wood Peckers.

WEDNESDAY 14th.

It rained part of the morning, as soon as the rain ceased we set off when it began again and continued raining until we reached another branch of the Tongue River, where we encamped. We went close along the mountain all the way for about 10 miles by a West Course crossing many small Creeks all running into the Tongue River, most of them were dry but thickly wooded with the Saule blanc; there was no Beaver work. I saw a few Cranes.

THURSDAY 15th.

Fine clear weather. I traded 8 Beavers and purchased a horse for which I paid a gun 200 balls, one flannel Robe, one shirt, one half axe, one battle do, one bow iron, one comb, one But Knife, one small do, 2 Wampam hair pipes, one . . . 2 axes, one Wampum shell, 40 B. Blue Beads, 2 Mass Barley Corn do and one fm W.S. Red Stroud. We left this place at 11 before noon and proceeded 9 miles in a North West Course and encamped on another branch of the Tongue River. Wind N.W. fine warm weather. The Indians Killed Buffaloes and a few Bears, the latter they hunt for pleasure only as they do not eat the flesh but in case of absolute necessity. Perhaps the whole nation is employed about a bear, whom they have caused to take refuge in a thicket, there they plague him a long while and then Kill him, he is seldom strip of his skin.

FRIDAY 16th.

I purchased a saddle and bridle for the horse I purchased yesterday for which I paid 40 shots Powder Being short of Balls. I gave 20 pounds Powder only for a Beaver 1 Knife, I sell 2 Beavers 10 String Blue Beads, 1 Beaver & so on. We proceeded along the mountain as usual by a N.W. Course about 15 miles, crossed 3 small Creeks emptying in the Tongue River where we arrived at one in the afternoon, we forded it and encamped on the north side, N. & N.E. is a small Mountain lying between this river and the large Horn River, they call it the Wolf Teeth. (Sela is in the Rocky Mountain language and Seja in the Big Belly's.) Fine weather wind N.W.

SATURDAY 17th.

The Indians having hunted yesterday we did not rise the Camp but remained here all day. There were many Bears here about, who are attracted by the quantity of Choak Cherries and other fruit there is here. The Woods along the Rivers are as thickly covered with Bears Dung as a Barn door is of that of the Cattle, large Cherry trees are broken down by them in Great number. The Indians Kill one or two almost every day. The Tongue River here is small being only about 20 feet broad with two feet water in the deepest part of the rapids. It receives many additional small stream in its way to the River Roches Jaunes. The points of the River are pretty large and well stocked with wood viz . . . & maple.

SUNDAY 18th.

At 7 o'clock we left our encampment and proceeded Northward; at noon we stopped on a branch of the small Horn River & the greatest part of the Indians went on to the small Horn River to hunt. At half past two in the afternoon we set off again and crossing the River we encamped on its Borders where we found the hunting party with their horses loaded with fresh meat. We travelled about 15 miles this day and are farther from the mountain than yesterday though still close to it.

MONDAY 19th.

Since we are close to the mountain many women have deserted with their lovers to their fine tents that are across the mountain, there are no Cattle in the mountain nor on the other side, so that they are lothe to go that way, while the desertion of their wives strongly Call them there. Harangues were twice made to rise the Camp, and counter order were given before the tents were thrown down. The reason of this is that the wife of the Spotted Crow who regulates our movements has deserted, he is for going one way while the Chief of the other bands are for following our old course. Horses have been Killed and women wounded since I am with them on the score of jealousy. Today a snake Indian shot his wife dead but it seems not without reason for it is said it was the third time he found her and the Gallant together. The Small Horn river runs East from the Mountain to this place here it makes a bend N by East and passing round of the wolf teeth it falls into the large Horn river. The bed of the River here is Rocks a continual rapid, the water clear and cold as Ice, the ground barren and the banks of the river thinly wooded with same Kind of wood as heretofore. I traded 6 Beavers.

TUESDAY 20th.

We flitted and encamped 3 miles higher up the River on a beautiful spot where there was plenty of fine grass for the horses, our Course West. I traded 3 Beavers.

WEDNESDAY 21st.

I made a present of a few articles to the Chief and a few other Considered Persons. We remained here all day. There is plenty of ash here. There were very few persons in the Camp that were not employed in making themselves horse whip handles with that wood; it was with that design they came here, as that wood is seldom found elsewhere. I saw some Beavers work on that River.

THURSDAY 22nd.

Water froze the thickness of paper last night in horse tracks. I was called to a Council in the Chiefs Brothers tent Lodge, where the Spotted Crow resigned his employment of regulating our marches, an other old man took the office upon himself and told me that he intended to pursue their old course to the River aux Roches Jaunes. I traded 8 Beavers with the Snake Indians in whose possession I saw a Kettle or Pot hewn out of a solid stone, it was about 11/ inch thick & contained about 6 or 8 quarts; it had been made with no other instrument but a piece of Iron.

FRIDAY 23rd.

We rose the Camp at 11 in the forenoon and followed a N.E. Course for one mile N.W. 6 de, & encamped on a branch of the . . . River, where there is a Beaver Dam and other work occasionally found. I traded 4 Beavers. Wind S.E. the only roads practicable to Cross the mountain are at the heads of this and the Tongue River.

SATURDAY 24th.

This morning we were alarmed by the report that three Indians had been seen on the first hill of the mountain and that three Buffaloes were in motion and that two shots had been heard towards the large Horn River. Thirty men saddled their horses and immediately went off to see what was the matter while all the other Kept in readiness to follow if necessary. In a few hours some came back and told us that they had seen 35 on foot walking on the banks of one of the branches of the Large Horn River. In less time than the Courier Could well tell his news no one remained in the Camp, but a few old men and women, all the rest scampered off in pursuit. I went along with them we did not all Set off together nor could we all Keep together as some horses were slower than others but the foremost stopped galloping on a hill, and continued on with a small trot as people came up. They did the dance when the Chief arrived, he and his band or part of it galloped twice before the main body of the people who still continued their trot intersecting the line of their course while one of his friends I suppose his aide de Camp harangued. They were all dressed in their best Cloths. Many of them were followed by their wives who carried their arms, and who were to deliver them at the time of Battle. There were likewise many children, but who could Keep their saddles. Ahead of us were some young men on different hills making signs with their Robes which way we were to go. As soon as all the Chiefs were come up and had made their harangue every one set off the way he liked best and pursued according to his own judgement. The Country is very hilly and full of large Creeks whose banks are Rocks so that the pursued had the advantage of being able to get into places where it was impossible to go with horses & hide themselves. All escaped but two of the foremost who being scouts of the party had advanced nearer to us than the others and had not discovered us, they were surrounded after a long race but Killed and scalped in a twinkling. When I arrived at the dead bodies they had taken but his scalp and the fingers of his right hand with which the outor was off. They borrowed my hanger with which they cut off his left hand and returned it the knife to me bloody as a mark of honor and desired me throw it at him. Men women and children were thronging to see the dead Bodies and taste the Blood. Everyone was desirous of stabbing the bodies to show what he would have done had he met them alive and insulted & frothed at them in the worst language they could give. In a short time the remains of a human body was hardly distinguishable. Every young man had a piece of flesh tied to his gun or lance with which he rode off to the Camp sing-ing and exultingly showing it to every young woman in his way, some women had whole limb dangling from their saddles. The sight made me Shudder with horror at such Cruelties and I returned home in quite a different frame from that in which I left it.

SUNDAY 25th.
The Scalp dance was danced all night and the scalps carried in procession through the day.

MONDAY 26th.
It rained in the morning as it did yesterday, at noon the Weather Clearing we set off Course S.W. wind S.E. fine weather. We encamped in the mountain 9 miles distant from our last encampment by a small Creek in which there was little running water, but an amazing number of Beaver Dams. I counted 6 in about 2 points of the River but most of them appeared to be old Dams. The young men paraded all day with the scalps tied to their horses bridles singing and keeping time with the Drum and Sheskequois or Rattle.

TUESDAY 27th.
We remained here all day, 10 Young Men were sent to observe the motions of those who were routed lately, they are afraid of being attacked having seen the road of a numerous body of people on the large Horn River. In the evening news came that the Buffaloes were in motion on the Large Horn River, and harangues were made to guard the Camp.

WEDNESDAY 28th.
Two hours before day light, all the Indians horses were saddled at their doors, they put all their young children on horse back & tied to the saddles, then they slept the remainder of the night. They likewise loaded some horses with the most valuable part of their property while they in the expectation of being attacked sat in the tents their arms ready & their horses saddled at the door. At broad day light nothing appearing they took in their children and unloaded their horses. At 9 in the morning 4 young men arrived and reported that they had seen nothing of the enemy, that there were parties of Buffaloes between the Large Horn and the River aux Roches Jaunes.

THURSDAY 29th.
We rose the Camp this morning and marched a Course West by North. The Indians hunted and saw Strange Indians. There was a Continual harangue by different Chiefs the whole night which with the singing and dancing of the scalp

prevented any Sleep being had. We pitched the tents on a small creek running into the large Horn River distant about 20 miles from our last encampment.

FRIDAY 30th.
We left the place and encamped on the Large Horn River close to the foot of the mountain and of very high Rocks. Course West about 5 miles.

SATURDAY 31st.
We remained at this place the whole day. Some young one who had been en découverte returned from a deserted camp of about 30 Lodges where they found Chief Coats N.B. strewed Wampoon shells and other articles, which it seems had been left by the people inhabiting those tents upon some panic. This is what these Indians say but it is my opinion that those goods are rather an offering to the supreme being which those Indians often make and leave in tree well wrapped up, and which our young men found. This River is broad deep and clear water strong current, bed stone and gravel about 1/2 mile above this encampment, the River runs between 2 big Rocks & loses 2/3 of its breadth but gains proportionally in depth. There is no beach at the foot of the Rocks, they are but perpendicular down to the water. It is awful to behold and makes one giddy to look down upon the river from the top of those Rocks. The River appears quite narrow and runs with great rapidity immediately under our feet, so that I did not dare to look down but when I could find a stone behind which I could keep & looking over it to see the foaming water without danger of falling in. This river does not take its rise in this mountain, it passes through the mountains and takes its water in the next range. There is a fall in this River 30 or 40 miles above this where presides a Manitoin or Devil. These Indians say it is a Man Wolf who lives in the fall and rises out of it to devour any person or beast that go to near. They say it is impossible to Kill him for he is ball proof. I measured a Ram's horn which I found when walking along the River, it was 5 spans in length and was very weighty, it seems to me that the animal who carried it died of old age for the small end of the horn was much worn and broke into small splinters, which was not the case in any of the animals I saw Killed, nor were their horns of that size neither.

The Mountain is here a solid Rock in most places bare and naked, in other places Clothed with a few Red Pine. The sides of some Coulé are as smooth and perpendicular as any wall, and of an amazing height; and in places there are holes in those perpendicular Rocks resembling much those niches in which statues are placed. Others like church doors & vaults, the tout ensemble is grand and striking. Beautiful prospects are to be had from some parts of those Rocks, but the higher places are inaccessible. The Large Horn River is seen winding through a level plain of about 3 miles breadth for a great distance almost to its conflux with the River aux Roches Jaunes.

SUNDAY, SEPTEMBER 1st.
We Left this place and pitched our tents about 3 miles lower down where we remained two days, while we were here a Snake Indian arrived, he had been absent since the Spring and had seen part of his nation who traded with the Spaniards, he brought a Spanish Bridle and Battle ax, a large thick blanket, striped white and black and a few other articles, such as Beads, etc. A Missouri Big Belly fished here and caught 14 Cat fish in a very short time.

We had much dancing at this place still for the scalps. There are Islands in the River here but most of them are heaps of sand. The Wooded points of the River do not join the open plain is seen between them but there is plenty of wood in some places. The leaves begin to fall.

WEDNESDAY 4th.
We left the encampment and proceeded N.W. by North about 15 miles and pitched the tents on a Small Creek running into the Large Horn River. Where we left the River we had a level plain for about 4 or 5 miles when the Country became hilly and barren.

THURSDAY 5th.
We Kept the same Course as yesterday and encamped on a most small Creek running as the former about the same nature.

FRIDAY 6th.
We rose the Camp early and at 11 before noon arrived at Mampoa or Shot stone River, from whence the Indians went out to hunt, there being plenty of Buffaloes on the road to this place, the mountains were as follows. The mountain along which we travelled from the Pine River lay S. E. another called

Amanchabé Clije south, the Boa [or Bod] Mountain S.W. but appeared faintly on account of a thick fog that covered it.

SATURDAY 7th.

We remained all day here, the Indian women being very busy to dry tongues and the best part of the meat and dressing skins for a great feast they are preparing while their war exploits are recapitulated.

SUNDAY 8th.

I set off early this morning with two Indians to visit the River aux Roches Jaunes and the adjacent part. I intended to return from this place as the Indians will take a very round about road to go there. We were not half ways, when we fell in with Buffalos, my guides were so bent upon hunting that they did not guide me where I wanted, and we returned at night to the tents with meat, but with rain as it rained from noon till night. The Indians showed me a mountain lying North West which they told me was in direct line to the Missouri falls and not far from it. We passed through two new raised Camps of strange Indians at the door of the largest tent were 7 heaps of sticks each containing 10 sticks denoting the number of lodges in the Camp, to have been 70.

MONDAY 9th.

I purchased a horse we had information that four strangers had been seen who likewise saw our people & hid themselves. At night a young man arrived who saw and conversed (I cannot say he spoke for the whole conversation was carried on by signs they not understanding one another language) with a fort de prairie Big Belly, they wanted to bring each other to their respective Camps but both were afraid and neither of them dared to go to the other Camp. The B.B. are encamped on the large Horn River behind the mountain and are come on peaceable terms they are 275 or 300 Lodges.

TUESDAY 10th.

We rose the Camp at 9 and took a N. West Course to the River aux Roches Jaunes where we arrived at two in the afternoon distant 16 miles we forded into a large Island in which we encamped. This is a fine large River in which there is a strong current, but the Indians say there are no falls. Fordable places are not easily found although I believe the water to be at its lowest. The bottoms are large and well wooded.

WEDNESDAY 11th.

5 Big Bellys arrived and came into our lodge being the Chief Lodge. They brought words of peace from their nation and say they came to trade horses. They were well received by the Indians and presents of different articles were made them. They told me they had traded last winter with Mr. Donald whom they made Known to me as crooked arm. I went round the Island in which we are encamped, it is about 5 miles in circumference and thickly wooded in some places all along the North Side of the Island. The Beaver has cut down about 50 feet of the wood. 9 Lodges of the people that were left in the Spring was joined in they are 15 tents at present, they encamped on the opposite side of the River.

THURSDAY 12th.

I traded six large Beavers from the Snake Indians. We crossed from the Island to the West side of the River & proceeded upward for about 9 miles south West and encamped in a point where they usually make their fall medicine.

FRIDAY 13th.

I bought a Horn Bow & a few Arrows a Saddle & pichimom, part of a tent and a few of those blue Glass Beads they have from the Spaniards, and on which they set such value that a horse is given for 100 grains.

SATURDAY 14th.

Having now full filled the instructions I received from Mr. Chaboillez, which were to examine the lands of the Crow Indians and see if there is Beaver as was reported, and I to invite them to hunt it, I now prepared to depart, I assembled the Chiefs in Council, and after having smoked a few pipes, I informed them that I was setting off, that I was well pleased with them and their behavior towards me, and that I would return to them next fall. I desired them to kill Beavers and Bears all winter for that I would come and trade with them and bring them their wants. I added many reasons to show them that it was their interest to hunt Beavers, and then proceeded to settle the manners of Knowing one another next fall, and how I am to find them which is as follows. Upon my arrival at the Island if I do not find them I am to go to the Mountain called Amanchabé Chije & then light 4 drift fires on 4 successive days, and they will Come to us (for it is very high and the fire can be seen at a great distance) in number 4 & not more, if more than four come to us we are to act upon the defensive for it will be other Indians. If we light less than 3 fires they will not come to us but think it is enemies. They told me that in winter they were always to be found at a Park by the foot of the Mountain a few miles from this or there abouts. In the spring and fall they are upon this River and in summer upon the Tongue and Horses River.

I have 122 Beavers 4 Bears and two otters which I traded not so much for their value (for they are all summer skins) as to show them that I set some value on the Beavers and our property. The presents I made them I thought were sufficient to gain their good will in which I think I succeeded. I never gave them any thing without finding means to let them know it was not for nothing. Had more been given they would have thought that goods were so common among us than to set no value upon them, for Indians that have seen few White men will be more thankful for a few articles given them than for great many, as they think that little or no value is attached to what is so liberally given. It was therefore I purchased their Bears and likewise as a proof that there is Beaver in those parts, besides it saved to distribute the good I had into the most deserving hands, that is the less lazy.

We departed about noon. 2 Chiefs accompanied us about 8 miles, we stopped and smoked a parting pipe, they embarrassed us, we shook hands & parted they followed us about one mile, at a distance gradually lessening their steps till we were almost out of sight and Crying or pretending to Cry they then turned their backs and went home. At parting they promised that none of their young men would follow us, they took heaven and earth to witness to attest their sincerity in what they had told us, and that they had opened their ears to my words and would do as I desired them, they made me swear by the same that I would return and that I told them no false words (and certainly I had no intention of breaking my oath nor have I still. If I do not keep them my word it certainly is not my fault).

Our course was N.E. 20 miles, a little before sun set we were overtaken by a storm which forced us into a point of the River where we encamped & passed the night during which our horses were frightened & it was with difficulty we could get them together again. We Kept watch by night.

SUNDAY 15th.

We followed a N.E. course and crossed the River Roches Jaunes at 9 and proceeded along the South side, at 10 we crossed Manpoa River at its entrance into River Roches Jaunes, Manpoa or the Shot Storm River is about 10 feet in breadth and with very little water it take its waters in Amanabe Chief at a short distance there is wood along its Banks, especially close to the mountain and Beaver on the east side of this River. Close to its discharge in the River Roches Jaunes is a Whitish perpendicular Rock on which is painted with Red earth a battle between three persons on horseback and 3 on foot. At 2 in the afternoon we arrived at a high hill on the side of the river called by the Natives Erpian Macolié where we stopped to refresh our horses & killed one Cow. An hour before sun set we set off again and encamped after dark making no fire for fear of being discovered by horse thieves or enemies. From Manpoa to this place our Course was east. Buffaloes and Elk we found in great plenty. Wind S.W.

MONDAY 16th.

It froze hard last night North, Weather Cloudy N.E. 9 miles and stopped to Cook victuals for the day as we make no fire at night. Elk and Buffaloes in the greatest plenty. It rained till 3 in the afternoon, when weather clearing we set

off and encamped at the Rocks of the large Horn River where we arrived at 8 in the evening.

TUESDAY 17th.
We crossed the river early in the morning, its points here are large & beautiful well stocked with wood, we passed through a most abominable Country and often despaired of being able to get clear of this place encountering Rocks which it was impossible to ascend or to go round so we were obliged often to go back on other road which presented us with the same difficulties. At last we ascended the hill but being on the top did not offer a more pleasing prospect, we were often obliged to unload the horses and carry baggage ourselves and the horses being light we made jump over . . . in the Rock and climb precipices, but were near losing them. At last at 3 in the afternoon we passed the whole of that bad road and arrived at the Border of Rocks where we could see a fine level country before us but the sun was set before we could find a practable road to come down to it, which we effected not without unloading the horses and carrying down their loads part of the way, while: the horses slided down upon their rumps about 25 yards. We broke some of our saddles, and arrived in the plain just as the day was setting and encamped further on by the side of the River. It is probable that had we had a guide with us we could have avoided those Rocks, while our ignorance of the Road made us enter into & once engaged among the difficulty was as great to return as to proceed. We Kept no regular course, but went on as we could to all points of the compass in order to extricate ourselves. We Killed one Elk.

WEDNESDAY 18th.
This morning we saw the points of wood where we encamped last night 9 miles south of us from which we were parted by the River on one side and the Rocks on the other. I heard the noise of the fall or Great Rapids yesterday, but now at too great a distance from the River and too busily engaged to go and see it. It froze hard last night, we left our encampment later our horses were tired, but after having set out did not stop till after sun set having followed for 22 miles a north East course wind South West. Fine weather plenty Elk and Buffaloes.

THURSDAY 19th.
Cold and Cloudy and followed the same course as last day for 22 miles stopped at 2 in the afternoon. and Killed a stag which was very poor being its Rutting Season. We resumed our course to the N. East for 8 miles and encamped for the night.

FRIDAY 20th.
We set this day early out, ascended the hills which are rugged and barren proceeding N.E. for 36 miles. Killed one large . . , fine weather with a N.E. wind.

SATURDAY 21st.
We had a very bad road. Came down to the River to see if we could find a better passage but it was impossible, the River striking the Rock at every bend and ascended the hill again and with difficulty made our way over Rocks. After sun set we encamped on the River a la Langue. Killed 2 Elks which were very fat. Course East for 18 miles wind N. E.

SUNDAY 22nd.
We crossed the River a la Langue and passed over a plain of about 9 miles in breadth where we came again to Rocks and precipices without number over which we jogged on without stopping till 2 hours before sun set when we encamped on the side of the River close to a Rapid. There is little or no wood here along the River except a few Liards scattered here and there and no grass at all. Course N.E. for about 18 miles. Wind S.W.

MONDAY 23rd.
We had a pretty level plain the whole of the day 12 miles West and 24 miles N. E. At 10 we crossed the Powder River, it has no wood on its bank here and is much shallower than when we crossed it going; its water is the same being still muddy, we encamped at night by a small Creek, having been unable to find grass for our horses throughout the day we were obliged to cut down three Liards and let the horses feed on the bark.

TUESDAY 24th.
Set off early, at 9 in the morning we found a place where there was grass where we stopped and let our horses eat. At three in the afternoon we saddled our

horses and went on until we encamped after sunset having followed an Eastern Course for 13 miles. Wind S.W. fine weather. It is 4 nights since it froze.

WEDNESDAY 25th.
We passed through a very uneven country, but there being no Rocks we had no very great difficulties and encamped at night in a very large point of wood in which there was plenty of Deer. Watched all night having seen something like a man Creeping on the beach. We had made this day 37 miles by a North Course. The fire is in the plains from which the wind brought columns of thick smoke in abundance so that we could barely see. We shoed our horses with raw deer hide as their hoofs are worn out to the flesh with continual walking since last Spring setting their feet on loose stones lames them & sometimes makes them bleed.

THURSDAY 26th.
What we saw last night and mistook for a man was a Bear whose tracks we found this morning. We set out at 8 and the plain being even we went on at a great rate, at 2 in the afternoon we stopped to Kill a cow, our provision being out, at three we set off again and met on our road a female bear eating. We killed her and took the skin it being good. At five we stopped for the night.

Here the River is divided into many channels forming so many islands, the banks and islands are thickly covered with woods, chiefly Liard, oak and maple. Our course was North which we followed for 39 miles having the wind ahead, which brought us thick smoke in abundance. We saw this day plenty Elk and Buffaloes.

FRIDAY 27th.
We crossed a plain of about 6 miles and arrived at a bend of the River where it was impossible to continue on the hill so that we were fain to descend to the River and Beach. We bemired 3 of our horses and got them out but with great difficulty. At one we stopped to let the horses eat. The wind was south and we had no appearance of smoke but the weather threatened rain. We encamped at sun set after having followed a North course for 24 miles and found plenty of grass.

SATURDAY 28th.

This whole day we travelled through a level country having fine weather. We made 30 miles in a Northerly direction and passed 3 Indian encampment of this summer, whom I suppose must have been occupied by warriors for they had no tents.

SUNDAY 29th.

We passed through a most beautiful and pleasant country, the river being well wooded. We found here more fine grass than in any place since I left the Missouri and of course the greatest number of Buffaloes. The wind was N.W. and the weather Cloudy and Cold. Having made 30 miles by a N.N.E. Course we encamped on a small creek round which the river passed.

MONDAY 30th.

We ascended the hill which produces plenty of fine grass; about 6 miles further we saw the forks of the River aux Roches Jaunes and the Missouri Course N.E. 27 miles and descended to the Missouri having but a bend. We had followed the River for 7 miles when we heard the report of a gun twice, and the voice of a woman as crying. We stopped and sent Morrison en decouverté and I and Souci remained to watch the horses and property. Morrison returned in about 2 hours and reported that what we had taken for a Woman's voice was that of a young Cub, and as to the gun we supposed it proceeded from trees thrown down by the wind, as it blew very hard, and the Buffaloes, Bears and Elk were very quiet in the wood and plain, so that there was no appearance of being any human Creature there about. We went on & ascended the hills to cut a large bend of the River following an east course for 11 miles and encamped in a large point of Elm trees for the night. The Wind was North West and very strong tearing down trees by their roots every moment.

TUESDAY OCTOBER 1st.

Weather Cloudy raining now and then, Wind N.W. very cold Course North 12 miles. Passing through a Coulé yesterday I found a lodge made in the form of those of the Mandans & Big Bellys (I suppose made by them) surrounded by a small Fort. The Lodge appears to have been made 3 or 4 years ago but was inhabited last winter. Outside of the fort was a Kind of Stable in which they kept their horses. There was plenty of Buffaloes heads in the Fort some of them painted red.

WEDNESDAY 2nd.
Strong N.W. wind Cold and Cloudy-Course N.E. 26 miles Killed a Cow. Country even plenty of grass.

THURSDAY 3rd.
Set off at 7 through a very hilly and bad country N.E. 20 miles east 15 and encamped on the River it rained part of the day Wind north West very Cold.

FRIDAY 4th.
It rained and was bad weather all night, at break of the day it began to snow and continued snowing very hard till 2 in the afternoon. Strong N.W. wind. We sought our horses all day without being able to find them till after sun set; the bad weather having drawn them in the woods.

SATURDAY 5th.
Set off early, fine weather Course S.E. by E. 26 miles plenty of Buffaloes on both sides of the River. Killed Cow.

SUNDAY 6th.
All the small Creeks and Ponds were frozen over this morning Course S. E. by S. 20 miles South. Passed through a thick wood of about 4 miles.

MONDAY 7th.
East 2 miles south 11 we arrived at the lesser Missouri which we crossed S.E. 3 miles saw many Bears and Skunks.

TUESDAY 8th.
Ascended the hills, Plains even 39 miles S.S.E. fine warm weather wind S.W.

WEDNESDAY 9th.
Proceeded on the hills through a fine Country course E. by S. 12 miles. South 2 miles and arrived at the Big Bellys who were encamped about 3 miles above their village. I found here a letter of Mr. Charles McKenzie to me.

THURSDAY 10th.

I remained here all day to refresh the horses before I proceed to the Assiniboines River. Among other news the Indians tell me that there are 14 American Crafts below who are ascending to this place. The Sioux have Killed 8 White men last spring upon St. Peters River & 3 Big Bellys here.

FRIDAY 11th.

I intended crossing over today but was prevented by the strength of the wind which blew all day with amazing violence from the North West. I got a few pair of shoes made and Corn pounded for provision, news came that the Sioux were seen encamped at a short distance below. Expecting to be attacked they [the Big Bellies] were under arms all night.

SATURDAY 12th.

About noon the weather being calm & warm we crossed the River; the horses swam the whole bredth of the River & were nearly spent. We met with 3 Assiniboines and their wives on the North side of the River who were going to the Big Bellys to trade. We went slowly on till sun set when we encamped on the side of a small lake in the Plains which are burning to the West. Course North.

SUNDAY 13th.

Fine weather, wind N.W. plenty of Buffaloes just arriving in the plain. Few being on all sides. The Buffaloes were in motion so that we could not get near enough to get a shot at them, & our horses so tired & fatigued that I did not chuse to run them. We crossed the fire at sun set and encamped by the side of a small lake whose borders had escaped the general Conflagration.

MONDAY 14th.

We watched our horses all that night for fear of Asssiniboines, of whom we had seen the tracks, in the evening; set off before sun rise and arrived at 10 in the forenoon at the River la Sourie where we stopped for the remainder of the day. The grass on either side of the river here is not burnt but the fire appears on both sides at a distance, West and north. Soon in the evening the Buffaloes were in motion on the North side of the River which made us fear for our horses.

TUESDAY 15th.

After dark last night we left our encampment and marched two and a half hours by star light, when Clouds gathering so as to obscure our sight of the stars and of course being unable to regulate our course we stopped in a Creek and there passed the night being free of anxiety.

In the morning we proceeded weather Cold and Cloudy wind N. W. We stopped for the Night on the deep River, which does not draw the name of a Riper, being a hallow in the plain in which there are small deep ponds communicating with each other in the spring and rainy seasons only, nor is there a single twig to be found about. At sun set it began to rain and continued so all night. We covered the property with part of a tent we had, and we passed the whole night Shivering by a small fire made of cow dung (which we had taken care to gather before the rain began) with the assistance of our saddle on our back, by the way of Cloaks.

Wednesday 16th. It snowed rained and hailed the whole day. Wind N.W. and amazing strong. We arrived after dark at the woods of one of the Elk Head Rivers, wet to the skin and quite benumbed with Cold.

Thursday 17th. Weather Cloudy and wind N.W. and very Cold so we were fain to stop, make a fire and warm ourselves, especially as we are not over and above well dressed to Keep off the Cold. We wrapped ourselves in Buffalo Robes and proceeded to the Grand Coulé and encamped on the very same spot where we had the quarrel last spring with the Assiniboines.

Friday 18th. In the morning we met with a few Assiniboines coming from the Fort, we stopped and smoked a pipe with them. They told us that Mount a la Bosse had been evacuated and that Mr. Falcon was building a house to winter in, about half ways between that and R. qu'il appelle Fort. We arrived at Mount a la Bosse Fort, where I found Mr. Charles McKenzie and 3 men taking care of the remaining property.

I remained here one day and then went to see Mr. Falcon at the Grand Bois about 15 miles above this, returned the next day and then sat out for River la Sourie Fort where I arrived the 22 October.

So ends my journal of my Journey to the Rocky Mountains.

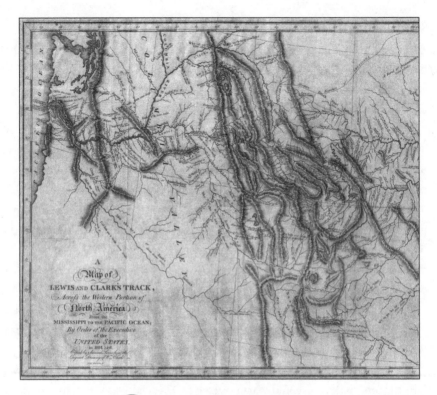

CHAPTER 3

TEN DAYS IN THE MOUNTAINS

with the Lewis and Clark Expedition

[Clark, October 13, 1804]

13th of October Saturday 1804 Newmon Confined for Mutinous expressions, proceeded on passed a Camp of Sioux on the S. S. those people did not Speak to us. passed a Creek on the S. S. 18 miles above the Ricaras I call Stone Idol Creek, this Creek heads in a Small lake at no great distance, near which there is a Stone to which the Indians asscribe great virtue &. &c. at 21 Miles passed a Creek 15 yds wide on the L. S. I call Pocasse, we observed great quantites of grapes, a fine

Breez from S E Camped on the L. S. Some rain thus evening, we formed a Court Martial of 7 of our party to Try Newmon, they Senteenced him 75 Lashes and banishment from the party—The river narrow current jentle & wood plenty on the Bottoms the up land is as usial Open divircified plains, generally rich & leavel.

[Clark, October 13, 1804]
13th of October Satturday 1804 one man J. Newmon Confined for mutinous expression Set out early proceeded on, passd. a Camp of Seauex on the S. S. those people only viewed us & did not Speak one word—The visiters of last evening all except one returned which is the Brother of the Chief we have on board passed (1) a Creek on the S. S. 13 yds. at 18 me. above the Town heading in Some Ponds a Short Diste. to the N. E we call Stone Idol C. (well to observe here that the Yankton or R Jacque heads at about 2 Days March of this place Easterly, the R de Seauex one Day further, the Chien a branch of R. Rouche Still beyond, and the River St. Peters 4 Days March from this place on the Same direction Informtn. of the Rickores). passed 2 large willow (2) & Sand Islands above the mouth of the last Creek—at 21 miles above the Village passed a (3) Creek about 15 yards wide on the L. S. we Call after 2d Chief Pocasse (or Hay) nearly opposit this creek a fiew miles from the river on the S. S. 2 Stones resembling humane persons & one resembling a Dog is Situated in the open Prarie, to those Stone the Rickores pay Great reverance make offerings whenever they pass (Infomtn. of the Chief & Intepeter) those people have a Curious Tradition of those Stones, one was a man in Love, one a Girl whose parents would not let marry, the Dog went to mourn with them all turned to Stone gradually, Commenceing at the feet. Those people fed on grapes untill they turned, & the woman has a bunch of grapes yet in her hand on the river near the place those are Said to be Situated, we obsd. a greater quantity of fine grapes than I ever Saw at one place.

The river about the Island on which the lower Rickores Village is Situated is narrow and Conts. a great propotion of Timber than below, the bottoms on both Sides is Covered with timber the up lands naked the Current jentle and Sand bars Confined to the points Generally.

We proceeded on under a fine Breeze from the S.E. and Camped late at the upper part of Some wood on the Starboard Side, Cold & Some rain this evening. we Sent out hunters Killed one Deer.

We Tried the Prisoner Newman last night by 9 of his Peers they did "Centence him 75 Lashes & Disbanded the party."

[Lewis and Clark, October 13, 1804]

Orders 13th of October 1804 A court Martial to Consist of nine members will set to day at 12 oClock for the trial of John Newman now under Confinement. Capt. Clark will attend to the forms & rules of a president without giveing his opinion

Detail for the Court Martial
Sert. John Ordaway
Sergeant Pat. Gass
Jo. Shields
H. Hall
Jo. Collins
Wm. Werner
Wm. Bratten
Jo. Shannon
Silas Goodrich
Meriwether Lewis
Capt. 1st U S. Regt. Infty.

Win Clark Capt
or E. N W D

In conformity to the above order the Court martial convened this day for the trial of John Newman, charged with "having uttered repeated expressions of a highly criminal and mutinous nature; the same having a tendency not only to distroy every principle of military discipline, but also to alienate the affections of the individuals composing this Detachment to their officers, and disaffect them to the service for which they have been so sacredly and solemnly engaged."—The Prisonar plead not guilty to the charge exhibited against him. The court after having duly considered the evidence aduced, as well as the defense of the said prisonor, are unanimously of opinion that the prisonar John Newman is guilty of every part of the charge exhibited against him, and do sentence him agreeably to the rules and articles of war, to receive seventy five lashes on his bear back, and to be henceforth discarded from the perminent party engaged for North Western discovery; two thirds of the Court concurring in the sum and nature of the punishment awarded. The commanding officers approve and confirm the sentence of the court, and direct the punishment take place tomorrow between the hours of one and two P.M.—The commanding officers further direct that John Newman in future be attatched to the mess and crew of the red Perogue as a labouring hand on board the same, and that he be deprived of his arms and accoutrements, and not be permited the honor of mounting guard untill further orders; the commanding officers further direct that in lieu of the guard duty from which Newman has been exempted by virtue of this order, that he shall be exposed to such drudgeries as they may think proper to direct from time to time with a view to the general relief of the detachment.

[Clark, October 14, 1804]
14th of October Sunday 1804 Some rain last night we Set out in the rain which continued all day passed a Creek on the L. S. Piaheto 15 yds Wide, halted on a Sand bar and had the punishmt inflicted on Newmon, which caused the indian Chieif to cry untill the thing was explained to him. Camped opposit an antient fortification which is on the L. S., when I explained to the Chief the Cause of whipping N—he observed that examples were necessary & that

he himself had made them by Death, but his nation never whiped even from their bearth.

[Clark, October 14, 1804]

14th of October Sunday 1804. Some rain last night all wet & Cold, we Set early the rain contind all Day at _____ miles we passed a Creek in the L. S. 15 yards wide this Creek we Call after the 3rd Chief Piaheto (or Eagles feather). At 1 oClock we halted on a Sand bar & after Dinner executed the Sentence of the Court Martial So far as giveing the Corporal punishment, & proceeded on a fiew miles. The wind a head from N. E. Camped in a Cove of the bank on the S. S. imediately opposit our Camp. On the L. Side I observe an antient fortification the walls of which appear to be 8 or 10 feet high, the evening wet and disagreeable, the river Something wider more timber on the banks.

The punishment of this day allarmd the Indian Chief verry much, he Cried aloud (or effected to Cry) I explained the Cause of the punishment and the necessity He thought examples were also necessary, & he himself had made them by Death, his nation never whiped even their Children, from their burth.

[Clark, October 15, 1804]

15th of October Rained all last night, passed a Ricara hunting camp on the S.S. & halted at another on the L.S. Several from the Camp visited us and gave meat as also those of the Camp we halted at, we gave them fish hooks Some beeds &c. as we proceeded on we Saw a number of Indians on both Sides all day, Saw L. S. some Curious Nnobs high and much the resemblance of a hiped rough house, we halted at a Camp of 10 Lodges of Ricaras on the S. S., we visited thier Lodges & were friendly recved by all—their women fond of our men—&c.

[Clark, October 15, 1804]

15th of October Monday 1804 rained all last night, we Set out early and proceeded on at 3 Miles passed an Ind. Camp on the S. S. we halted above and about 30 of the Indians came over in their Canoos of Skins, we eate with them, they give us meat, in return we gave fishhooks & Some beeds, about a mile higher we came too on the L. S. at a Camp of Ricres of about 8 Lodges, we also eate & they gave Some meat, we proceded on Saw numbers of Indians on both Sides passing a Creek, Saw many Curious hills, high and much the resemblance of a house with a hiped roof. At 12 oClock it Cleared away and the evening was pleasent, wind from the N. E.—at Sunset we arrived at a Camp of Ricares of 10 Lodges on the S. S. we Came too and Camped near them Capt Lewis & my Self went with the Chief who accompanis us, to the Huts of Several of the men all of whome Smoked & gave us Something to eate also Some meat to take away, those people were kind and appeared to be much plsd. at the attentioned paid them.

Those people are much pleased with my black Servent—Their womin verry fond of carressing our men. &.

[Clark, October 16, 1804]

16th of October Tuesday 1804 Some rain this morning 2 Squars verry anxious to accompany us we Set out with our Chief on Board by name Ar ke tar nar shar (or Chief of the Town) a little above our Camp on the L. S. passed an old Shyenne Village, which appears to have been Serounded with a wall of earth; this is the retreat & first Stand of this nation after being reduced by the Sioux and drove from their Countrey on the heads of red River of L Winipic where they Cultivated the landspassed a Creek I call So-harch or Girl Creek L. S. 2 miles higher passed Woman Crreek or Char-parts passed an Island Situated in a bend to the S. S. at the lower point of this Island a Creek comes in Called Kee-tooth.

Sar-kar-nar—or the place of Beaver above the Island a Small River on the Same S. Side Called War-re-Con nee Elk shed their horns, this river is 35 yards wide & heads near the River au Jacque, Carp Island wind hard a head from the N W. Saw great numbers of goats or Antelope on Shore, Capt Lewis one man & the Ricara Chief walked on Shore, in the evening I discovered a number of Indians on each Side and goats in the river or Swiming & on Sand bars, when I came near Saw the boys in the water Swiming amongst the goats & Killing them with Sticks, and then hauling them to the Shore. Those on Shore Kept them in the water, I saw 58 Killed in this way and on the Shore, the hunter with Cap Lewis Shot 3 goats I came to and Camped above the Ricara Camp on the L. S. Several Indians visited us duereing the night Some with meat, Sang and were merry all night.

[Clark, October 16, 1804]

16th October Tuesday 1804 Some rain this morning, 2 young Squars verry anxious to accompany us, we Set out with our Chief on board by name Ar ke tar na Shar or Chief of the Town, a little above our Camp on the L. S. passed a Circular work, where the, Shar ha (or Chien, or Dog Indians) formerly lived, a Short distance abov passed a Creek which we Call Chien Creek, above is a willow Island Situated near (i) the L. Side a large Sand bar above & on both Sides (2) passed a Creek above the Island on the L. S. call So-harch (or Girls) Creek, at 2 miles higher up (3) passed a Creek on L. S. call Char part (or womins) Creek passed (5) an Island Situated in a bend to the S. S. this Isd. is about 11/2 miles long, Covered with timber Such as Cotton wood, opsd. the lower point a creek coms in on the S. S. called by the Indians Kee tooth Sar kar nar (or place of Beavr) above the Island a Small river about 35 yards wide corns in Called War re con ne or (Elk Shed their horns). The Island is Called Carp Island by Ivens. wind hard from the N. W. Saw great numbers of Goats on the Shore S. S. proceeded on Capt. Lewis & the Indian Chief walked on Shore, Soon after I discovered Great numbers of Goats in the river, and Indians on the Shore on each Side, as I approached or got nearer I discovered boys in the water Killing the Goats with Sticks and halling them to Shore, Those on the banks Shot them with arrows and as they approachd. the Shore would turn them back of this Gangue of Goats I counted 58 of which they had killed & on the Shore, one of our hunters out with Cap Lewis killed three Goats, we passed the Camp on the S. S. and proceeded 1/2 mile and Camped on the L. S. many Indians came to the boat to See, Some Came across late at night, as they approach they hollowed and Sung, after Staying a Short time 2 went for Some meat, and returned in a Short time with fresh & Dried Buffalow, also goat, those Indians Strayed all night, They Sung and was verry merry the greater part of the night.

[Lewis, October 16, 1804]

October 16th This day took a small bird alive of the order of the ____ or goat suckers. it appeared to be passing into the dormant state. on the morning of the 18th the murcury was at 30 above 0. the bird could scarcely move.—I run my penknife into it's body under the wing and completely distroyed it's lungs and heart—yet it lived upwards of two hours this fanominon I could not account for unless it proceeded from the want of circulation of the blood—the recarees call this bird to'-na it's note is at-tah-to'-nah'; at-tah'to'-nah'; to-nah, a nocturnal bird, sings only in the night as does the whipperwill.—it's weights oz 17 Grains Troy.

[Clark, October 17, 1804]
17th of October 1804 Wind S. W. I walked on Shore with the Ricara Chief and an Inteprieter, they told me maney extroadenary Stories, I Killed 3 Dear & a Elk, the Chief Killed a Deer and our hunters Killed 4 Deer, in my absenc the wind rose So high that the Boat lay too all Day; Latd 46° 23' 57" N, I caught a Small uncommon whiperwill we observe emence herds of Goats, or Antelopes flocking down from the N E Side & Swiming the River, the Chief tels me those animals winter in the Black Mountain, and in the fall return to those mounts from every quarter, and in the Spring disperse in the planes, those emence herds we See all of which is on the N E Side of the River is on their way to the mountain, and in the Spring they will be as noumeroes on their return (some ganges winter on the Missouri)—camped on the L. S. note from the Ricares to the River Jacque near N. E. is about 40 mes. to the Chien a fork of R Rogue 20 passing the Sioux River near the Chien this from information of Mr. Graveline who passed through this Countrey.

[Clark, October 17, 1804]
17th October Wednesday 1804. Set out early a fine morning the wind from the N W. after brackfast I walked on Shore with the Indian Chief & Interpeters, Saw Buffalow Elk and Great numbers of Goats in large gangues (I am told by Mr. G. that those Animals winter in the Black mountains and this is about the Season they Cross from the East of the Missouris to go to that Mountain, they return in the Spring and pass the Missourie in Great numbers). This Chief tells me of a number of their Treditions about Turtles, Snakes, &. and the power of a perticiler rock or Cave on the next river which informs of everr thing none of those I think worth while mentioning—The wind So hard a head the boats Could not move aftr 10 oClock, Capt Louis Took the altitude of the Sun Laid. 46° 23'57" I Killed 3 Deer and the hunters with me killed 3 also the Indian Shot one but Could not get it—I Scaffeled up the Deer & returned & met the boat after night on the L. S. about 6 miles above the place we Camped last night— one of the men Saw a number of Snakes, Capt Lewis Saw a large Beaver house S. S. I Cought a Whipprwill Small & not Common. the leaves are falling fast. the river wide and full of Sand bars. Great numbers of verry large Stone on the Sides of the hills & Some rock of a brownish Colour in the Ld. Bend below this.

Great numbers of Goats are flocking down to the S. Side of the river on their way to the Black Mountains where they winter those animals return in the Spring in the Same way & Scatter in different directions.

[Clark, October 18, 1804]
18th of October 1804. at 6 miles passed the mouth of La Bullet or Cannon Ball River on the L. Side about 140 yards Wide, and heads near the Black Mountains above the mouth of this River, in and at the foot of the Bluff, and in the water is a number of round Stones, resembling Shells and Cannon balls of Different Sises, and of excellent grit for Grindstons—the Bluff continus for about a mile, The water of this River is confined within 40 yards—we met 2 french men in a Canoe, who informed us they wer trapping near the mandans and were robed of 4 Traps, & part of their Skins and Several other articles by Indians he took to be Mandans those men return with us, Saw emence numbers of Goats all Day S. S. our hunters Kill Sevral passed a large Creek Called Che wah or fish Creek on the S. S. 28 yds. wide, passed a Small Creek at 2 m on the L. S. Camped on the L. S. Saw a no of Buffalow, & in one gangue 248 Elk our hunters Killed 6 Deer & 4 Elk this evening. The Countrey is leavel and fine Some high Short hills, and ridges at a Distance, Bottoms fine and Partially timbered with Cotton wood principally Some ash & Elm.

[Clark, October 18, 1804]
18th of October Thursday 1804 Set out early proceeded on at 6 mes. passed the mouth of (1) la Boulet (or Cannon Ball River) about 140 yards wide on the L. S. this river heads in the Court not over Black mountains) (a fine Day) above the mouth of this river Great numbers of Stone perfectly round with fine Grit are in the Bluff and on the Shore, the river takes its name from those Stones which resemble Cannon Balls.—The water of this river is Confined within 40 yards. We met 2 french men in a perogue Desending from hunting, & complained of the Mandans robing them of 4 Traps ther fur & Seeveral othr articles Those men were in the imploy of our Ricaree interpeter Mr. Gravelin they turned & followered us.

Saw Great numbers of Goats on the S. S. Comeing to the river our hunters Killed 4 of them Some run back and others crossed & prosceed on their journey to the Court Noir, at (3) passed a Small River Called Che wah or fish river on the S. S. this river is about 28 yards wide and heads to the N. E, passed a

Small creek on the L. S. 1 mile abov the last, and Camped on a Sand bar on the L. S. opposit to us we Saw a Gangue of Buffalow bulls which we did not think worth while to kill—our hunters Killd. 4 Goats 6 Deer 4 Elk & a pelican & informs that they Saw in one Gang 248 Elk, (I walked on Shore, in the evining with a view to See Some of those remarkable places mentioned by evens, none of which I could find,) The Countrey in this quarter is Generally leavel & fine Some high Short hills, and some ragid ranges of Hills at a Distans.

The ricara Indians inform us that they find no black tail Deer as high up as this place, those we find are of the fallow Deer Kind.

The Ricareis are not fond of Spiritous liquers, nor do they apper to be fond of receiveing any or thank full for it.

[Clark, October 19, 1804]

19th of October Friday 1804. Set out early under a gentle Breeze from the S. E. more timber than Common in the bottoms passed a large Pond on the S. S. I walked out on the high land L. Side and observed great numbers of Buffalows, I counted in view at one time 52 gangues of Buffalow & 3 of Elk, besides Deer & goats &c. all the Streems falling from the hills or high lands So brackish that the water Can't be Drank without effecting the person making use of it as Globesalts. I saw in my walk Several remarkable high Conocal hills, one 90 feet, one 60 and others Smaller-the Indian Chief Say that the Callemet Bird live in the hollows of those hills, which holes are made by the water passing from the top & &. I also Saw an old Village fortified Situated on the top of a high Point, which the Ricarra Chief tels me were Mandans, we Camped on the L. S. I Killed a Deer & Saw Swans &c. our hunters Killed 4 Elk and 6 Deer to Day

[Clark, October 19, 1804]

19th October Friday 1804 a fine morning wind from the S. E. we Set out early under a gentle Breeze and proceeded on verry well, more timber than Common on the banks on this part of the river—passed a large Pond on the S. S.—I walked out on the Hills & observed Great numbers of Buffalow feedeing on both Sides of the river I counted 52 Gangues of Buffalow & 3 of Elk at one view, all the runs which come from the high hills which is Generally about one or 2 miles from the water is brackish and near the Hills (the Salts are) and the Sides of the Hills & edges of the Streems, the mineral salts appear. I saw Som remarkable round hills forming a Cone at top one about 90 foot one 60 & Several others Smaller, the Indian Chief Say that the Callemet bird live in the holes of those hills, the holes form by the water washing thro Some parts in its passage Down from the top—near one of those holes, on a point of a hill 90 feet above the lower plane I observed the remains of an old village, which had been fortified, the Indian Chief with us tels me, a party of Mandans lived there, Here first saw ruins of Mandan nation we proceeded on & Camped on the L. S. opposit the upper of those Conocal hills our hunters killed 4 Elk 6 Deer & a pelican, I saw Swans in a Pond & Killed a fat Deer in my walk, Saw above 10 wolves. This day is pleasent.

[Clark, October 20, 1804]

20th of October 1804 wind from the S E, I walked out to view those remarkable places pointed out by Evens, and continud all day Saw an old Village of the Mandans below the Chess chi ter R. appear to have been fortified above the village on the Same L. S. is a coal bank where we Campd. passed a Small Creek on the S. S. and an Island on the L. S. Covered with willows Small Cotton. the Countrey thro which I passed this day is Delightfull, Timber in the bottoms, Saw great nos. of Buffalow Elk Goats & Deer as we were in want of them I Killed 3 Deer, our hunters 10 Deer and wounded a white Bear. I Saw Several fresh tracks of that animal double the Sise of the largest track I ever Saw, great numbers of wolves, those animals follow the buffalow and devour, those that die or are Killed, and those too fat or pore to Keep up with the gangue.

[Clark, October 20, 1804]

20th of October Satterday 1804 Set out early this morning and proceeded on the wind from the S. E after brackfast I walked out on the L. Side to See those remarkable places pointed out by Evins, I saw an old remains of a villige on the Side of a hill which the Chief with us Too ne tels me that nation lived in a number villages on each Side of the river and the Troubleson Seauex caused them to move about 40 miles higher up where they remained a fiew years & moved to the place they now live, (2) passed a Small Creek on the S. S. (3) and one on the L. S. passed (4) a Island Covered with willows laying in the middle of the river no current on the L. S. Camped on the L. S. above a Bluff containing Coal (5) of an inferior quallity, this bank is imedeately above the old village of the Mandans—The Countrey is fine, the high hills at a Distanc with gradual assents, I Kild 3 Deer The Timber Confined to the bottoms as usial which is much larger than below. Great numbers of Buffalow Elk & Deer, Goats. our hunters killed 10 Deer & a Goat to day and wounded a white Bear I saw Several fresh track of those animals which is 3 times as large as a mans track—The wind hard all Day from the N. E. & East, great numbers of buffalow Swiming the river.

I observe near all large gangues of buffalow wolves and when the buffalow move those Anamals follow and feed on those that are killed by accident or those that are too pore or fat to Keep up with the gangue.

[Lewis, October 20, 1804]
20th October Peter Crusat this day shot at a white bear he wounded him, but

being alarmed at the formidable appearance of the bear he left his tomahalk and gun; but shortly after returned and found that the bear had taken the oposite rout.—soon after he shot a buffaloe cow broke her thy, the cow pursued him he concealed himself in a small raviene.

[Clark, October 21, 1804]
21t of October Sunday 1804 a verry Cold night wind hard from the N. E. Some rain in the night which freesed as it fell, at Day began to Snow and

Continued all the fore part of the day, at 1/4 of a mile passed the Mouth of Chess-che tar (or Heart) River L. S. 38 yards wide, this river heads near Turtle mountain with Knife River on this River is a Smothe Stone which the Indians have great fath in & Consult the Stone on all great occasions which they Say Marks or Simblems are left on the Stone of what is to take place &c. An old Mandan Village above the mouth of this Little River, I saw a Single tree in the open Plains which the Mandans formerly paid great Devotion to run Cords thro their flesh & tie themselves to the tree to make them brave, passed an old Village on a Small run on the S. S. one on the bank L. and Camped, I Killed a fat Buffalow this evening—Little gun all my hunting.

[Clark, October 21, 1804]

21st October Sunday 1804 a verry Cold night wind hard from the N. E Some rain in the night which frosed up it fell at Day light it began to Snow and Continud all the fore part of the Day passed just above our Camp (1) a Small river on the L. S. Called by the Indians Chiss-Cho-tar this river is about 38 yards wide Containing a good Deel of water Some Distance up this River is Situated a Stone which the Indians have great fath in & Say they See painted on the Stone, "all the Calemites & good fortune to hapin the nation & partes who visit it"—a tree (an oak) which Stands alone near this place about 2 miles off in the open prarie which has with Stood the fire they pay Great respect to, make Holes and tie Strings thro the Skins of their necks and around this tree to make them brave (all this is the information of Too ne is a whipper will) the Chief of the Ricares who accompanied us to the Mandins, at 2 miles (2) passed the 2nd Villages of the Manden, which was in existance at the Same time with the 1st this village is at the foot of a hill on the S. S. on a butifull & extensive plain—at this time Covered with Buffalow—a Cloudy afternoon, I killed a fine Buffalow, we Camped on the L. S. verry Cold ground Covered with Snow.

[Clark, October 22, 1804]

22nd of October 1804 last night at about 1 oClock I was violently attacked with Rhumetism in my neck, which was so violently I could not move, Cap L. applied a hot Stone raped in flannel which gave temperry ease, we passed a War party of Tetons on their way as we Supposed to the Mandans of 12 men on the L. S. We gave them nothing and refused to put them across the river, passed 2 old Villages at the mouth of a large Creek L. S and a Small Island at the head of which is a bad place, an old Village on the S. S. and the upper of the 6 Villages the Mandans occupied about 25 years ago. This village was entirely cut off by the Sioux & one of the others nearly, the Small Pox distroyed great Numbers.

[Clark, October 22, 1804]
22nd October Monday 1804 last night at 1 oClock I was violently and Suddinly attacked with the Rhumitism in the neck which was So violent I could not move Capt. applied a hot Stone raped in flannel, which gave me some temporry ease,-. we Set out early, the morning Cold at 7 oClock we Came too at a Camp of Teton Seaux on the L. S. those people 12 in number were naikd and had the appearanc of war, we have every reason to believ that they are going or have been to Steel horses from the Mandans. They tell two Stories, we gave them nothing after takeing brackfast proceeded on—my Neck is yet verry painfull at times Spasms.

Camped on the L. Side, passed an Island Situated on the L. Side at the head of which & Mandans village S. S. we passd a bad place—The hunters kil-led a buffalow bull, they Say out of about 300 buffalow which they Saw, they did not See one Cow. Great Deel of Beaver Sign. Several Cought every night.

CHAPTER 4

COULTER'S RUN

By John Bradbury

This man came to St. Louis in May 1810, in a small canoe, from the head waters of the Missouri, a distance of three thousand miles, which he traversed in thirty days; I saw him on his arrival, and received from him an account of his adventures after he has separated from Lewis and Clark's party: one of these, from its singularity, I shall relate.

On the arrival of the party on the headwaters of the Missouri, Coulter, observing an appearance of abundance of beaver being there, he got permission to remain and hunt for some time, which he did in company with a man of the name of Dixon, who had traversed the immense tract of country from St. Louis to the head waters of the Missouri alone. Soon after he separated from Dixon and trapped in company with a hunter named Potts; and aware of the hostility of the Blackfeet Indians, one of whom had been killed by Lewis, they set their traps at night, and took them up early in the morning, remaining concealed during the day.

They were examining their traps early one morning, in a creek about six miles from that branch of the Missouri called Jefferson's Fork, and were ascending in a canoe, when suddenly they heard a great noise, resembling the trampling of animals; but they could not ascertain the fact, as the perpendicular banks on each side of the river impeded their view. Coulter immediately pronounced it to be occasioned by Indians, and advised an instant retreat, but was accused of cowardice by Potts, who insisted that the noise was caused by buffalo, and they proceeded on. In a few minutes after their doubts were removed, by a party of Indians making their appearance on both sides of the creek, to the amount of five or six hundred, who beckoned them to come ashore.

As retreat was now impossible, Coulter turned the head of the canoe to the shore; and at the moment of its touching, and Indian seized the rifle belonging to Potts; but Coulter, who is a remarkably strong man, immediately retook it, and handed it to Potts, who remained in the canoe, and on receiving it, pushed off into the river. he had scarcely quitted the shore when an arrow was shot at him, and he cried out, *"Coulter, I am wounded."*

Coulter remonstrated with him on the folly of attempting to escape, and urged him to come ashore. Instead of complying, he instantly leveled his rifle at an Indian, and shot him dead on the spot. This conduct, situated as he was, may appear to have been an act of madness, but it was doubtless the effect of sudden, but sound reasoning; for if taken alive, he must have expected to be tortured to death, according to their custom. He was instantly pierced with arrows so numerous, that, to use the language of Coulter, "he was made a riddle of."

They now seized Coulter, stripped him entirely naked, and began to consult on the manner in which he should be put to death. They were first inclined to set him up as a mark to shoot at; but the chief interfered, and seizing him by the shoulder, asked him if he could run fast. Coulter, who had been some time amongst the Kee-kat-sa, or Crow Indians, had in considerable degree acquired the Blackfoot language, and was also well acquainted with Indian customs, he knew he now had to run for his life, with the dreadful odds of five or six hundred against him, and these armed Indians; he therefore cunningly replied that he was a very bad runner, although he was considered by the hunters as remarkably swift.

The chief now commanded the party to remain stationary, and led Coulter out on the prairie three or four hundred yards, and released him, bidding him *to save himself if he could.* At that instant the horrid war whoop sounded in the ears of poor Coulter, who, urged with hope of preserving his life, ran with a speed at which he was himself surprised.

He ran nearly half way across the plain before he ventured to look over his shoulder, when he perceived that the Indians were very much scattered, and that he had gained ground to a considerable distance from the main body; but one Indian, who carried a spear was very much before all the rest, and not more than a hundred yards from him.

A faint gleam of hope now cheered the heart of Coulter; he derived confidence from the belief that escape was within the bounds of possibility, but that confidence was nearly fatal to him, for he exerted himself to such a degree, that the blood gushed from his nostrils, and soon almost covered the fore part of his body.

He now arrived within a mile of the river, when he distinctly heard the appalling sound of footsteps behind him, and every instant expected to feel the spear of his pursuer. Again he turned his head and saw the savage not twenty yards from him. Determined if possible to avoid the expected blow, he suddenly stopped, turned around and spread out his arms.

The Indian, surprised by the suddenness of his action, and perhaps at the bloody appearance of Coulter, also attempted to stop, but exhausted with running, he fell whilst endeavoring to throw his spear, which stuck in the ground, and broke in his hand. Coulter instantly snatched up the pointed part, with which he pinned him to the earth, and then continued his flight.

The foremost of the Indians, on arriving at the place, stopped until the others came up to join them, when they set up a hideous yell. Every moment of this time was improved by Coulter, who, though fainting and exhausted, succeeded in gaining the skirting of the cotton wood trees, on the borders of the fork, on which he ran, and plunged into the river. Fortunately for him, a little below this place there was an island, against the upper point of which a raft of drift timber had lodged. He dived under the raft, and after several efforts, got his head above water amongst the trunks of trees, covered over with smaller wood to the depth of several feet.

Scarcely had he secured himself, when the Indians arrived on the river, screeching and yelling, as Coulter expressed it, "like so many devils." They were frequently on the raft during the day, and were even seen through the chinks by Coulter, who was congratulating himself on his escape, until the idea arose that they might set the raft on fire. In horrible suspense he remained until night, when hearing no more of the Indians, he dived under the raft, and swam silently down the river to a considerable distance, when he landed, and travelled all night.

Although happy in having escaped from the Indians, his situation was still dreadful: he was completely naked, under a burning sun: the soles of his feet were entirely filled with the thorns of the prickly pear; he was hungry, and had no means of killing game, although he saw abundance around him, and was at least seven days journey from Lisa's Fort, on the Bighorn branch of the Roches Jaunes river. These were circumstances under which almost any man but an American hunter would have despaired. He arrived at the fort in seven days, having subsisted on a root much esteemed by the Indians of the Missouri, now know by naturalists as *Psoralea esculenta.*

CHAPTER 5

BONNEVILLE IN THE MOUNTAINS

from *The Adventures of Captain Bonneville*

By Washington Irving

It was on the 20th of July that Captain Bonneville first came in sight of the grand region of his hopes and anticipations, the Rocky Mountains. He had been making a bend to the south, to avoid some obstacles along the river, and had attained a high, rocky ridge, when a magnificent prospect burst upon his sight. To the west rose the Wind River Mountains, with their bleached and snowy summits towering into the clouds. These stretched far to the north-northwest, until they melted away into what appeared to be faint clouds, but which the experienced eyes of the veteran hunters of the party recognized for the rugged mountains of the Yellowstone; at the feet of which extended the wild Crow country: a perilous, though profitable region for the trapper.

To the southwest, the eye ranged over an immense extent of wilderness, with what appeared to be a snowy vapor resting upon its horizon. This, however, was pointed out as another branch of the Great Chippewyan, or Rocky chain; being the Eutaw Mountains, at whose basis the wandering tribe of hunters of the same name pitch their tents. We can imagine the enthusiasm of the worthy captain when he beheld the vast and mountainous scene of his adventurous enterprise thus suddenly unveiled before him. We can imagine with what feelings of awe and admiration he must have contemplated the Wind River Sierra, or bed of mountains; that great fountainhead from whose springs, and lakes, and melted snows some of those mighty rivers take their rise, which wander over hundreds of miles of varied country and clime, and find their way to the opposite waves of the Atlantic and the Pacific.

The Wind River Mountains are, in fact, among the most remarkable of the whole Rocky chain; and would appear to be among the loftiest. They form, as it were, a great bed of mountains, about eighty miles in length, and from twenty to thirty in breadth; with rugged peaks, covered with eternal snows, and deep, narrow valleys full of springs, and brooks, and rock-bound lakes. From this great treasury of waters issue forth limpid streams, which, augmenting as they descend, become main tributaries of the Missouri on the one side, and the Columbia on the other; and give rise to the Seeds-ke-dee Agie, or Green River, the great Colorado of the West, that empties its current into the Gulf of California.

The Wind River Mountains are notorious in hunters' and trappers' stories: their rugged defiles, and the rough tracts about their neighborhood, having been lurking places for the predatory hordes of the mountains, and scenes of rough encounter with Crows and Blackfeet. It was to the west of these mountains, in the valley of the Seeds-ke-dee Agie, or Green River, that Captain Bonneville intended to make a halt for the purpose of giving repose to his people and his horses after their weary journeying; and of collecting information as to his future course. This Green River valley, and its immediate neighborhood, as we have already observed, formed the main point of rendezvous, for the present year, of the rival fur companies, and the motley populace, civilized and savage, connected with them. Several days of rugged travel, however, yet remained for the captain and his men before they should encamp in this desired resting-place.

On the 21st of July, as they were pursuing their course through one of the meadows of the Sweet Water, they beheld a horse grazing at a little distance. He showed no alarm at their approach, but suffered himself quietly to be taken, evincing a perfect state of tameness. The scouts of the party were instantly on the look-out for the owners of this animal; lest some dangerous band of savages might be lurking in the vicinity. After a narrow search, they discovered the trail of an Indian party, which had evidently passed through that neighborhood but recently. The horse was accordingly taken possession of, as an estray; but a more vigilant watch than usual was kept round the camp at nights, lest his former owners should be upon the prowl.

The travellers had now attained so high an elevation that on the 23d of July, at daybreak, there was considerable ice in the waterbuckets, and the thermometer stood at twenty-two degrees. The rarefy of the atmosphere continued to affect the wood-work of the wagons, and the wheels were incessantly falling to pieces. A remedy was at length devised. The tire of each wheel was taken off; a band of wood was nailed round the exterior of the felloes, the tire was then made red hot, replaced round the wheel, and suddenly cooled with water. By this means, the whole was bound together with great compactness.

The extreme elevation of these great steppes, which range along the feet of the Rocky Mountains, takes away from the seeming height of their peaks, which yield to few in the known world in point of altitude above the level of the sea.

On the 24th, the travellers took final leave of the Sweet Water, and keeping westwardly, over a low and very rocky ridge, one of the most southern spurs of the Wind River Mountains, they encamped, after a march of seven hours and a half, on the banks of a small clear stream, running to the south, in which they caught a number of fine trout.

The sight of these fish was hailed with pleasure, as a sign that they had reached the waters which flow into the Pacific; for it is only on the western streams of the Rocky Mountains that trout are to be taken. The stream on which they had thus encamped proved, in effect, to be tributary to the Seeds-ke-dee Agie, or Green River, into which it flowed at some distance to the south.

Captain Bonneville now considered himself as having fairly passed the crest of the Rocky Mountains; and felt some degree of exultation in being the first individual that had crossed, north of the settled provinces of Mexico, from the waters of the Atlantic to those of the Pacific, with wagons. Mr. William Sublette, the enterprising leader of the Rocky Mountain Fur Company, had, two or three years previously, reached the valley of the Wind River, which lies on the northeast of the mountains; but had proceeded with them no further.

A vast valley now spread itself before the travellers, bounded on one side by the Wind River Mountains, and to the west, by a long range of high hills. This, Captain Bonneville was assured by a veteran hunter in his company, was the great valley of the Seeds-ke; and the same informant would have fain persuaded him that a small stream, three feet deep, which he came to on the 25th, was that river. The captain was convinced, however, that the stream was too insignificant to drain so wide a valley and the adjacent mountains: he encamped, therefore, at an early hour, on its borders, that he might take the whole of the next day to reach the main river; which he presumed to flow between him and the distant range of western hills.

On the 26th of July, he commenced his march at an early hour, making directly across the valley, toward the hills in the west; proceeding at as brisk a rate as the jaded condition of his horses would permit. About eleven o'clock in the morning, a great cloud of dust was descried in the rear, advancing directly on the trail of the party. The alarm was given; they all came to a halt, and held a council of war. Some conjectured that the band of Indians, whose trail they had discovered in the neighborhood of the stray horse, had been lying in wait for them in some secret fastness of the mountains; and were about to attack them on the open plain, where they would have no shelter. Preparations were immediately made for defence; and a scouting party sent off to reconnoitre. They soon came galloping back, making signals that all was well. The cloud of dust was made by a band of fifty or sixty mounted trappers, belonging to the American Fur Company, who soon came up, leading their pack-horses. They were headed by Mr. Fontenelle, an experienced leader, or "partisan," as a chief of a party is called in the technical language of the trappers.

Mr. Fontenelle informed Captain Bonneville that he was on his way from the company's trading post on the Yellowstone to the yearly rendezvous, with reinforcements and supplies for their hunting and trading parties beyond the mountains; and that he expected to meet, by appointment, with a band of free trappers in that very neighborhood. He had fallen upon the trail of Captain Bonneville's party, just after leaving the Nebraska; and, finding that they had frightened off all the game, had been obliged to push on, by forced marches, to avoid famine: both men and horses were, therefore, much travel-worn; but this was no place to halt; the plain before them he said was destitute of grass and water, neither of which would be met with short of the Green River, which was yet at a considerable distance. He hoped, he added, as his party were all on horseback, to reach the river, with hard travelling, by nightfall: but he doubted the possibility of Captain Bonneville's arrival there with his wagons before the day following. Having imparted this information, he pushed forward with all speed.

Captain Bonneville followed on as fast as circumstances would permit. The ground was firm and gravelly; but the horses were too much fatigued to move rapidly. After a long and harassing day's march, without pausing for a noontide meal, they were compelled, at nine o'clock at night, to encamp in an open plain, destitute of water or pasturage. On the following morning, the horses were turned loose at the peep of day; to slake their thirst, if possible, from the dew collected on the sparse grass, here and there springing up among dry sand-banks. The soil of a great part of this Green River valley is a whitish clay, into which the rain cannot penetrate, but which dries and cracks with the sun. In some places it produces a salt weed, and grass along the margins of the streams; but the wider expanses of it are desolate and barren. It was not until noon that Captain Bonneville reached the banks of the Seeds-ke-dee, or Colorado of the West; in the meantime, the sufferings of both men and horses had been excessive, and it was with almost frantic eagerness that they hurried to allay their burning thirst in the limpid current of the river.

Fontenelle and his party had not fared much better; the chief part had managed to reach the river by nightfall, but were nearly knocked out by the exertion; the horses of others sank under them, and they were obliged to pass the night upon the road.

On the following morning, July 27th, Fontenelle moved his camp across the river; while Captain Bonneville proceeded some little distance below, where there was a small but fresh meadow yielding abundant pasturage. Here the poor jaded horses were turned out to graze, and take their rest: the weary journey up the mountains had worn them down in flesh and spirit; but this last march across the thirsty plain had nearly finished them.

The captain had here the first taste of the boasted strategy of the fur trade. During his brief, but social encampment, in company with Fontenelle, that experienced trapper had managed to win over a number of Delaware Indians whom the captain had brought with him, by offering them four hundred dollars each for the ensuing autumnal hunt. The captain was somewhat astonished when he saw these hunters, on whose services he had calculated securely, suddenly pack up their traps, and go over to the rival camp. That he might in some measure, however, be even with his competitor, he dispatched two scouts to look out for the band of free trappers who were to meet Fontenelle in this neighborhood, and to endeavor to bring them to his camp.

As it would be necessary to remain some time in this neighborhood, that both men and horses might repose, and recruit their strength; and as it was a region full of danger, Captain Bonneville proceeded to fortify his camp with breastworks of logs and pickets.

These precautions were, at that time, peculiarly necessary, for the bands of Blackfeet Indians which were roving about the neighborhood. These savages are the most dangerous banditti of the mountains, and the inveterate foe of the trappers. They are Ishmaelites of the first order, always with weapon in hand, ready for action. The young braves of the tribe, who are destitute of property, go to war for booty; to gain horses, and acquire the means of setting up a lodge, supporting a family, and entitling themselves to a seat in the public councils. The veteran warriors fight merely for the love of the thing, and the consequence which success gives them among their people.

They are capital horsemen, and are generally well mounted on short, stout horses, similar to the prairie ponies to be met with at St. Louis. When on a war party, however, they go on foot, to enable them to skulk through the country with greater secrecy; to keep in thickets and ravines, and use more adroit subterfuges and stratagems. Their mode of warfare is entirely by ambush, surprise, and sudden assaults in the night time. If they succeed in causing a panic, they dash forward with headlong fury: if the enemy is on the alert, and shows no signs of fear, they become wary and deliberate in their movements.

Some of them are armed in the primitive style, with bows and arrows; the greater part have American fusees, made after the fashion of those of the Hudson's Bay Company. These they procure at the trading post of the American

Fur Company, on Marias River, where they traffic their peltries for arms, ammunition, clothing, and trinkets. They are extremely fond of spirituous liquors and tobacco; for which nuisances they are ready to exchange not merely their guns and horses, but even their wives and daughters. As they are a treacherous race, and have cherished a lurking hostility to the whites ever since one of their tribe was killed by Mr. Lewis, the associate of General Clarke, in his exploring expedition across the Rocky Mountains, the American Fur Company is obliged constantly to keep at that post a garrison of sixty or seventy men.

Under the general name of Blackfeet are comprehended several tribes: such as the Surcies, the Peagans, the Blood Indians, and the Gros Ventres of the Prairies: who roam about the southern branches of the Yellowstone and Missouri Rivers, together with some other tribes further north.

The bands infesting the Wind River Mountains and the country adjacent at the time of which we are treating, were Gros Ventres of the *Prairies*, which are not to be confounded with Gros Ventres of the *Missouri*, who keep about the *lower* part of that river, and are friendly to the white men.

This hostile band keeps about the headwaters of the Missouri, and numbers about nine hundred fighting men. Once in the course of two or three years they abandon their usual abodes, and make a visit to the Arapahoes of the Arkansas. Their route lies either through the Crow country, and the Black Hills, or through the lands of the Nez Perces, Flatheads, Bannacks, and Shoshonies. As they enjoy their favorite state of hostility with all these tribes, their expeditions are prone to be conducted in the most lawless and predatory style; nor do they hesitate to extend their maraudings to any party of white men they meet with; following their trails; hovering about their camps; waylaying and dogging the caravans of the free traders, and murdering the solitary trapper. The consequences are frequent and desperate fights between them and the "mountaineers," in the wild defiles and fastnesses of the Rocky Mountains.

The band in question was, at this time, on their way homeward from one of their customary visits to the Arapahoes; and in the ensuing chapter we shall treat of some bloody encounters between them and the trappers, which had taken place just before the arrival of Captain Bonneville among the mountains.

* * *

Leaving Captain Bonneville and his band ensconced within their fortified camp in the Green River valley, we shall step back and accompany a party of the Rocky Mountain Fur Company in its progress, with supplies from St. Louis, to the annual rendezvous at Pierre's Hole. This party consisted of sixty men, well mounted, and conducting a line of packhorses. They were commanded by Captain William Sublette, a partner in the company, and one of the most active, intrepid, and renowned leaders in this half military kind of service. He was accompanied by his associate in business, and tried companion in danger, Mr. Robert Campbell, one of the pioneers of the trade beyond the mountains, who had commanded trapping parties there in times of the greatest peril.

As these worthy compeers were on their route to the frontier, they fell in with another expedition, likewise on its way to the mountains. This was a party of regular "down-easters," that is to say, people of New England, who, with the all-penetrating and all-pervading spirit of their race, were now pushing their way into a new field of enterprise with which they were totally unacquainted. The party had been fitted out and was maintained and commanded by Mr. Nathaniel J. Wyeth, of Boston. This gentleman had conceived an idea that a profitable fishery for salmon might be established on the Columbia River, and connected with the fur trade. He had, accordingly, invested capital in goods, calculated, as he supposed, for the Indian trade, and had enlisted a number of Eastern men in his employ, who had never been in the Far West, nor knew anything of the wilderness. With these, he was bravely steering his way across the continent, undismayed by danger, difficulty, or distance, in the same way that a New England coaster and his neighbors will coolly launch forth on a voyage to the Black Sea, or a whaling cruise to the Pacific.

With all their national aptitude at expedient and resource, Wyeth and his men felt themselves completely at a loss when they reached the frontier, and found that the wilderness required experience and habitudes of which they were totally deficient. Not one of the party, excepting the leader, had ever seen an Indian or handled a rifle; they were without guide or interpreter, and totally unacquainted with "wood craft" and the modes of making their way among savage hordes, and subsisting themselves during long marches over wild mountains and barren plains.

In this predicament, Captain Sublette found them, in a manner becalmed, or rather run aground, at the little frontier town of Independence, in Missouri, and kindly took them in tow. The two parties travelled amicably together; the frontier men of Sublette's party gave their Yankee comrades some lessons in hunting, and some insight into the art and mystery of dealing with the Indians, and they all arrived without accident at the upper branches of the Nebraska or Platte River.

In the course of their march, Mr. Fitzpatrick, the partner of the company who was resident at that time beyond the mountains, came down from the rendezvous at Pierre's Hole to meet them and hurry them forward. He travelled in company with them until they reached the Sweet Water; then taking a couple of horses, one for the saddle, and the other as a pack-horse, he started off express for Pierre's Hole, to make arrangements against their arrival, that he might commence his hunting campaign before the rival company.

Fitzpatrick was a hardy and experienced mountaineer, and knew all the passes and defiles. As he was pursuing his lonely course up the Green River valley, he descried several horsemen at a distance, and came to a halt to reconnoitre. He supposed them to be some detachment from the rendezvous, or a party of friendly Indians. They perceived him, and setting up the war-whoop, dashed forward at full speed: he saw at once his mistake and his peril—they were Blackfeet. Springing upon his fleetest horse, and abandoning the other to the enemy, he made for the mountains, and succeeded in escaping up one of the most dangerous defiles. Here he concealed himself until he thought the Indians had gone off, when he returned into the valley. He was again pursued, lost his remaining horse, and only escaped by scrambling up among the cliffs. For several days he remained lurking among rocks and precipices, and almost famished, having but one remaining charge in his rifle, which he kept for self-defence.

In the meantime, Sublette and Campbell, with their fellow traveller, Wyeth, had pursued their march unmolested, and arrived in the Green River valley, totally unconscious that there was any lurking enemy at hand. They had encamped one night on the banks of a small stream, which came down from the Wind River Mountains, when about midnight, a band of Indians burst upon their camp, with horrible yells and whoops, and a discharge of guns and arrows. Happily no other harm was done than wounding one mule, and causing several horses to break loose from their pickets. The camp was instantly in arms; but the Indians retreated with yells of exultation, carrying off several of the horses under cover of the night.

This was somewhat of a disagreeable foretaste of mountain life to some of Wyeth's band, accustomed only to the regular and peaceful life of New England; nor was it altogether to the taste of Captain Sublette's men, who were chiefly Creoles and townsmen from St. Louis. They continued their march the next morning, keeping scouts ahead and upon their flanks, and arrived without further molestation at Pierre's Hole.

The first inquiry of Captain Sublette, on reaching the rendezvous, was for Fitzpatrick. He had not arrived, nor had any intelligence been received concerning him. Great uneasiness was now entertained, lest he should have fallen into the hands of the Blackfeet who had made the midnight attack upon the camp. It was a matter of general joy, therefore, when he made his appearance, conducted by two half-breed Iroquois hunters. He had lurked for several days among the mountains, until almost starved; at length he escaped the vigilance of his enemies in the night, and was so fortunate as to meet the two Iroquois hunters, who, being on horseback, conveyed him without further difficulty to the rendezvous. He arrived there so emaciated that he could scarcely be recognized.

The valley called Pierre's Hole is about thirty miles in length and fifteen in width, bounded to the west and south by low and broken ridges, and overlooked to the east by three lofty mountains, called the three Tetons, which domineer as landmarks over a vast extent of country.

A fine stream, fed by rivulets and mountain springs, pours through the valley toward the north, dividing it into nearly equal parts. The meadows on its borders are broad and extensive, covered with willow and cotton-wood trees, so closely interlocked and matted together as to be nearly impassable.

In this valley was congregated the motley populace connected with the fur trade. Here the two rival companies had their encampments, with their retainers of all kinds: traders, trappers, hunters, and half-breeds, assembled from all quarters, awaiting their yearly supplies, and their orders to start off in new directions. Here, also, the savage tribes connected with the trade, the Nez Perces or Chopunnish Indians, and Flatheads, had pitched their lodges beside the streams, and with their squaws, awaited the distribution of goods and finery. There was, moreover, a band of fifteen free trappers, commanded by a gallant leader from Arkansas, named Sinclair, who held their encampment a little apart from the rest. Such was the wild and heterogeneous assemblage, amounting to several hundred men, civilized and savage, distributed in tents and lodges in the several camps.

The arrival of Captain Sublette with supplies put the Rocky Mountain Fur Company in full activity. The wares and merchandise were quickly opened, and as quickly disposed of to trappers and Indians; the usual excitement and revelry took place, after which all hands began to disperse to their several destinations.

On the 17th of July, a small brigade of fourteen trappers, led by Milton Sublette, brother of the captain, set out with the intention of proceeding to the southwest. They were accompanied by Sinclair and his fifteen free trappers; Wyeth, also, and his New England band of beaver hunters and salmon fishers, now dwindled down to eleven, took this opportunity to prosecute their cruise in the wilderness, accompanied with such experienced pilots. On the first day, they proceeded about eight miles to the southeast, and encamped for the night, still in the valley of Pierre's Hole. On the following morning, just as they were raising their camp, they observed a long line of people pouring down a defile of the mountains. They at first supposed them to be Fontenelle and his party, whose arrival had been daily expected. Wyeth, however, reconnoitred them with a spy-glass, and soon perceived they were Indians. They were divided into two parties, forming, in the whole, about one hundred and fifty persons, men, women, and children. Some were on horseback, fantastically painted and arrayed, with scarlet blankets fluttering in the wind. The greater part, however, were on foot. They had perceived the trappers before they were themselves discovered, and came down yelling and whooping into the plain. On nearer approach, they were ascertained to be Blackfeet.

One of the trappers of Sublette's brigade, a half-breed named Antoine Godin, now mounted his horse, and rode forth as if to hold a conference. He was the son of an Iroquois hunter, who had been cruelly murdered by the Blackfeet at a small stream below the mountains, which still bears his name. In company with Antoine rode forth a Flathead Indian, whose once powerful tribe had been completely broken down in their wars with the Blackfeet. Both of them, therefore, cherished the most vengeful hostility against these marauders of the mountains. The Blackfeet came to a halt. One of the chiefs advanced singly and unarmed, bearing the pipe of peace. This overture was certainly pacific;

but Antoine and the Flathead were predisposed to hostility, and pretended to consider it a treacherous movement.

Is your piece charged?" said Antoine to his red companion.

"It is."

"Then cock it, and follow me."

They met the Blackfoot chief half way, who extended his hand in friendship. Antoine grasped it.

"Fire! " cried he.

The Flathead levelled his piece, and brought the Blackfoot to the ground. Antoine snatched off his scarlet blanket, which was richly ornamented, and galloped off with it as a trophy to the camp, the bullets of the enemy whistling after him. The Indians immediately threw themselves into the edge of a swamp, among willows and cotton-wood trees, interwoven with vines. Here they began to fortify themselves; the women digging a trench, and throwing up a breastwork of logs and branches, deep hid in the bosom of the wood, while the warriors skirmished at the edge to keep the trappers at bay.

The latter took their station in a ravine in front, whence they kept up a scattering fire. As to Wyeth, and his little band of "downeasters," they were perfectly astounded by this second specimen of life in the wilderness; the men, being especially unused to bushfighting and the use of the rifle, were at a loss how to proceed. Wyeth, however, acted as a skilful commander. He got all his horses into camp and secured them; then, making a breastwork of his packs of goods, he charged his men to remain in garrison, and not to stir out of their fort. For himself, he mingled with the other leaders, determined to take his share in the conflict.

In the meantime, an express had been sent off to the rendezvous for reinforcements. Captain Sublette, and his associate, Campbell, were at their camp when the express came galloping across the plain, waving his cap, and giving the alarm; "Blackfeet! Blackfeet! a fight in the upper part of the valley! to arms! to arms!"

The alarm was passed from camp to camp. It was a common cause. Every one turned out with horse and rifle. The Nez Perces and Flatheads joined. As fast as horseman could arm and mount he galloped off; the valley was soon alive with white men and red men scouring at full speed.

Sublette ordered his men to keep to the camp, being recruits from St. Louis, and unused to Indian warfare. He and his friend Campbell prepared for action.

Throwing off their coats, rolling up their sleeves, and arming themselves with pistols and rifles, they mounted their horses and dashed forward among the first. As they rode along, they made their wills in soldier-like style; each stating how his effects should be disposed of in case of his death, and appointing the other his executor.

The Blackfeet warriors had supposed the brigade of Milton Sublette all the foes they had to deal with, and were astonished to behold the whole valley suddenly swarming with horsemen, galloping to the field of action. They withdrew into their fort, which was completely hid from sight in the dark and tangled wood. Most of their women and children had retreated to the mountains. The trappers now sallied forth and approached the swamp, firing into the thickets at random; the Blackfeet had a better sight at their adversaries, who were in the open field, and a half-breed was wounded in the shoulder.

When Captain Sublette arrived, he urged to penetrate the swamp and storm the fort, but all hung back in awe of the dismal horrors of the place, and the danger of attacking such desperadoes in their savage den. The very Indian allies, though accustomed to bushfighting, regarded it as almost impenetrable, and full of frightful danger. Sublette was not to be turned from his purpose, but offered to lead the way into the swamp. Campbell stepped forward to accompany him. Before entering the perilous wood, Sublette took his brothers aside, and told them that in case he fell, Campbell, who knew his will, was to be his executor. This done, he grasped his rifle and pushed into the thickets, followed by Campbell. Sinclair, the partisan from Arkansas, was at the edge of the wood with his brother and a few of his men. Excited by the gallant example of the two friends, he pressed forward to share their dangers.

The swamp was produced by the labors of the beaver, which, by damming up a stream, had inundated a portion of the valley. The place was all overgrown with woods and thickets, so closely matted and entangled that it was impossible to see ten paces ahead, and the three associates in peril had to crawl along, one after another, making their way by putting the branches and vines aside; but doing it with caution, lest they should attract the eye of some lurking marksman. They took the lead by turns, each advancing about twenty yards at a time, and now and then hallooing to their men to follow. Some of the latter gradually entered the swamp, and followed a little distance in their rear.

They had now reached a more open part of the wood, and had glimpses of the rude fortress from between the trees. It was a mere breastwork, as we have said, of logs and branches, with blankets, buffalo robes, and the leathern covers of lodges, extended round the top as a screen. The movements of the leaders, as they groped their way, had been descried by the sharp-sighted enemy. As Sinclair, who was in the advance, was putting some branches aside, he was shot through the body. He fell on the spot. "Take me to my brother," said he to Campbell. The latter gave him in charge to some of the men, who conveyed him out of the swamp.

Sublette now took the advance. As he was reconnoitring the fort, he perceived an Indian peeping through an aperture. In an instant his rifle was levelled and discharged, and the ball struck the savage in the eye. While he was reloading, he called to Campbell, and pointed out to him the hole; "Watch that place," said he, "and you will soon have a fair chance for a shot." Scarce had he uttered the words, when a ball struck him in the shoulder, and almost wheeled him around. His first thought was to take hold of his arm with his other hand, and move it up and down. He ascertained, to his satisfaction, that the bone was not broken. The next moment he was so faint that he could not stand. Campbell took him in his arms and carried him out of the thicket. The same shot that struck Sublette wounded another man in the head.

A brisk fire was now opened by the mountaineers from the wood, answered occasionally from the fort. Unluckily, the trappers and their allies, in searching for the fort, had got scattered, so that Wyeth, and a number of Nez Perces, approached the fort on the northwest side, while others did the same on the opposite quarter. A cross-fire thus took place, which occasionally did mischief to friends as well as foes. An Indian was shot down, close to Wyeth, by a ball which, he was convinced, had been sped from the rifle of a trapper on the other side of the fort.

The number of whites and their Indian allies had by this time so much increased by arrivals from the rendezvous, that the Blackfeet were completely overmatched. They kept doggedly in their fort, however, making no offer of surrender. An occasional firing into the breastwork was kept up during the day. Now and then, one of the Indian allies, in bravado, would rush up to the fort, fire over the ramparts, tear off a buffalo robe or a scarlet blanket, and return with it in triumph to his comrades. Most of the savage garrison that fell, however, were killed in the first part of the attack.

At one time it was resolved to set fire to the fort; and the squaws belonging to the allies were employed to collect combustibles. This however, was abandoned; the Nez Perces being unwilling to destroy the robes and blankets, and other spoils of the enemy, which they felt sure would fall into their hands.

The Indians, when fighting, are prone to taunt and revile each other. During one of the pauses of the battle, the voice of the Blackfeet chief was heard.

"So long," said he, "as we had powder and ball, we fought you in the open field: when those were spent, we retreated here to die with our women and children. You may burn us in our fort; but, stay by our ashes, and you who are so hungry for fighting will soon have enough. There are four hundred lodges of our brethren at hand. They will soon be here—their arms are strong—their hearts are big—they will avenge us!"

This speech was translated two or three times by Nez Perce and Creole interpreters. By the time it was rendered into English, the chief was made to say that four hundred lodges of his tribe were attacking the encampment at the other end of the valley. Every one now was for hurrying to the defence of the rendezvous. A party was left to keep watch upon the fort; the rest galloped off to the camp. As night came on, the trappers drew out of the swamp, and remained about the skirts of the wood. By morning, their companions returned from the rendezvous with the report that all was safe. As the day opened, they ventured within the swamp and approached the fort. All was silent. They advanced up to it without opposition. They entered: it had been abandoned in the night, and the Blackfeet had effected their retreat, carrying off their wounded on litters made of branches, leaving bloody traces on the herbage. The bodies of ten Indians were found within the fort; among them the one shot in the eye by Sublette. The Blackfeet afterward reported that they had lost twenty-six warriors in this battle. Thirty-two horses were likewise found killed; among them were some of those recently carried off from Sublette's party, in the night; which showed that these were the very savages that had attacked him. They proved to be an advance party of the main body of Blackfeet, which had been upon the trail of Sublette's party. Five white men and one halfbreed were killed, and several wounded. Seven of the Nez Perces were also killed, and six wounded. They had an old chief, who was reputed as invulnerable. In the course of the action he was hit by a spent ball, and threw up blood; but his skin was unbroken. His people were now fully convinced that he was proof against powder and ball.

A striking circumstance is related as having occurred the morning after the battle. As some of the trappers and their Indian allies were approaching the fort through the woods, they beheld an Indian woman, of noble form and features, leaning against a tree. Their surprise at her lingering here alone, to fall into the hands of her enemies, was dispelled, when they saw the corpse of a warrior at her feet. Either she was so lost in grief as not to perceive their approach; or a proud spirit kept her silent and motionless. The Indians set up a yell, on discovering her, and before the trappers could interfere, her mangled body fell upon the corpse which she had refused to abandon. We have heard this anecdote discredited by one of the leaders who had been in the battle: but the fact may have taken place without his seeing it, and been concealed from him. It is an instance of female devotion, even to the death, which we are well disposed to believe and to record.

After the battle, the brigade of Milton Sublette, together with the free trappers, and Wyeth's New England band, remained some days at the rendezvous, to see if the main body of Blackfeet intended to make an attack; nothing of the kind occurring, they once more put themselves in motion, and proceeded on their route toward the southwest. Captain Sublette having distributed his supplies, had intended to set off on his return to St. Louis, taking with him the peltries collected from the trappers and Indians. His wound, however obliged him to postpone his departure. Several who were to have accompanied him became impatient of this delay. Among these was a young Bostonian, Mr. Joseph More, one of the followers of Mr. Wyeth, who had seen enough of mountain life and savage warfare, and was eager to return to the abodes of civilization. He and six others, among whom were a Mr. Foy, of Mississippi, Mr. Alfred K. Stephens, of St. Louis, and two grandsons of the celebrated Daniel Boone, set out together, in advance of Sublette's party, thinking they would make their way through the mountains.

It was just five days after the battle of the swamp that these seven companions were making their way through Jackson's Hole, a valley not far from the three Tetons, when, as they were descending a hill, a party of Blackfeet that lay in ambush started up with terrific yells. The horse of the young Bostonian, who was in front, wheeled round with affright, and threw his unskilled rider. The young man scrambled up the side of the hill, but, unaccustomed to such wild scenes, lost his presence of mind, and stood, as if paralyzed, on the edge of a bank, until the Blackfeet came up and slew him on the spot. His comrades had fled on the first alarm; but two of them, Foy and Stephens, seeing his danger, paused when they got half way up the hill, turned back, dismounted, and hastened to his assistance. Foy was instantly killed. Stephens was severely wounded, but escaped, to die five days afterward. The survivors returned to the camp of Captain Sublette, bringing tidings of this new disaster. That hardy leader, as soon as he could bear the journey, set out on his return to St. Louis, accompanied by Campbell. As they had a number of pack-horses richly laden with peltries to convoy, they chose a different route through the mountains, out of the way, as they hoped, of the lurking bands of Blackfeet. They succeeded in making the frontier in safety. We remember to have seen them with their band, about two or three months afterward, passing through a skirt of woodland in the upper part of Missouri. Their long cavalcade stretched in single file for nearly half a mile. Sublette still wore his arm in a sling. The mountaineers in their rude hunting dresses, armed with rifles and roughly mounted, and leading their pack-horses down a hill of the forest, looked like banditti returning with plunder. On the top of some of the packs were perched several half-breed children, perfect little imps, with wild black eyes glaring from among elf locks. These, I was told, were children of the trappers; pledges of love from their squaw spouses in the wilderness.

* * *

The blackfeet warriors, when they effected their midnight retreat from their wild fastness in Pierre's Hole, fell back into the valley of the Seeds-ke-dee, or Green River where they joined the main body of their band. The whole force amounted to several hundred fighting men, gloomy and exasperated by their late disaster. They had with them their wives and children, which incapacitated them from any bold and extensive enterprise of a warlike nature; but when, in the course of their wanderings they came in sight of the encampment of Fontenelle, who had moved some distance up Green River valley in search of the free trappers, they put up tremendous war-cries, and advanced fiercely as if to attack it. Second thoughts caused them to moderate their fury. They recollected the severe lesson just received, and could not but remark the strength of Fontenelle's position; which had been chosen with great judgment.

A formal talk ensued. The Blackfeet said nothing of the late battle, of which Fontenelle had as yet received no accounts; the latter, however, knew the hostile and perfidious nature of these savages, and took care to inform them of the encampment of Captain Bonneville, that they might know there were more white men in the neighborhood. The conference ended, Fontenelle sent a Delaware Indian of his party to conduct fifteen of the Blackfeet to the camp of Captain Bonneville. There was at that time two Crow Indians in the captain's camp, who had recently arrived there. They looked with dismay at this deputation from their implacable enemies, and gave the captain a terrible character of them, assuring him that the best thing he could possibly do, was to put those Blackfeet deputies to death on the spot. The captain, however, who had heard nothing of the conflict at Pierre's Hole, declined all compliance with this sage counsel. He treated the grim warriors with his usual urbanity. They passed some little time at the camp; saw, no doubt, that everything was conducted with military skill and vigilance; and that such an enemy was not to be easily surprised, nor to be molested with impunity, and then departed, to report all that they had seen to their comrades.

The two scouts which Captain Bonneville had sent out to seek for the band of free trappers, expected by Fontenelle, and to invite them to his camp, had been successful in their search, and on the 12th of August those worthies made their appearance.

To explain the meaning of the appellation, free trapper, it is necessary to state the terms on which the men enlist in the service of the fur companies. Some have regular wages, and are furnished with weapons, horses, traps, and other requisites. These are under command, and bound to do every duty required of them connected with the service; such as hunting, trapping, loading and unloading the horses, mounting guard; and, in short, all the drudgery of the camp. These are the hired trappers.

The free trappers are a more independent class; and in describing them, we shall do little more than transcribe the graphic description of them by Captain Bonneville. "They come and go," says he, "when and where they please; provide their own horses, arms, and other equipments; trap and trade on their own account, and dispose of their skins and peltries to the highest bidder. Sometimes, in a dangerous hunting ground, they attach themselves to the camp of some trader for protection. Here they come under some restrictions; they have to conform to the ordinary rules for trapping, and to submit to such restraints, and to take part in such general duties, as are established for the good order and safety of the camp. In return for this protection, and for their camp keeping, they are bound to dispose of all the beaver they take, to the trader who commands the camp, at a certain rate per skin; or, should they prefer seeking a market elsewhere, they are to make him an allowance, of from thirty to forty dollars for the whole hunt."

There is an inferior order, who, either from prudence or poverty, come to these dangerous hunting grounds without horses or accoutrements, and are furnished by the traders. These, like the hired trappers, are bound to exert themselves to the utmost in taking beaver, which, without skinning, they render in at the trader's lodge, where a stipulated price for each is placed to their credit. These though generally included in the generic name of free trappers, have the more specific title of skin trappers.

The wandering whites who mingle for any length of time with the savages have invariably a proneness to adopt savage habitudes; but none more so than the free trappers. It is a matter of vanity and ambition with them to discard everything that may bear the stamp of civilized life, and to adopt the manners, habits, dress, gesture, and even walk of the Indian. You cannot pay a free trapper a greater compliment, than to persuade him you have mistaken him for an Indian brave; and, in truth, the counterfeit is complete. His hair suffered to attain to a great length, is carefully combed out, and either left to fall carelessly over his shoulders, or plaited neatly and tied up in otter skins, or parti-colored ribands. A hunting-shirt of ruffled calico of bright dyes, or of ornamented leather, falls to his knee; below which, curiously fashioned legging, ornamented with strings, fringes, and a profusion of hawks' bells, reach to a costly pair of moccasons of the finest Indian fabric, richly embroidered with beads. A blanket of scarlet, or some other bright color, hangs from his shoulders, and is girt around his waist with a red sash, in which he bestows his pistols, knife, and the stem of his Indian pipe; preparations either for peace or war. His gun is lavishly decorated with brass tacks and vermilion, and provided with a fringed cover, occasionally of buckskin, ornamented here and there with a feather. His horse, the noble minister to the pride, pleasure, and profit of the mountaineer, is selected for his speed and spirit, and prancing gait, and holds a place in his estimation second only to himself. He shares largely of his bounty, and of his pride and pomp of trapping. He is caparisoned in the most dashing and fantastic style; the bridles and crupper are weightily embossed with beads and cockades; and head, mane, and tail, are interwoven with abundance of eagles' plumes, which flutter in the wind. To complete this grotesque equipment, the proud animal is bestreaked and bespotted with vermilion, or with white clay, whichever presents the most glaring contrast to his real color.

Such is the account given by Captain Bonneville of these rangers of the wilderness, and their appearance at the camp was strikingly characteristic. They came dashing forward at full speed, firing their fusees, and yelling in Indian style. Their dark sunburned faces, and long flowing hair, their legging, flaps, moccasons, and richly-dyed blankets, and their painted horses gaudily caparisoned, gave them so much the air and appearance of Indians, that it was difficult to persuade one's self that they were white men, and had been brought up in civilized life.

Captain Bonneville, who was delighted with the game look of these cavaliers of the mountains, welcomed them heartily to his camp, and ordered a free allowance of grog to regale them, which soon put them in the most braggart spirits. They pronounced the captain the finest fellow in the world, and his men all *bons garçons*, jovial lads, and swore they would pass the day with them. They did so; and a day it was, of boast, and swagger, and rodomontade. The prime bullies and braves among the free trappers had each his circle of novices, from among the captain's band; mere greenhorns, men unused to Indian life; *mangeurs de lard*, or pork-eaters; as such new-comers are superciliously called by the veterans of the wilderness. These he would astonish and delight by the hour, with prodigious tales of his doings among the Indians; and of the wonders he had seen, and the wonders he had performed, in his adventurous peregrinations among the mountains.

In the evening, the free trappers drew off, and returned to the camp of Fontenelle, highly delighted with their visit and with their new acquaintances, and promising to return the following day. They kept their word: day after day their visits were repeated; they became "hail fellow well met" with Captain Bonneville's men; treat after treat succeeded, until both parties got most potently convinced, or rather confounded, by liquor. Now came on confusion and uproar. The free trappers were no longer suffered to have all the swagger to themselves. The camp bullies and prime trappers of the party began to ruffle up, and to brag, in turn, of their perils and achievements. Each now tried to out-boast and out-talk the other; a quarrel ensued as a matter of course, and a general fight, according to frontier usage. The two factions drew out their forces for a pitched battle. They fell to work and belabored each other with might and main; kicks and cuffs and dry blows were as well bestowed as they were well merited, until, having fought to their hearts' content, and been drubbed into a familiar acquaintance with each other's prowess and good qualities, they ended the fight by becoming firmer friends than they could have been rendered by a year's peaceable companionship.

While Captain Bonneville amused himself by observing the habits and characteristics of this singular class of men, and indulged them, for the time, in all their vagaries, he profited by the opportunity to collect from them information concerning the different parts of the country about which they had been accustomed to range; the characters of the tribes, and, in short, everything important to his enterprise. He also succeeded in securing the services of several to guide and aid him in his peregrinations among the mountains, and to trap for him during the ensuing season. Having strengthened his party with such valuable recruits, he felt in some measure consoled for the loss of the Delaware Indians, decoyed from him by Mr Fontenelle.

CHAPTER 6

STORIES OF JED SMITH AND THE ASHLEY-HENRY MEN

from *The Splendid Wayfaring: Jedediah Smith and the Ashley-Henry Men*

By John G. Neihardt

JED WRESTLES WITH DEATH

It was now time for the fall hunt to begin, and accordingly it was decided that a small party should strike southward along the eastern border of the Crow country, locating the richest beaver streams and trapping on the way, while the main body should move on up the Yellowstone to the mouth of the Big Horn, there to establish winter quarters. At the mouth of the Powder sixteen men were told off for this undertaking, William L. Sublette being one of the number. Jed Smith and Thomas Fitzpatrick were placed in command.

Bidding farewell to their comrades, these pushed southward up the valley of the Powder. Beaver sign was fairly plentiful. Traps set in the evening generally yielded satisfactory returns in the morning; and the better part of each afternoon was spent in skinning the catch and preparing the pelts. Travelling leisurely thus through a region where fresh meat could be procured with little difficulty, the men worked contentedly toward the Big Horn Mountains that at length began to lift clearer and clearer in the southwest. Here indeed was life such as these young fellows had dreamed of in the humdrum of the settlements. Autumn brooded goldenly on the vast land of no restraint. How glorious to be young and free!

For a week the party kept together; then Smith, with five men, struck out westward. Fitzpatrick, with the balance of the trappers, kept on up the valley, hoping to fall in with the Crow nation then on its fall buffalo hunt in the region between the headwaters of the Powder and the North Fork of the Platte. Smith was to explore the country westward, trapping on the upper reaches of the Tongue and Rosebud as he went, and meet Fitzpatrick returning by way of the Big Horn, whence the reunited bands should proceed to winter quarters on the Yellowstone.

For several days Smith and his men worked slowly up a small tributary stream that came down from the divide between the Powder and the Tongue, and the hunting was good. Then one evening Jed met with an accident that seemed likely to end his dream of the great mysterious. white spaces beyond the Rockies. He had been setting a trap at the margin of the creek and was pushing up through the brush that fringed the bank, when a huge hairy form towered growling above him.

There followed a period of torturing dreams; and when he awoke it was night and he was lying beside a fire with his shadowy comrades leaning over him. There was a roaring ache in his head, and at intervals a stabbing pain shot through one of his hips. He had been felled with a blow from the paw of a grizzly, his thigh had been badly mangled, and he was in a fair way to be rubbed out when his comrades, who were setting traps in the vicinity, had rushed to his rescue and killed the bear.

As in the case of old Hugh Glass, it was plain enough that Jed, though conscious, would be unable to travel for many days; and that night it was decided that three of the party should go in pursuit of Fitzpatrick, the two others remaining to watch over the wounded man. For several days after the departure of the three, things went well enough in the camp by the nameless creek; and though it was evident that Jed's recovery would be slow, and though signs of approaching winter were not lacking, there seemed to be little reason for uneasiness. The Rees and Blackfeet were far away, and the Gros Ventres were doubtless hunting buffalo on the plains bordering the Missouri. Deer and antelope abounded in the broken country round about; so there would be no lack of fresh meat, and Jed's companions could profitably spend the time of waiting in collecting beaver pelts.

But one evening, a half hour or so after the two men had gone up-stream to set their traps, leaving their horses staked near the camp, Jed heard a number of shots, fired in rapid succession, and a medley of wild cries. The sounds came from the direction in which his comrades had gone. Considering the number of shots and voices, there was but one conclusion to draw. Seizing his rifle and powder-horn, Jed, at the cost of excruciating pain, dragged himself into the midst of a thicket nearby and waited breathlessly. Very soon there was a crashing of the brush up-stream, and a dozen Indians in war paint came cantering down the creek. Catching sight of the camp and the three grazing horses, the band halted, dismounted, and, gabbling excitedly in a tongue that Jed did not recognize, proceeded to appropriate the animals and whatever articles of equipment that struck their fancy.

During this time several were poking about in the brush with the muzzles of their guns, and Jed had decided that his last hour on earth was about to end, when, at a command from one of the party, they all leaped upon their horses and galloped off down stream. But during the few moments when the camp was being looted, the wounded man in the brush had seen that which told a tragic story—two dripping scalps, the hair of which he recognized only too well!

The dusk fell with a penetrating chill and the long and terrible night began. Jed crawled out of his hiding place, and after much patient industry, accompanied by torture, he managed to gather together a small heap of dry twigs. But though he had a flint and steel he struck no fire, lest the Indians, camping in the vicinity, might return. The blankets had gone with the rest of the equipment, and there in that chill immensity the sick man shivered, thinking of his dead comrades and haunted with the most gloomy forebodings. Would Fitzpatrick return that way before it was too late? How many days would it take to die of starvation? How many nights like this could one endure? Why endure the cold any longer? Why fear sudden death at the hands of savages, with that slow death waiting at the end of many days and nights of suffering?

By and by in the wee hours of the morning he made a fire, and heartened by its cheerful glow and warmth, he thanked God that, for all his woe, he had not only his rifle, knife, and flint and steel, but, what was more, the much worn copy of the Bible which he always carried in a pocket of his hunting shirt—a practice which had occasioned considerable sly merriment among his less pious comrades.

For awhile now he strove to read by the dancing light, and his memory supplied what he could not follow with his eyes. "He is chastened also with pain upon his bed, and the multitude of his bones with strong pain . . . Yea, his soul draweth near to the grave, and his life to the destroyers . . . His flesh shall be fresher than a child's; he shall return to the days of his youth. He shall pray unto God and He will be favorable unto him...."

Jed fell into an uneasy sleep. When he awoke, the fire was out, but the dawn had come. In the new light the old sustaining faith came on him like a revelation. God was in the world as much as ever, and He would provide. Yonder ran pure water—a tremendous blessing. As for food, doubtless his comrades had set traps nearby, and there is much poorer food than beaver flesh.

Having prayed earnestly for strength to endure the pain he was about to suffer, he dragged himself along the bank, keeping a sharp lookout for traps. The first was empty, and the second also. Appalled at the pain that his venture was costing him, he lay still for some time, nursing the forebodings of the night. But at length prayer strengthened him, and he began to drag himself again. The third trap contained a beaver; but it was an hour before Jed succeeded in bringing it ashore by means of a forked branch cut from the brush.

It was nearly noon when he finished his breakfast; and for hours he lay exhausted, dreading the passing of the day. Then at length, when the sun was nearing the western horizon, he began to collect fuel for the night.

The next day he fasted, for he found no beaver; and still another day came and went without food. Game seemed suddenly to have deserted the region, that his trial might be the greater. He turned to the Book for courage. "I will lift up mine eyes unto the hills, from whence cometh my help. My help cometh from the Lord which made heaven and earth. . . . The Lord shall preserve thee from evil...."

In the early morning of the third day of fasting Jed's prayers were answered. He wakened suddenly, rubbed his eyes, and saw a buck deer drinking at the stream an easy rifle-shot away. Without lifting his head he reached for the loaded gun that lay beside him, and turning on his side, took careful aim just behind the shoulder of the buck. At the roar of the gun it went down, floundering in the mud, and then was still.

Praising the goodness of God, he feasted that day; and having feasted, he dragged himself up the torturing slope of a nearby hillock, and lying there, he searched the empty distances all day long. Nothing appeared but a flock of crows.

But answered prayer had enormously strengthened the old faith in him. What if Fitzpatrick did not return? No man who knows God can be alone, and a way would be made. Doubtless his hip would heal enough before the winter set in so that he might make his way alone to the mouth of the Big Horn.

For three days he fed from the flesh of the buck, keeping constant watch over a flock of crows that were bent upon robbing his larder, and frightening them away whenever they swooped down. Then what remained of the meat went putrid, and the crows, in a noisy black cloud, soon stripped the bones clean. Jed watched them and wondered how long it would be before they should be feasting on human flesh.

He spent the two following days upon the hillock without food. Once a herd of antelope appeared a half mile away. For hours they remained in sight, peacefully grazing; then they disappeared. The third day after his meat supply had failed, he did not attempt to climb out of the creek bottom, and somehow his prayers seemed feeble. He thought much now of the home folks back in Ashtabula, Ohio, and there were times when he visualized them all with a startling clearness. Would he ever see them with his eyes again?

"The Lord is my shepherd," he read; "I shall not want. He maketh me to lie down in green pastures; he leadeth me beside the still waters. Yea, though I walk through the valley of the shadow of death, I will fear no evil; for Thou art with me." These words, oft repeated, added power to his prayers; and during the fourth day after the crows had picked the carcass, God seemed to hear again, for three deer came down to the creek to drink some two hundred yards away. But when Jed took aim, the mark danced about giddily. He fired. A jet of water arose ten yards short of the drinking animals, that crashed through the brush and disappeared. He turned to the Book for strength with which to bear this disappointment. "Thou preparest a table before me in the presence of mine enemies...."

Was he being mocked? What had he done that the Almighty should desert him? Earnestly now he implored forgiveness for his sins that he might die in peace; and a soothing quiet came upon him.

The next day Colonel Keemle of the Missouri Fur Company, led by the three who had gone in search of Fitzpatrick, came riding up the creek with a band of trappers. These were the survivors of the Blackfoot disaster on Pryor's Fork of the Yellowstone during the previous spring, when Jones and Immel had been slain.

By securing a blanket across two poles, the ends of which were fastened to the pack saddles of two of the more docile horses, a litter was made for Jed, whose wounds, despite his lack of food, had healed sufficiently to admit of travel. Pushing westward across the upper waters of the Tongue, Keemle's party came to the camp of a roving band of Cheyennes, and there, in a few days, came Fitzpatrick and his men. They had met and travelled for some days with the Crows who would soon return to the mouth of the Big Horn for the winter.

Fitzpatrick had conceived a big idea during his absence; and, riding beside the horse-litter as the party travelled down the valley of the Little Big Horn toward winter quarters, he and Jed eagerly discussed plans for a spring expedition. A Crow chief had told how, following up the Sweetwater, which flows into the North Fork of the Platte, one would come to a break in the Wind River Mountains through which one might travel as easily as over open prairie down to the Siskadee Agie, as the Indians called Green River, So plentiful were the beaver yonder, the Crow chief had said, that traps were not needed; one could knock over all one wanted with a club!

How this story must have fired the imagination of the wounded man! Here, at last, was news from the mysterious white spaces! The gates to the world of his dream were about to swing wide!

A keen northwind was bringing the winter when they reached the Yellowstone. There near the mouth of the Big Horn, and not far from the abandoned post that Manuel Lisa had built sixteen years before, snug winter quarters had been erected by Henry's men. Shortly after the arrival of Smith and Fitzpatrick, a party that had been sent northwest into the country of the Blackfeet returned with more thrilling tales than beaver.

Thus united again, Henry's men settled down for the winter, trapping the streams of the region and trading with the Crows, who had come up from the south and pitched their skin lodges nearby.

THE GHOST

THE new year, 1824, arrived in the midst of tremendous blizzards, and for weeks the trappers had nothing to do but to eat, sleep, sing, clog to a *voyagenr's* fiddling, and to swap yarns. The latter occupation offered the best avenue of escape from tedium; for man is so constituted that he is never really happy

except when creative, and yarning, as these men understood it, was, at its best, certainly much more than a memory exercise! The craving for sensation during those shut-in days and nights, together with the keen spirit of rivalry that grew up among the storytellers, often spurred them on to splendid mendacities. The old veteran from the Southwest was perhaps the most successful practitioner of this primitive art, owing partly, no doubt, to a native talent for being quite unashamed, and partly to the fact that his alleged adventures were sufficiently remote both in time and space to give his imagination the proper focal length for seeing large.

Was there anyone present who had never heard of that terrible beast called the carcagne? Well, the old veteran from the Southwest had seen one with his own eyes, and could describe it in every particular. Not only had he seen one, but once when he and a companion were roasting a goat away down yonder near the Spanish Peaks, a carcagne had come bounding into camp, seized the meat from the fire and disappeared—all with incredible speed. With every question from his audience, the old man's memory seemed to grow richer, until the original version of the incident was no more than the simple musical theme which the winds and strings and brasses chase wildly through the intricate mazes of an involved orchestration, And what was the carcagne like? Well, its hair was long, coarse, and black, and had the peculiar property of growing longer, coarser, and blacker upon closer scrutiny. As to general appearance, this strange beast was a perfect wolf from the tip of its nose to its shoulders, and thereafter it was a bear, though it was far bigger than any bear the deponent had ever seen. Its cry was indescribable, and was such as to strike terror into the stoutest heart.

However, marvelous as the carcagne, upon repeated examination, proved to be, the telling of this tale was the merest preliminary exercise for the old veteran. His memory became more athletic, and he recalled the Munchies. And what were the Munchies? Why, they were a tribe of white Indians—whiter than Americans—living away down yonder beyond the Gila country. The old veteran had met a man who had seen the Munchies; in fact, the old veteran had seen them with his own eyes. He had not only seen them; he had lived in one of their huge cities for some months, and he could testify to the fact that they were a highly civilized people.

It happened in this way. Perhaps the youngsters present hadn't heard of McKnight, Baird and Chambers; but doubtless the older men would remember how those gentlemen had set out from St Louis on a trading expedition to Santa Fe in the spring of 1812, Well, anyway, the speaker had been induced by those gentlemen to accompany the party as hunter, his great skill in that line having already rendered him famous, as one might say. Upon entering the Mexican country, the party, consisting of twelve men, was seized by the Spanish authorities and sent to prison in Chihuahua, there to remain until death, it would appear. But the speaker, being an exceedingly clever man, had contrived to escape—in three or four distinct ways, as the highly circumstantial narrative seemed to indicate. Once outside the prison, the hero of his own story fled to the mountains to evade his pursuers.

For weeks he wandered about, lost in the wilderness of mountains; and, having no weapon, it began to appear that he would surely die of starvation. Then, one day, summoning all his power in a last desperate effort, he climbed to the top of a very high mountain. And what did his hearers suppose he saw?

The old veteran was a master of dramatic pauses, which served, doubtless, the double purpose of intensifying the interest of his audience and giving the narrator an opportunity to recall any episode that, owing to the well-known carelessness of Chance, might have failed to happen.

Well, on its further side, that mountain range dropped sheer a thousand feet or more to a fertile cup-like valley apparently hemmed in on all sides by a giddy precipice. And lo, spread out on the valley floor was a vast city with spires and domes that shone in the sun! Yonder was food at last—but how to reach it? All the rest of that day the narrator of the tale sought in vain for a means of descent; and next day he continued his search, until in mid-afternoon he came to a ragged fissure in the cliff, down which, by dint of native cleverness and prodigious strength, he managed to make his way. He found the plain to be far vaster in extent than he had supposed (and the city itself proportionately larger), so that it was not until the next morning that he reached his destination, though he continued to travel most of the night.

The Munchies (for it was their city that had been seen from the top of the mountain) appeared to be unaware that any other human beings existed, and they received the starved trapper as a god. Processions and feasts were the order of the day. Housed in a huge temple, where he was daily adored by thousands, the old trapper grew fat and dissatisfied. Had he only been treated as a human being, he might have been there yet, the contented father of a brood of Munchies. But being a god soon wearied him, and he began to yearn for the old free life. Accordingly, one dark night, he made his escape, reaching the fissure in the cliff just at the white of dawn. He climbed all that day, and when, at sunset, he stood on the crest of the mountain, he could see the whole Munchie population rushing wildly about the plain like a colony of agitated ants.

The narrator had, at the time, intended to return; not alone, to be sure, but with a dozen hardy fellows properly armed. The Munchies were rich beyond calculation, even the poorest citizens eating from plates of solid gold. Furthermore, being vegetarians, because there were no wild animals in their valley, and having no word for "enemy" in their vocabulary, they were without weapons of any sort.

The business possibilities there were certainly very inviting!

And why hadn't the old veteran gone back? Well, he had tried to go back two years later, and a score of others with him. For months he and his companions had climbed lofty peaks, looking for the city of the Munchies, but in vain.

Who were the Munchies and whence came they? That was indeed a puzzling matter; but the narrator, having brought a Munchie coin away with him, once showed the same to a priest who declared that the inscription thereon was in the best Latin. Doubtless the Munchies were descendants of a small band of Roman adventurers who, having crossed the Atlantic something like 1,500 years before Columbus, had been lost in the wilderness!

The coin? The old veteran regretted exceedingly to report that he had lost the coin some years back under circumstances involving a clash with hostile Indians—which reminded him of another story well calculated to discourage any further questioning with reference to the mysterious city, lost forever in the wilds of Chihuahua.

So, mounting to the greater audacity by way of the lesser, the old veteran often reached dizzy pinnacles of improvisation, entertaining himself quite as much as his comrades. But there is in this cosmos of ours a story-making agency that at times, though working only in the raw stuff of facts, outdoes man's boldest fictions, That agency is generally known as Chance. The least sensitive prevaricator feels it incumbent upon himself to give even his wildest yarns some semblance of plausibility, which is a matter of logical sequences. But Chance, being unhuman, is under no compulsion to be plausible, and is apparently subject only to that weird super-logic of events, the course of which is non-predictable by any mental process, A story thus created does not woo credence step by step; it simply overwhelms incredulity with the impossible accomplished, and leaves the critic grasping the broken chain of his logic.

Now a masterpiece of this order had been in preparation ever since the westbound party had passed the forks of the Grand River during the previous August; and so audaciously improbable was the tale, that had it been told by the old veteran of the Southwest, it would probably have been received with hilarious laughter, for all the sadness of it.

It happened thus. The blizzards that had ushered in the new year, 1824, had ceased at last, and a great white calm had fallen on the wilderness. It was now nearly February. The men were beginning to look forward to the renewed activity of the spring hunt, and Fitzpatrick's plans for pushing westward through the pass, of which the Crows had told him, into the mysterious beaver country whence all streams sought the Pacific, furnished an enthralling topic for conversation. Even the Crows had not penetrated far into the region now about to be visited. It seemed somewhat like planning a trip to the other side of the moon.

Night had fallen, and the hush of intense cold was upon the white waste. A merry fire roared on the hearth in the big trading room where the men were lounging. Old Baptiste was making the Major's fiddle laugh and weep, and often when his bow swung into some old Southern jig tune, the younger fellows would step it lively, aping the Negro dancers away down yonder on the plantations that used to be home. By and by, in a momentary hush, the stockade gate was heard to rattle at its bar as though a sudden wind had shaken it; yet there was no wind. The men listened awhile, but heard only the howling of the wolves and the fort timbers popping in the great freeze.

The music began again, and a youth, swinging into an extravagant Negro clog, aroused a roar of laughter. Again the music stopped; and scarcely had the silence returned, when a wild hoarse cry arose outside. Some Crow Indian was there at the gate, no doubt; but what could he want? A trapper got up, went out into the snow that whined under his moccasins, and, followed by the candle-glimmer that spilled through the open door, went to the gate and raised the wicket through which trading was sometimes carried on. Immediately those inside heard the wicket clatter down, and with a look of terror on his face the trapper dashed back into the room and slammed the door.

"I—I—saw—" he stammered.

"Saw what?" asked the Major.

"Old Glass!" whispered the trapper "—all white—his ghost! "

"Fiddlesticks!" said the Major. Getting up from his bench by the fire, he went out into the starlit silence, and the men thronged to the door. The dry snow fifed to his stride. The chain clanked; the gate swung wide. And then the impossible came to pass! The men saw Henry walking backward, and after him came no other than Hugh Glass who had died yonder at the forks of the Grand and was buried there! His hair that swept his shoulders and his long gray beard matted upon his chest were ghostly with his frozen breath. The men gave way at the door, and Henry backed in, followed by the spectre. And what a face it had—grotesquely blurred as though seen reflected in ruffled water!

The old man stalked boldly into the middle of the room with his long rifle under his arm and stared about him.

"My God!" gasped the Major; "two men saw you die at the forks of the Grand!"

The old man's chest rumbled with unpleasant laughter.

"Show me these men who have seen so much," he said, "Either they lie here or I lie there! I'm not half sure myself."

"Yonder is one," said Henry.

Hugh turned to where a trapper crouched against the wall with abject terror in his eyes. For a brief moment the ruined face of the old man was as though a blizzard swept across it. He set the trigger of his gun and clicked the lock. Then his face softened, and, easing the hammer down, he strode over to the grovelling man and kicked him lightly.

"Get up and wag your tail," said he; "I wouldn't kill a pup. Where's the other one who saw me die?"

The other one had gone to Fort Atkinson with despatches before the snows had come; and the other one proved to be a youth whom Hugh had loved and befriended.

"Well, well," remarked the man who had just returned from the grave; "It's a long way I've travelled if yonder gentleman has spoken truth. So put on the pot and you will see what an appetite a ghost can have!" And having eaten with a wolfish hunger, the old man told the story of his resurrection.

He could not say how long he had lain there by the spring; but by and by he awoke and managed to get his eyes open. It was some time before he could realize what had happened to him. Then he knew by the footprints of horses all about him that the main party had been there and gone on. The ash-heap of an old fire, however, showed that Major Henry had not intended to desert him. Some of his comrades had been left behind to care for him; but where were they? And where were his "fixins"? Not even so much as a knife had been left him.

The more he thought about the matter the greater grew his anger, and he swore that he would live that he might avenge that treachery. Deliberately he set about the difficult business of getting well enough to travel, The spring furnished plenty of good water, and over it hung a bush full of ripe bullberries. Also, with his teeth he was able to tear flesh from the gashed body of the bear; but the meat had begun to spoil and soon he had only the fruit and what bread-root he could find in the vicinity.

After some days of waiting he decided that his leg, which seemed to have been broken, was hardly likely to carry him for some weeks; so he thought it well to begin his journey at once by crawling. Fort Kiowa, the nearest post on the Missouri, was over a hundred miles away. After weeks of well nigh incredible hardships, sorely wounded and without weapons, he had succeeded in reaching the post. Shortly afterward, still intent upon revenge, he had joined a keelboat party bound for the mouth of the Yellowstone; but at the Mandan villages the ice had closed in. Still driven by his wrath, he had pushed on alone through the winter wilderness; and here he was at the mouth of the Big Horn!

The wrath that had given him strength to survive was now concentrated upon the friend who had robbed and deserted him; and within a few weeks he set out again, riding southward by way of the Powder to the Platte, eastward to the Niobrara, down that stream to its mouth, and thence by the valley of the Missouri to Fort Atkinson. But the treacherous friend had gone up stream, and Hugh followed.

If, when the long pursuit was ended, Hugh had wrought vengeance upon his youthful betrayer, his adventure would have been little more than an astonishing exhibition of brute endurance and ferocity; but in the end the Graybeard forgave, and that fact raises his story to the level of sublimity.

ASHLEY'S LONG WINTER TRAIL

ON November 3rd, 1824, General Ashley left Fort Atkinson for the far off Green River, intending to proceed by way of the Platte, the North Fork of the Platte, the Sweetwater, and South Pass, which Fitzpatrick had discovered during the spring of that year, In mid-afternoon of the second day out he came to the mouth of the Loup River where the greater portion of his party had been encamped since his return to St. Louis during the early summer. There were twenty-five men in this band, and they had in charge fifty pack-horses, together with all the necessary impedimenta of a trapping expedition. During the summer and early fall they had fared well enough, having succeeded in collecting a considerable quantity of beaver both by trapping and by trading with occasional bands of Indians, However, during the recent weeks they had been rather poorly fed, as wild game, upon which they were forced to depend for food, had become scarce in that region. Great was their disappointment when, after looking forward to Ashley's coming with supplies, they learned that he had brought nothing with him, but planned to purchase from the Pawnees, whose village was located some fifty miles up the Loup valley, a sufficient quantity of provisions to last until the buffalo herds should be reached. Certainly the long and hazardous journey was not beginning well. There was no singing in camp that night, and no one was in a mood for telling stories. Winter in a wild land lay ahead of these men, and there was no telling how far away the bison might be.

Of the twenty six men who sat in camp that night at the mouth of the Loup, only nine are remembered by name: General Ashley, Thomas Fitzpatrick, Robert Campbell, James P. Beckwourth, Moses Harris (generally known as "Black" Harris), one Clement (or Claymore), Baptiste La Jeunesse, one Le Brache, and one Dorway. The first three are great names in the annals of the Early West. Beckwourth, then on his first trip to the mountains, later became a chief of the Crow tribe and won great distinction among his adopted people in their many battles with the Blackfeet. At one time he was celebrated from the Missouri to the Pacific for his yarns, in all of which he figured as the hero. He is said to have been poisoned by the Crows in 1867 at a farewell dog-feast on the eve of his intended departure for his new home on Cherry Creek, Colorado; for the Crows attributed their former success in the Blackfoot wars to their white chief and wished to keep his bones among them if they could not have the living man. "Black" Harris seems to have been another well known spinner of yarns, in his day, and greatly in love with the marvelous. He must have been more than ordinarily courageous and dependable, for Sublette more than once chose him for a companion on his long winter journeys. Of the last four, Clement (or Claymore) is remembered vaguely as a leader of one of the Ashley parties on Green River during the spring and summer of 1825; La Jeunesse is only a name, recorded by Beckwourth as that of his youthful friend; Le Brache did nothing more important than to get himself killed by Indians during the next summer; and Dorway, who according to Beckwourth was a Frenchman and a good swimmer, has left us nothing but his name, and even that is evidently misspelled!

Early in the morning of November 6th the party broke camp and moved up the Loup River in the direction of the Pawnee Loup village, three couriers having been sent in advance to inform the Indians that Ashley was coming to trade with them. During the afternoon it began to snow heavily from the Northeast. All night the snow fell, and all the next forenoon the string of men and horses pushed on through a white world, soundless but for the muffled footfall of the pack-animals and the whispering of the great tumbling flakes, By noon the Northwest wind began to blow, and by dusk it was a howling fury.

During this time the rations of the men consisted of a half pint of flour per day for each man; and now that the grass was covered two feet deep, the horses were fed on cottonwood bark whenever the edible variety could be found. However, the men struggled on in fairly good spirits, looking forward to a plenteous supply of food in the Indian town.

The 8th day of November dawned windless and bitter cold, and the men labored on patiently through the drifts up the Loup valley, thinking of the feasts they were going to have when they reached the Pawnee Loups. It was mid-forenoon when the three couriers were seen returning along the rise that flanked the river, and these were hailed with a great cry in which the horses joined. But it was not good news that the couriers brought; for the Pawnee Loups had already left their village for their wintering ground at the Forks of the Platte.

That evening the poorest of the horses was killed for meat.

Two weeks passed by, during which frequent attempts were made to advance; but the cold was intense, the snow deep, and most of the time a blizzard wind was blowing. From the day when the first horse was killed until the 21st of November, the party was able to advance only about twelve miles. By this time many of the animals were enfeebled with hunger and cold, and several had died, their carcasses filling the kettles of the half starved men.

On the 22nd of November, the desperate party struck out across country southward and managed to reach the valley of the Platte fifteen miles away. There, by good fortune, they found an abundance of game for themselves and a good supply of rushes for the horses. Having spent all the next day in feasting about cozy fires in the protection of the timber that covered the bottom lands, they set out once more on the morning of the 24th. For ten days they toiled on up the valley of the Platte, which yielded plenty of fuel and horse feed, and their hunters kept them well supplied with the flesh of deer and elk. On December 3rd they reached Plumb Point, near the site of the present city of Kearney; and there the Grand Pawnees were encamped, being on the way to their wintering ground on the Arkansas River.

These Indians strongly advised Ashley to give up his original intention and to winter at the Forks of the Platte, which, they said, was the only place between Plumb Point and the mountains where fuel and horse feed could be found in sufficient quantities. Though the weather was now extremely cold and stormy, Ashley resumed the march next morning. About midday the party overtook the tribe of Pawnee Loups, whose deserted village on the Loup River had so keenly disappointed the half starved trappers during the second week of November. For eight days Ashley's men travelled in company with these Indians, reaching the latter's wintering place at the Forks of the Platte on December 12th. The suffering of the men during those eight days of blizzard weather had been intense, and half of the horses had fallen by the way. So Ashley decided to spend a fortnight at this place in order to purchase horses and supplies, and to prepare his party for the difficult journey that lay ahead, for he had been told that little wood was to be found within the next two hundred miles.

The weather now turned fine, and though the hill-lands were still covered with two feet of snow, the valleys in many places had been swept bare by the great winds and afforded plenty of dry grass and rushes for the horses, "The day after our arrival at the Forks," writes Ashley, "the chiefs and principal men of the Loups assembled in council for the purpose of learning my wants and to devise means to supply them. I made known to them that I wished to procure twenty five horses and a few buffalo robes, and to give my men an opportunity of providing more amply for the further prosecution of the journey, I requested that we might be furnished with meat to subsist upon while we remained with them, and promised that a liberal remuneration should be made for any services they might render me. After their deliberations were closed, they came to this conclusion that notwithstanding they had been over-taken by unusually severe weather before reaching their wintering ground, by which they had lost a great number of horses, they would comply with my requisition in regard to horses and other necessaries as far as their means would admit. Several speeches were made by the chiefs during the council, all expressive in the highest degree of their friendly disposition toward our government, and their conduct in every particular manifested the sincerity of their declarations."

As a result of these negotiations, Ashley procured twenty three horses and a liberal supply of beans, dried pumpkin, corn, cured meat "and other necessary things." Ten days spent in resting and feasting served to put men and horses in fine spirits.

"And now," says Beckwourth, "everything being ready for departure, our general intimated to Two Axe (Chief of the Loups) his wish to get on. Two Axe objected. 'My men are about to surround the buffalo,' he said; 'if you go now, you will frighten them. You must stay four days, then you may go.' His word was law, so we stayed accordingly, Within the four days appointed they made the surround. There were engaged in this hunt from one to two thousand Indians, some mounted and some on foot. They encompass a large space where the buffalo are contained, and closing in around them on all points, form a complete circle. Their circle, as first enclosed, may measure perhaps six miles in diameter with an irregular circumference determined by the movements of the herd. When the surround is formed, the hunters radiate from the main body to the right and left until the ring is entire. The chief then gives the order to charge, which is communicated along the ring with the speed of lightning. Every man then rushes to the center, and the work of destruction is begun. . . . The slaughter generally lasts two or three hours.... The field over the surround presents the appearance of one vast slaughter house. He who has been most successful in the work of devastation is celebrated as a hero, and receives the highest honors from the fair sex, while he who has been so unfortunate as not to kill a buffalo is jeered and ridiculed by the whole band. Flaying, dressing and preserving the meat next engages their attention and affords them full employment for several weeks."

Arrangements for departure were made by Ashley's men on the 23rd of December, and on the morning of the 24th, bidding goodbye to their friends, the Pawnee Loups, they began the westward march again. It had been Ashley's intention to follow Fitzpatrick's route up the North Platte and the Sweetwater through South Pass; but the Loups had informed him that the North Fork afforded less wood than the South Fork, and accordingly he had decided to ascend the latter stream. "The weather was fine," writes the General, "the valleys literally covered with buffalo, and everything seemed to promise a safe and speedy movement to the first grove of timber on my route, supposed to be about ten days' march." Christmas day dawned clear, and the party continued to make good progress in the golden winter weather. During the afternoon they were overtaken by a band of Loups who had been sent out as envoys to the Arapahoes and Kiowas in the hope that they might be able to establish friendly relations between those tribes and their own people.

The next day was cloudy and bitter cold. In the afternoon it began to snow and blow again, and the night was terrible. The blizzard continued to rage until sundown of the 27th; and on the morning of the 28th four of the horses so far gone with the cold that even when they were lifted to their feet they could not stand. Abandoning the poor brutes to the wolves, the party labored on. So deep was the snow now that had it not been for the large herds of bison moving down the river, progress would have been impossible. These not only broke trail for the party, but also, in searching for food, pawed the snow away in many places, thus making it possible for the horses to graze. "We continued to move forward without loss of time," writes Ashley," hoping to be able to reach the wood described by the Indians before all our horses should become exhausted. On the 1st of January, 1825, I was exceedingly surprised and no less gratified at the sight of a grove of timber, in appearance distant some two or three miles on our front. It proved to be a grove of cottonwoods of the sweet-bark kind, suitable for horse food, located on an island offering, among other conveniences, a good situation for defence. I concluded to remain here several days for the purpose of recruiting my horses."

At this point the five Loups bade farewell to the white men and, each carrying on his back a small bundle of faggots for fuel, struck southward toward the Arkansas where they expected to find the villages of the Arapahoes and Kiowas. Ten days were spent on the island, during which time a strict guard was kept, as Ashley had been told that his old enemies, the Rees, were among the Arkansas Indians. Standing guard, the general tells us, "was much the most severe duty my men had to perform, but they did it with alacrity and cheerfulness, as well as all other services required at their hands. Indeed, such was their pride and ambition in the discharge of their duties, that their privations in the end became sources of amusement to them."

On the 11th of January, most of the cottonwood bark having been consumed, and the horses now being in fair condition, the party moved on up the river. Small sticks of driftwood and some occasional willow brush served for fuel, but no edible cottonwood was found until the 20th, when they came to another island and camped. Here, near the site of Fort Morgan, Colorado, they had their first view of the Rocky Mountains, which the General judged to be about sixty miles away.

Ashley had been informed by the Indians that it would be impossible for him to cross the mountains during the winter; so he decided to move to their base and make a fortified camp, from which trapping could be carried on while small bands were exploring the country in search of a pass through which the whole party might be taken later on. After spending two days on the island, that the horses might recuperate, they continued their journey up the South Platte until they reached a stream coming in from a northwesterly direction. Ascending this tributary (doubtless the Cache La Poudre), they camped on the 4th of February "in a thick grove of cottonwood and willows" among the foot hills of the Front Range. Long's Peak loomed huge to southward, seeming to Ashley no more than six or eight miles away, though the distance must have been at least thirty-five miles.

After leaving the camp of January 20th, game had become scarcer and scarcer, and the party had been forced to rely almost entirely upon the provisions that had been procured from the Loups at the Forks of the Platte.

The main body remained in camp here for three weeks, during which time small detachments were busily engaged in exploring. Finally, on the 26th of February, Ashley began the passage of the foothills, though the country was still "enveloped in one mass of snow and ice." "Our passage across the first range of mountains, which was exceedingly difficult and dangerous," so runs the General's narrative, "employed us three days, after which the country presented a different aspect. Instead of finding the mountains more rugged as I advanced towards their summit and everything in their bosom frozen and torpid, affording nothing on which an animal could possibly subsist, they assumed quite a different character. The ascent of the hills (for they do not deserve the name of mountains) was so gradual as to cause but little fatigue in traveling over them. The valleys and south sides of the hills were but partially covered with snow, and the latter presented already in a slight degree the verdure of spring, while the former were filled with numerous herds of buffalo, deer and antelope."

The party had now crossed from the country drained by the South Platte to that drained by the North Platte. Travelling slowly northwest by west for nine days through a region almost destitute of wood, they came on the 10th of March to a stream "about one hundred feet wide, meandering north-eastwardly through a beautiful and fertile valley about ten miles in width." This was the Laramie River, and here two days were spent in camp, as the valley furnished a fairly good supply of dry grass for the horses and an abundance of fuel.

Moving again on the 12th of March, the party camped in the evening at the foot of the Medicine Bow Mountains, which Ashley attempted to cross on the 14th and 15th; but finding the snow from three to five feet deep, he gave up the attempt and returned to his former camping place. Having rested a day, the party set out on the 17th, travelling northwardly along the base of the range. "As I thus advanced," writes the General, "I was delighted with the variegated scenery presented by the valleys and mountains, which were enlivened by innumerable herds of buffalo, antelope and mountain sheep grazing on them; and what added no small degree of interest to the whole scene were the many small streams issuing from the mountains, bordered with a thin growth of small willows and richly stocked with beaver. As my men could profitably employ themselves on these streams, I moved slowly along, averaging no more than five or six miles per day, and sometimes remained two days at the same encampment."

On the 21st of March, the appearance of the country seemed to justify another attempt to cross the mountains; and on the afternoon of the 23rd, after struggling through a "rough and broken country generally covered with snow," the party camped "on the edge of a beautiful plain," with the Medicine Bow range behind them.

Moving westward across the plain on the 24th, they camped for the night on the North Platte, a few miles south of the point where the Union Pacific Railroad now crosses that stream. The 25th and 26th days of March were spent in passing over an "elevated rough country entirely destitute of wood and affording no water save what could be procured by the melting of snow." Sage brush was used for fuel.

During the next five days the party pushed across the Great Divide Basin, "which appeared to have no outlet," and succeeded in crossing the Continental Divide at a point that later came to be known as Bridger's Pass.

During the night of the 2nd of April, a party of Crow Indians, returning from an expedition against the Snakes, drove off seventeen of the white men's horses and mules, leaving the party in a "dreadful condition," as the General tells us. With one man, Ashley boldly pursued the thieves and recovered three of the animals that had strayed from the stolen herd. On the 4th of April, nine men were sent out in pursuit of the Crows, while Ashley, with the balance of the party, laden with the packs of the stolen horses, "proceeded in search of a suitable encampment at which to await the return of the horse-hunters." On the 6th, Ashley's weary band reached a small stream running northwest, which is now called Morton Creek. Here they found the first running water and the first wood since leaving their camp of March 24th on the North Platte. About ten miles farther on down stream they reached another creek, later known as the Big Sandy, down which Fitzpatrick had led his men just one year before. Here they remained in camp until the 9th of April, when the nine men, who had been sent in pursuit of the Crows, returned without horses. On the 12th the party started down the Sandy, making no more than eight miles a day, for the men were heavily laden and the weather was snowy and raw. After travelling down the stream for six days, they struck across country to the westward, and in the evening of April 18th, 1825, they went into camp on the banks of "a beautiful river running south." They had reached the Green one hundred sixty-six days after leaving Fort Atkinson on the Missouri!

Thus ended one of the most remarkable journeys in the annals of the West. Commenting thereon, Harrison Clifford Dale says: "In 1824–25, Ashley plotted the first section of the central overland route to the Pacific. . . . He was the first white man *to* travel this route in the dead of winter, and the first to use that variation of South Pass, called by the name of one of his employees, James Bridger. He was the first American to investigate the mountains of northern Colorado, the first to enter the Great Divide Basin, to cross almost the entire length of southern Wyoming, and the first to navigate the dangerous canyons of Green River."[1]

The latter exploit will be considered in the following chapter.

DOWN GREEN RIVER

After a whole winter of difficult travel through a wild country, much of which no white man had ever seen before, Ashley had reached the chosen trapping ground with his party afoot and heavily burdened. Obviously, men who were playing the rôle of the pack-horse could not be expected to explore a wide scope of country in search of furs, and it became necessary to cache the merchandise at some convenient place, that the horses, which the Crows had failed to drive off, might be used by the trappers. However, the point at which Ashley was then camped was too far north for his purposes; for he wished to explore the country to the southward which no white man had yet penetrated. The General therefore decided to build a bullboat, descend the Green to "some eligible point about one hundred miles below," there to deposit the greater portion of the merchandise, "and make such marks as would designate it as a place of general rendezvous."

Three days were spent in camp, during which some of the men were engaged in making a frame for the boat, while others were sent out to procure down bison hides for the covering. When the boat was completed and loaded with the packs, Ashley divided his party into four bands. One of six men was to proceed to the sources of the Green; another of seven was to explore the region of the Bear River range to the westward; and a third group of six was to push southward toward the Uinta Mountains. The leaders of the bands, only two of whom are known—Fitzpatrick and one Clement (or Claymore)—"were instructed to endeavor to fall in with" the parties of Jedediah Smith and William Sublette who, as we have noted, had set out for the country beyond South Pass at the time when Fitzpatrick began his disastrous voyage down the Sweetwater. All the Ashley men then in the mountains were to assemble by the 10th of July at a point to be marked by the General farther down the Green.

All preparations having been made, the three bands, with the horses, left camp on Thursday, April 21 st, 1825; and Ashley, with the six remaining men, began his voyage.

"After making about fifteen miles," so runs the narrative, "we passed the mouth of the creek which we had left on the morning of the 18th, and to which we gave the name of Sandy." Thus was named a stream destined to become famous in the great days of the California and Oregon Trail, when migrating thousands should pour down upon it through South Pass.

Soon after pushing off that morning, it had become evident to Ashley's little band that the boat was too heavily laden for safety, if, as might be expected, there should be rapids ahead. So, having decided to build another boat, they went into camp at four o'clock in the afternoon some twenty five miles below the Sandy. The new craft was finished by the evening of the 23rd, and on Sunday morning, the 24th, they were off again, making thirty miles before they tied up for the night.

During the 25th, they drifted rapidly through twenty miles of "mountain-ous country," passed the mouth of "a beautiful, bold-running stream about fifty yards wide" (now called Black's Fork), and camped on an island "after making about twenty five miles." For five days thereafter they moved on down stream in a leisurely fashion "without observing any remarkable difference in the appea-rance of the river or the surrounding country." On the last day of April they "arrived at the base of a lofty mountain, the summit of which was covered with snow," and camped at the mouth of "a creek sixty feet wide" (now known as Henry's Fork), that entered from the west. "This spot," says Ashley, "I selected as a place of general rendezvous, which I designated by marks in accordance with the instruction given to my men,"

Thus far no difficulty had been encountered in the descent of the river, for the channel, in the most shallow places, had been no less than four feet deep. Game had been abundant, for bison were at that time "travelling from the west in great numbers."

Having spent the 1st of May at the mouth of Henry's Fork, they pushed off again on the 2nd, and had proceeded only about a half mile when the moun-tains closed in on either side of the river, rising perpendicularly to a height of one thousand five hundred feet. The channel narrowed to half its former width; the current became swifter; and the moaning sound of shadowy waters filled the winding gorge into which the boatmen now rushed, ignorant of what might lie ahead and unable to stop had they wished to do so. At length, rounding a bend, the boats swept out into a place where the huge walls fell back, leaving a pleasant little park along the margins of the stream. But scarcely had the boatmen felt relief from dread, when, swerving sharply to the left, the moaning current swirled them into a second fearsome gorge cut sheer through a lofty mountain. Once again they emerged into an open space, and once again the dark waters swept them onward through an overhanging canyon. And when they emerged again into an open space some ten miles below the mouth of Henry's Fork, they decided to call it a day, and camped. They had that day passed through the three canyons now called Flaming Gorge, Horseshoe, and Kingfisher.

Putting off in the morning of the 3rd of May, which was Sunday, they found the river "remarkably crooked with more or less rapids every mile, caused by rocks which had fallen from the sides of the mountain," and these made brisk work for the crews. They had made about twenty miles from their last camp when, hearing a deep roar of waters in the defile ahead of them, they hastily rowed to shore. Cautiously working their way along the bank, they "descended to the place from whence the danger was to be apprehended. It proved to be a perpendicular fall of ten or twelve feet produced by large fragments of rocks which had fallen from the mountain and settled in the river, extending entirely across the channel and forming an impregnable barrier to the passage of loaded watercraft." So they were obliged to unload their boats and let them down over the falls by means of long lines which they had provided for that purpose. It was sunset when this operation had been completed and the boats reloaded. Dropping down stream about a mile, they camped for the night. The falls over which they had passed have been given the name of their discoverer.

During his stop at this point, Ashley painted his name and the year on a huge bowlder that had fallen from the canyon wall, and the first three letters were still visible when the Kolb Brothers passed that way in 1911. The inscription was seen by William L. Manly in 1840, and by J. W. Powell in 1869.

During the 4th of May the boats sped safely onward in the midst of lofty heights "almost entirely composed of strata of rock of various colors (mostly red) and partially covered with a dwarfish growth of pine and cedar." In the morning of the 5th, having dropped six miles down stream, they came to a place where "the mountains gradually recede from the water's edge, and the river expands to the width of two hundred fifty yards, leaving the bottoms on each side from one to three hundred yards wide, interspersed with clusters of small willows." This little valley, surrounded by lofty mountain walls, later came to be known as Brown's Hole. There Ashley's party remained in camp until the morning of the 7th of May, when, descending ten miles, they camped "on a spot of ground where several thousand Indians had wintered. Many of their lodges remained as perfect as when occupied. They were made of poles two or three inches in diameter, set up in circular form, and covered with cedar bark."

The adventurers had proceeded but two miles on the 8th when once again they were swept into a narrow winding canyon (now called Lodore), the sides of which rose gloomily to a tremendous height Says Ashley: "As we passed along between these massy walls, which in a great degree excluded from us the rays of heaven and presented a surface as impassable as their body was impregnable, I was forcibly struck with the gloom which spread over the countenances of my men. They seemed to anticipate (and not far distant too) a dreadful termination of our voyage, and I must confess that I partook in some degree of what I supposed to be their feelings, for things around us had truly an awful appearance. We soon came to a dangerous rapid which we passed over with a slight injury to our boats. A mile lower down, the channel became so obstructed by the intervention of large rocks over and between which the water dashed with such violence as to render our passage in safety impracticable. The cargoes of our boats were therefore a second time taken out and carried about two hundred yards, to which place, after much labor, our boats were scended by means of cords." About fifteen miles farther down stream they passed the mouth of the Tampa, which Ashley named Mary's River.

Within the next few days the party succeeded in reaching the mouth of the Uinta River (which, according to Ashley, the Indians called the Tewinty), having run the rapids of Whirlpool Canyon, "where the mountains again close to the water's edge and are more terrific than any seen during the whole voyage." There, near the site of the present town of Ouray, Utah, Ashley's men cached the cargoes of their boats, as the General had decided to ascend the Uinta River to its source on the return trip to the place of rendezvous. They then continued the descent of the Green River, passing through Desolation Canyon to a point about fifty miles below the mouth of the Uinta, the river being bounded all the way "by lofty mountains heaped together in the greatest disorder, exhibiting a surface as barren as can be imagined."

They had been travelling for three weeks down the Green River (never before navigated by white men), and now coming to the conclusion that nothing was to be gained by continuing the voyage, they abandoned their boats and started back afoot for their cache at the mouth of the Uinta. Within a few days they fell in with a friendly band of Utah Indians. "I understood by signs from them," says Ashley, "that the river which I had descended, and which I supposed to be the Rio Colorado of the West, continued its course as far as they had any knowledge of it, southwest through a mountainous country. They also informed me that all the country known to them south and west from the Tewinty River was almost entirely destitute of game, that the Indians inhabiting that region subsist principally on roots, fish and horses."

Having procured horses from the Utahs, the white men pushed on to the mouth of the Uinta, loaded their animals with the merchandise that had been cached there, and proceeded up the Uinta to the mouth of the Duchesne, which they followed through a mountainous and sterile country to its headwaters. From thence they crossed the Uinta Mountains and came upon the upper tributaries of the Weber River, which Ashley took to be the Buenaventura, a mythical stream then supposed to flow into the Bay of San Francisco! After travelling sixty miles down the Weber, they fell in with a portion of the band that had set out with Smith and Sublette from the camp on the Sweetwater during the previous summer. With this band were twenty nine men who had deserted from the Hudson Bay Company and were now bringing their furs to the rendezvous of the American trappers. From these and from a band of Utahs recently encountered, Ashley gained the impression that the stream he had been following emptied into a lake, from the western end of which a great river flowed westward to the sea. "The necessity of my unremitted attention to my business" writes Ashley, "prevented me from gratifying a great desire to descend the river to the ocean, which I ultimately declined with the greatest reluctance." It will be noted from this remark how little was then known of the vast central country between the Continental Divide and the Pacific. Ashley could not guess that he was then seven hundred miles distant from the ocean by an air-line route, and that in all the vast triangular space between the Snake and the Colorado no river rising in the Rockies reached the sea.

From the camp on the Weber, the combined parties set out for the appointed place of rendezvous.

THE RENDEZVOUS

Ten weeks had elapsed since Ashley's party had separated into four bands and struck out in as many directions from the camp on the Green River fifteen miles above the Sandy's mouth; and now all the trappers employed by Ashley in that country, including the parties of Smith and Sublette who had wintered west of the Divide, began to arrive at the place of rendezvous, their pack-animals laden with the precious spoils of many a beaver stream. By the 1st of July, 1825, one hundred twenty men, including the twenty-nine who had deserted from the Hudson Bay Company, were encamped on the Green at the mouth of Henry's Fork. Beckwourth tells us that many of the Frenchmen had their squaws and children with them, and that the encampment was "quite a little town."

When all had come in, the General opened his goods, "consisting of flour, sugar, coffee, blankets, tobacco, whisky, and all other articles necessary for that region." Whereupon, so Beckwourth assures us, the jubilee began. Some of these men had left St. Louis with Henry in the spring of 1822 and had been in the wilderness ever since. Many had not tasted sugar or coffee for many months, having lived entirely on the game of the country, and tobacco and whisky were luxuries not to be despised. These articles were purchased at enormous prices, and many a trapper not only swallowed in a day of ease what he had earned in a year of constant danger and hardship, but when the rendezvous broke up found himself indebted to his employer for his next year's outfit. Storytelling,

gambling, drinking, feasting, horse-racing, wrestling, boxing, and target-shooting, were the order of the day—"all of which were indulged in with a heartiness that would astonish more civilized societies," says Beckwourth.

The free trappers, who were not paid by the year as were the hired trappers, but, being their own masters, trapped where they pleased and sold their furs at the annual rendezvous, were the "cocks of the walk." These boasted freely with the naïvete of children—or Homeric heroes. As Joseph Meek tells us: "They prided themselves on their hardihood and courage; even on their recklessness and profligacy. Each claimed to own the best horses; to have had the wildest adventures; to have made the most narrow escapes; to have killed the greatest number of bears and Indians; to be the greatest favorite with the Indian belles: the greatest consumer of alcohol; and to have the most money to spend—that is, the largest credit on the books of the company. If his hearers did not believe him, he was ready to run a race with them, to beat them at 'cold sledge,' or to fight, if fighting were preferred—ready to prove what he affirmed in any way the company pleased."

While this orgy proceeds and the year's business is being transacted, let us see what of permanent value these men had accomplished in their wanderings; for it is not because they brought back much beaver that we remember them now.

A year has passed since we last saw Jedediah Smith and William L. Sublette. They were then pushing westward up the Sweetwater with a string of pack-horses and about fifty men, and they had just said farewell to Fitzpatrick bound by boat for Fort Atkinson with the proceeds of his spring hunt. Having crossed South Pass and followed the Little and Big Sandys down to the Green, the party was divided into three bands—one under Sublette, one under Etienne Provost, and one, consisting of only six men, under Jedediah Smith. From this point Smith turned northward, moving slowly and trapping as he went, following the course of the Green River to the mouth of Horse Creek, which comes in from the west at a point slightly south of the 43rd parallel. Ascending this stream to its source, he crossed over to the headwaters of Hoback's River which he descended to the Snake River. After travelling about one hundred miles down the latter stream, he turned northward, striking across country in the direction of Clark's Fork of the Columbia. He was now well into the territory that was being worked by the roving bands of the Hudson Bay Company, operating from various posts, the chief of which was Fort Vancouver on the lower Columbia. Previous to leaving the Snake River, he had been travelling practically the same route that had been followed by the eastbound Astorians under Robert Stuart just twelve years before. Buffalo were plentiful all along the way, so that the little party suffered no want. Also, many streams rich in beaver had been found, and by the end of summer Smith's horses were fairly well loaded with pelts.

Then one day in early fall a band of Iroquois Indians, led by a Canadian half-breed named Pierre, came to Smith's camp in a most wretched condition. They were without horses and guns, and were on the verge of starvation. Smith learned from them that they had started during February of that year from Spokane House on the Spokane River, a branch of the upper Columbia, with a party of Hudson Bay Company men under Alexander Ross, bound for the buffalo country at the headwaters of the Missouri and Yellowstone. They had crossed the Bitter Root Mountains and the Continental Divide with Ross during the winter, had hunted in the region of the Three Forks of the Missouri during the spring, and then, swinging southward and westward through what is now called the Yellowstone National Park, had begun to trap on the upper waters of the Snake. During June they had been detached from the main party and sent southward. All summer long they had wandered about, taking many beaver; but a week or two before falling in with the Americans, they had been attacked by a band of Snake Indians and had been robbed of horses, guns, and most of their peltry. However, they still had nine hundred skins, worth at that time in St. Louis not less than $5,000.

Now Smith was both a Christian and a Yankee. Being a Christian, he could do no less than give succor to those in distress; being a Yankee, he drove a hard bargain at the same time. He would escort the Iroquois to Pierre's Hole where Alexander Ross was thought to be encamped with the main party, and for such services he would accept the nine hundred skins in advance! At least, such was the story the Indians told to Ross. The unfortunate Indians, having accepted Smith's proposition, all the furs thus far acquired were cached, and the two parties started for Pierre's Hole. They had travelled only a few days when they met a band of Hudson Bay men who had been sent out to find the missing Iroquois, and by these Smith was guided to Ross's camp on the Salmon River near the mouth of the Pashimari.It was now the middle of October, 1824— about the time when Ashley at Fort Atkinson on the Missouri was preparing for his long winter journey up the Platte and across the Rockies to the Green River. Alexander Ross was ready to start for Flathead House, a Hudson Bay Company post on the upper waters of Clark's Fork of the Columbia, and Smith decided to accompany him, being eager to view the country and wishing to learn as much as possible about the doings of the British traders in that region. Surely our hero did not lack audacity!

On November 1st Ross's party, with their self- invited American guests, crossed the Bitter Root Mountains, by the same route that Lewis and Clark had taken nineteen years before and reached Flathead House on November 26th. On the same day Peter Skeene Ogden, one of the greater leaders of the Hudson Bay Company, arrived from Spokane House with an expedition bound for the Snake River country. Ogden remained there until December 20th, when he started for the spring trapping grounds. It is believed that Smith, having gathered all the information possible during his month's sojourn at Flathead House, accompanied Ross southward up the Bitter Root River to its source, thence across the divide to the Salmon River.

Early in the spring of 1825 Smith and his men, after recovering the peltry they had cached during the previous fall, arrived in Cache Valley slightly below the point where the Bear River, flowing southward, crosses the Utah line. Here they met Sublette's party, and it is easy to imagine with what eagerness the reunited comrades told of their adventures and wanderings.

Sublette and his men had been on a wild goose chase, though they too had succeeded in taking much fur by the way. Striking south and west from the mouth of the Sandy, where they had said farewell to the parties under Provost and Smith during the summer of 1824, they had come upon the upper waters of the Bear River which they took to be the Buenventura. They had followed this river throughout the remainder of the summer, trapping as they went. Rounding the Wasatch Mountains on the north and following the stream westward and southward, they had reached Cache Valley late in the fall, and finding it a sheltered place with plenty of wood, they had decided to winter there,

During the winter there had been much discussion among Sublette's men as to what would be found at the mouth of the stream upon which they were encamped, and by way of settling the discussion James Bridger, then but twenty years old, had descended Bear River to its mouth, where, quite naturally, he had found salt water! Returning to winter quarters, he reported to his companions what he had discovered, and it was believed that he had actually reached an arm of the Pacific Ocean!

The party under Provost, after parting from their comrades at the Sandy's mouth, had pushed southward for a considerable distance along the Green during the late summer of 1824; then turning westward, they had crossed the upper waters of the Bear and reached the Weber, which also empties into Salt Lake, but by a much more direct route than that of the Bear. Believing that he was on the Buenaventura, Provost descended the Weber; but how far he proceeded before going into winter quarters is unknown. There seems to be some reason to suspect that he may have reached Great Salt Lake in the fall of 1824, and that he spent the winter there near the Weber's mouth, thus antedating Bridger's discovery by a few months; but proof is wanting. At least it is known that Provost's band was at the mouth of the Weber early in the spring. Also, Jedediah Smith, so Ashley tells us in his letter to General Atkinson, had fallen "on the waters of the Grand Lake of Buenaventura" (meaning Great Salt Lake) on his return from Flathead House before he reached Cache Valley.

Thus, within a few months, three of the Ashley bands had reached Great Salt Lake by different routes. However, James Bridger is generally considered the discoverer.

During the spring hunt of 1825 a band of Hudson Bay men, that had been sent southward by Ogden from the upper Snake River country where he was then operating, fell in with a small detachment of Ashley men under Johnson Gardner on the Bear River. Gardner induced the British trappers to desert their employer and bring their catch (worth a fortune) to the American rendezvous. These were the men whom Ashley met, in company with one of his own bands, on the upper reaches of the Weber during June. Happily, Gardner's right to be remembered does not rest wholly upon this rather questionable transaction. His name goes linked with that of Hugh Glass; for in the winter of 1832 when Glass was killed by his old enemies, the Rees, on the frozen Yellowstone, not far below the mouth of the Big Horn, it was Johnson Gardner who, according to the famous traveller, Maximilian, Prince of Wied-Neuwied, followed the murderers and "killed two of them with his own hands."

And now all the Ashley men, who had been widely scattered in seven bands, were reunited on the Green River at the mouth of Henry's Fork, having explored the country bordering the Rockies on the west from the upper waters of Clark's Fork of the Columbia in latitude 47° 30', to a point slightly below latitude 40° on the Green River. Let us note the significance of what these men were doing.

In 1792 Captain Gray of the Boston trading ship, *Columbia*, had discovered the mouth of the great river which he named after his vessel. In 1805 Lewis and Clark had crossed the Continental Divide from the headwaters of the Missouri River and had descended the Columbia to the Pacific. In the fall of 1810 Major Andrew Henry, as we have noted, had crossed the Continental Divide and built a trading post on Henry's Fork of the Snake River, but owing to the hostility of the Blackfeet he had been forced to abandon his position the next year. In 1811 John Jacob Astor's men had founded the fur-trading establishment of Astoria at the Columbia's mouth. Thus by right of discovery, exploration, and occupation, the Americans claimed the great Oregon country lying west of the Rockies and north of latitude 42°, the northern boundary of the Spanish domain. But *possession* was quite another matter. In 1814, as a result of the war with England, Astor's great enterprise had failed, and the British Northwest Company had taken possession of Astoria, renaming it Fort George. Since that time English traders—first the Northwest Company, then the Hudson Bay Company—had been "the lords of the land," although an agreement had been made in 1818 whereby the British and the Americans were to have equal rights in the Oregon country. But so long as the Americans knew no overland route save those that had been followed by Lewis and Clark and by the Astorians, "joint occupancy" virtually meant British occupancy; for the northern passes across the Rockies were very difficult to cross, and the inveterate hostility of the Blackfeet made that way extremely hazardous. Had not a more advantageous road been found across the Continental Divide during those early years, it is most probable that the English would have become permanently established throughout the territory drained by the Columbia system; for always the flag follows the trader.

Thomas J. Parnham, who travelled overland to Oregon in 1839–40, when the stream of emigration was already beginning to flow across the Rockies, made the following just observations regarding the great central route to the Pacific: "The Platte, therefore, when considered in relation to our intercourse with the habitable countries of the Western Ocean, assumes an unequalled importance among the streams of the Great Prairie wilderness. But for it, it would be impossible for man or beast to travel those arid plains, destitute, alike, of wood, water, and grass, save what of each is found along its course. Upon the headwaters of the North Fork too is the only way or opening in the Rocky Mountains at all practicable for a carriage road through them. That travelled by Lewis and Clark is covered with perpetual snow; that near the debouchure of the South Fork of the river is over high and nearly impassable precipices; that travelled by myself, farther south, is, and ever will be impassable for wheel carriages. But the Great Gap (South Pass) seems designed by nature as the great gateway between the nations on the Atlantic and Pacific Oceans."

Dr. John McLoughlin, factor of the Hudson Bay Company's post, Fort Vancouver, used to say: "For all coming time we and our children will have uninterrupted possession of this country, as it can never be reached by families but by water around Cape Horn." And upon being told that he would live to see the coming of the Yankees, he would answer: "As well might they undertake to go to the moon!" He was thinking of the northern passes.

But now Ashley's men under Fitzpatrick had found a great natural road leading up the valleys of the Platte and the Sweetwater, over the scarcely noticeable Divide at South Pass; and Ashley himself had travelled a variation of this route by way of the South Platte and Bridger's Pass. The gateway of the mountains had swung open at last, and henceforth there would be no lack of Americans in the country west of the Rockies. It was the beginning of the invasion of the Far West. In course of a few years the settlers would follow the trail of the trappers in ever increasing numbers, until, when the river of humanity should be in full flood forty years later, ten thousand wagons, bound for Oregon and California, would trundle up that way in a single season.

Down from the North as far as Snake River had come the English. Up from the South, penetrating the wilderness as far as Utah Lake, and spreading up the coast of California, had come the Spaniards. Between the countries known to the British and the Spanish lay an unknown land. And now, at the Green River rendezvous in July, 1825, already were gathered together some of those who, within the next two years, were destined to lift the veil of mystery from that vast triangular space.

CHAPTER 7

JOE MEEK: THE MERRY MOUNTAIN MAN

By Stanley Vestal

One of the companions of Leonard in his trapping and trading expeditions in the Rocky Mountains was the versatile Joe Meek, who has frequently been mentioned in connection with this work. They were together at the battle of Pierre's Hole, he being in the employ of Milton Sublette at this time. The following year he with some companions joined the California expedition under Walker, when it reached Bear River. He gives a very meager and rather unreliable account of this overland voyage, in Mrs. Victor's *River of the West* in which he states that they returned by way of the Moquis villages, in northern Arizona and became involved in a disgraceful affair and murdered some of these half-civilized Indians. This is, no doubt, a mistake, and if not, the party must have separated, and only a portion followed this route.

Meek continued in the mountains until the decline of the fur trade in the early forties, at which time the emigration to Oregon by the overland route had increased to such a degree that thousands started from the western frontier of Missouri, in the spring, as soon as the grass was sufficiently advanced, the journey taking the whole of the summer, and when they arrived in Oregon in the fall they were, as a rule, in a very sad plight, having but little to carry them through the winter, and no crops could be planted or harvested until the following year.

Meek was indeed as poor as the poorest, and no better off than when, he went to the mountains many years before, a mere boy. He had an Indian wife and children. After due consideration he decided to join the emigrants and settle down on a claim in Oregon, as did also many other mountain-men. A neighbor of his was Judge Burnett, afterwards governor of California, who came to Oregon as poor as Meek; this gentleman tells an amusing story of himself which illustrates their poverty. When he arrived in Oregon he was allowed to occupy a school building, which was then only used for church purposes, and in payment of rent, was required to have the building in a condition to hold services when desired. His wardrobe, as may be imagined, was not very extensive, in fact, he went without shoes much of the time, but on these church occasions felt it duty bound to appear in his best; he found one shoe but was unable to find its mate; he thought, however, that by hiding his other foot under the seat, and exposing the one with the shoe, he would present a respectable appearance. Everything went well until about the middle of the sermon, when the minister, becoming thirsty, requested Judge Burnett to get him a glass of water; he said there was no refusing such a modest request, and hobbled to do the errand with but one shoe on, much to the amusement of the congregation. Meek was a hale fellow, good-natured and jovial, remarkably good at telling stories, which he could stretch to any magnitude, and not particularly fond of work, much to the disgust of good Doctor McLaughlin. Settlers were entitled to six hundred and forty acres of land if they had families; and if they had the facilities and inclination to work the same, the extremely rich soil soon returned them a competence.

They organized a provisional government, and Joe Meek, the future envoy, was elected marshal; his principal duty was to collect the taxes, which were paid in wheat at sixty cents a bushel, it being the legal tender of the country. He resigned this office, and was elected to the legislature, about 1846; was re-elected the following year, when he swam out to a wessel lying at the mouth of the Willamette, to get liquor to treat his constituents.

About this time the troublesome northwest boundary was settled, and Oregon became a part of the United States. Shortly after an Indian uprising, known as the "Cayuse War," occurred, and Doctor Whitman and his family, with others about the mission at Waiilatpu, were massacred. It was necessary under these circumstances to inform the United States government of the condition of affairs in Oregon at once, and ask for assistance. In view of this necessity it was resolved in the legislature to send a messenger to carry the intelligence of the massacre to Governor Mason in California, and through him to the commander of the United States squadron in the Pacific that a vessel of war might be sent into the Columbia River, and arms and ammunition borrowed for the present emergency, from the nearest arsenal.

For this duty was chosen Jesse Applegate, Esq., a gentleman who combined in his character and person the ability of the statesman with the sagacity and strength of the pioneer. Mr. Applegate with a party of brave men set out in midwinter to cross the mountains into California, but such was the depth of the snow they encountered that traveling became impossible, even after abandoning their horses, and they were compelled to return.

The messenger elected to proceed to the United States was Joseph L. Meek, whose Rocky Mountain experience eminently fitted him to encounter the dangers of such a winter journey, and whose manliness, firmness, and ready wit stood him instead of statesmanship. On December 17, 1847, Meek resigned his seat in the House in order to prepare for the discharge of his duty as messenger to the United States. On January 4, armed with his credentials from the Oregon legislature, and bearing despatches from that body and the Governor to the President, he set out on the long and perilous journey, having for travelling companions Mr. John Owens and Mr. George Ebbarts, the latter having formerly been a mountain-man like himself. At the Dalles they found the first regiment of Oregon riflemen, under Major Lee, of the newly created army of Oregon. From the reports which the Dalles Indians brought in of the hostility of the Indians beyond the Des Chutes River it was thought best not to proceed before the arrival of the remainder of the army, when all the forces would proceed at once to Waiilatpu. Owing to various delays, the army, consisting of about five hundred men, under Colonel Gilliam, did not reach the Dalles until late in January, when the troops proceeded at once to the seat of war. Arriving at Waiilatpu, the friends and acquaintances of Doctor Whitman were shocked to find that the remains of the victims were still unburied, although a little earth had been thrown over them. Meek, to whom Mrs. Whitman had seemed all that was noble and captivating, ever since his meeting with her in the train of the fur-trader, on their way out, had the melancholy satisfaction of bestowing, with others, the last sad rite of burial upon such portions of her once fair person as murderer and the wolves had not destroyed. Some tresses of golden hair were severed from the brow so terribly disfigured, to be given to her friends in the Willamette Valley as a last and only memorial. Among the state documents at Salem, Oregon, may still be seen one of these relics of the Waiilatpu tragedy. Not only had Meek to discover and inter the remains of the Whitmans, but also of his little girl, who was being educated at the mission, with a daughter of his former leader, Bridger.

This sad duty performed, he immediately set out, escorted by a company of one hundred men under Adjutant Wilcox, who accompanied him as far as the foot of the Blue Mountains. Here the companies separated, and Meek went on his way to Washington. Meek's party now consisted of himself, Ebbarts, Owens, and four men, who, desirous of returning to the states, took this opportunity. However, as the snow proved to be very deep on the Blue Mountains, and the cold severe, two of these four volunteers became discouraged and concluded to remain at Fort Boise, then a small trading-post of the Hudson Bay Company.

In order to avoid trouble with the Indians he might meet on the western side of the Rocky Mountains, Meek had adopted the red belt and Canadian cap of the employes of the Hudson Bay Company; and to this precaution was due the fact that he passed safely through the country now all raging with hostility caught from the Cayuses. About three days' travel beyond Fort Boise, the party met a village of Bannock Indians, who at once made warlike demonstrations, but on seeing Meek's costume, and receiving an invitation to hold a "talk," desisted, and received the travelers in a friendly manner. Meek informed the chief, with all the gravity which had won for him the name of "Shiamshuspusia" among the Crows in former years, that he was going on the business of the Hudson Bay Company to Fort Hall; and that Thomas McKay was a day's march behind with a large trading-party and plenty of goods. On the receipt of this good news, the chief ordered the braves to fall back, and permit the party to pass. Yet, fearing the deception might be discovered, they thought it prudent to travel day and night until they reached Fort Hall.

At this post of Hudson Bay Company, in charge of Mr. Grant, they were kindly received, and, stopped for a few hours of rest, Mr. Grant being absent, his wife provided liberally for the refreshment of the party, who were glad to find themselves even for a short interval under a roof, beside a fire, and partaking of freshly cooked food. But they permitted themselves no unnecessary delay. Before night, they were once more on their way, though snow had now commenced to fall afresh, rendering traveling very difficult. For two days they struggled on, their horses floundering in the soft drifts, until further progress in this manner became impossible. The only alternative was to abandon their horses and proceed on snow-shoes, which were readily constructed of willow sticks. Taking only a blanket and their rifles, and leaving the animals to find their way back to Fort Hall, the little party pushed on.

Meek was now on familiar ground, and the old mountain spirit which had once enabled him to endure hunger, cold, and fatigue without murmuring possessed him now. It was not without a certain sense of enjoyment that he found himself reduced to the necessity of shooting a couple of pole-cats to furnish a supper for himself and party. How long the enjoyment of feeling want would have lasted is uncertain, but probably only long enough to whet the appetite for plenty. To such a point had the appetites of all the party been whetted, when, after several days of scarcity and toil, followed by nights of emptiness and cold, Meek had the agreeable surprise of falling in with an old mountain comrade on the identical ground of many former adventures, the head-waters of Bear River. This man, whom Meek was delighted to meet, was Peg-leg Smith, one of the most famous of many well-known mountainmen; he received this name by having lost his leg when fighting with the Crows, and had a wooden leg which he had a way of unstrapping when in a fight, and it proved a weapon not to be despised. He was engaged in herding cattle in the valley of Thomas Fork, where the tall grass was not quite buried under snow, and had with him a party of ten men. Meek was as cordially received by his former comrade as the unbounded hospitality of mountain manners rendered it certain he would be. A fat cow was immediately sacrificed, which, though not buffalo meat, as in former times it would have been, was very good beef, and furnished a luxurious repast to the pole-cat eaters of the last few days.

Smith thought to celebrate the occasion by a grand entertainment. Accordingly, after a great deal of roast beef had been disposed of, a dance was called for, in which white men and Indian women joined with far more mirth and jollity than grace or ceremony. Thus passed some hours of the night, the bearer of despatches seizing, in true mountain style, the passing moments of pleasure, so long as it did not interfere with the punctilious discharge of his duty. And to the honor of our hero be it said, nothing was ever allowed to interfere with that. Refreshed and provided with rations for a couple of days, the party started on again the next morning, still on snow-shoes, and traveled up Bear River to the head-waters of Green River, crossing from the Muddy Fork over to Fort Bridger, where they arrived very much fatigued, but quite well, after a little more than three days' travel.

Here it was Meek's good fortune to again meet with his former leader, Bridger, to whom he related what had befallen him since turning pioneer. The meeting was joyful on both sides, clouded only by the remembrance of what had brought it about, and the reflection that both had personal wrongs to avenge in bringing about the punishment of the Cayuse murderers. Once more Meek's party were generously fed and furnished with such provisions as they could carry about their persons. In addition to this, Bridger presented them with four good mules, by which means the travelers were mounted four at a time, while the fifth took exercise on foot; so that by riding and walking, in turns, they were enabled to get on very well as far as the South Pass. Here for some distance the snow was very deep, and two of their mules were lost in it. Their course lay down the Sweetwater River, past many familiar hunting and camping grounds, to the Platte River. Owing to the deep snows, game was very scarce, and a long day of toil was frequently closed by a supperless sleep under shelter of some rock or bank, with only a blanket for covering. At Red Buttes they were so fortunate as to find and kill a single buffalo, which, separated from a distant herd, was left by Providence in the path of the famishing travelers.

On reaching the Platte River they found the traveling improved, as well as the supply of game, and proceeded with less difficulty as far as Fort Laramie, a trading-post in charge of a French trader named Papillion. Fresh mules were obtained, and the little party treated in the most hospitable manner. In parting from his entertainer, Meek was favored with this brief counsel: "There is a village of Sioux, of about six hundred lodges, a hundred miles from here. Your course will bring you to it. Look out for yourself, and don't make a Grey muss of it." The latter clause referred to the affair of 1837, when the Sioux had killed the Indian escort of Mr. Grey. When the party arrived at Ash Hollow, which they meant to have passed in the night, on account of the Sioux village, the snow was again falling so thickly that the party had not perceived their nearness to the village until they were fairly in the midst of it. It was now no safer to retreat than to proceed; and after a moment's consultation, the word was given to keep on. In truth, Meek thought it doubtful whether the Sioux would trouble themselves to come out in such a tempest, and if they did so. the blinding snowfall was rather in his favor. Thus reasoning, he was forcing his mule through the drifts as rapidly as the poor worried animal could make its way, when a head was protruded front a lodge door, and "Hello, Major," greeting his ear in an accent not altogether English. On being thus accosted, the party came to a halt, and Meek was invited to enter the lodge, with his friends. His host on this occasion was a French trader named Le Bean, who, after offering the hospitalities of the lodge, and learning who were his guests, offered to aecompany the party a few miles on his way. This he did saying by way of explanation of this act of courtesy, "The Sioux are a bad people; I thought it best to see you safely out of the villiage." Receiving the thanks of the travelers, he turned back at nightfall, and they continued on all night without stopping to camp, going some distance south of their course before turning east again, in order to avoid any possible pursuits.

Without further adventures, and by dint of almost constant travel, the party safely arrived at St. Joseph, Mo., in a little over two months, from Portland, Oregon. Soon afterwards, when the circumstances of this journey became known, a steamboat built for the Missouri River trade was christened the "Joseph L. Meek," and bore for a motto, on her pilot-house, "The quickest trip yet," in reference both to Meek's overland journey and her own steaming qualities. As Meek approached the settlements, and knew that he must soon be thrown into the society of the heighest officials, and be subjected to ordeals which he dreaded far more than Indian fighting, or even traveling across a continent of snow, the subject of how he was to behave in these new and trying positions very frequently occurred to him. He, an uneducated man, trained to mountain life and manners, without money, or even clothes, with nothing to depend on but the importance of his mission and his own mother-wit, felt far more keenly than his careless appearance would suggest, the difficulties and awkwardness of his position. "I thought a great deal about it," confessed Col. Joseph L. Meek later, "and I finally concluded that as I had never tried to act like anybody but myself, I would not make myself a fool by beginning to ape other folks now. So I said, 'Joe Meek you always have been, and Joe Meek you shall remain; go ahead, Joe Meek.'"

In fact, it would have been rather difficult putting on fine gentleman-like airs, in that old worn-out hunting suit of his, and with not a dollar to bless himself. On the contrary, it needed just the devil-may-care temper which naturally belonged to our hero, to carry him through the remainder of his journey to Washington. To be hungry, ill-clad, dirty, and penniless, is sufficient in itself for the subduing of most spirits; how it affected the temper of the messenger from Oregon we shall now learn. When the weary little party arrived in St. Joseph, they repaired to a hotel, and Meek requested that a meal should be served to all, but frankly confessed that they had no money to pay. The landlord, however, declined furnishing guests of his style upon such terms, and our travelers were forced to go into camp below the town. Meek now bethought himself of his letters of introduction. It chanced that he had one from two young men among the Oregon volunteers, to their father in St. Joseph. Stopping a negro who was passing his camp, he inquired whether such a gentleman was known to him; and on learning that he was, had him deliver the letter from the sons. This movement proved successful. In a short space of time the gentleman presented himself, and learning the situation of the party, provided generously for their present wants, and promised any assistance which might be required in future. Meek, however, chose to accept only that which was imperatively needed, namely, something to eat, and transportation to some point on the river where he could take a steamer for St. Louis. A portion of his party chose to remain in St. Joseph, and a portion accompanied him as far as Independence, whither this same St. Joseph gentleman conveyed them in a carriage, While Meek was stopping at Independence, he was recognized by a sister, whom he had not seen for nineteen years; who, marrying and emigrating from Virginia, had settled on the frontier of Missouri. But he gave himself no time for family reunion and gossip. A steamboat that had been frozen up in the ice all winter, was just about starting for St. Louis, and on board of this he went, with an introduction to the captain, which secured for him every privilege the boat afforded, together with the kindest attention of its officers. When the steamer arrived at St. Louis, by one of those fortunate circumstances so common in our hero's career, he was met at the landing by Campbell, a Rocky Mountain trader who had formerly belonged to the St. Louis Company. This meeting relieved him of any care about his night's entertainment in St. Louis, and it also had another effect, that of relieving him of any further care about the remainder of his journey; for, after hearing Meek's story of the position of affairs in Oregon and his errand to the United States, Campbell had given the same to the newspaper reporters, and Meek, like Byron, awoke next morning to find himself famous.

Having telegraphed to Washington, and received the president's order to come on, the previous evening, our hero wended his way to the levee the morning after his arrival in St. Louis. There were two steamers lying side by side, both up for Pittsburg, with runners for each, striving to out-do each other in securing passengers. A bright thought occurred to the moneyless envoy— he would earn his passage. Walking on board one of the boats, which bore the name of the "Declaration," himself a figure which attracted all eyes by his size and outlandish dress, he mounted to the hurricane deck and began to harangue the crowd upon the levee, in the voice of a Stentor: "This way, gentlemen, if you please. Come right on board the 'Declaration.' I am the man from Oregon, with despatches to the president of these United States, that you all read about in this morning's paper. Come on board, ladies and gentlemen, if you want to hear the news from Oregon. I have just come across the plains, two months from the Columbia River, where the Injuns are killing your missionaries. Those passengers who come aboard the 'Declaration' shall hear all about it before they get to Pittsburg. Don't stop thar, looking at my old wolfskin cap, but just come aboard, and hear what I've got to tell." The novelty of this sort of solicitation operated capitally. Many persons crowded on board the "Declaration" only to get a closer look at this picturesque personage who invited them, and many more because they were really interested to know the news from the far-off young territory which had fallen into trouble. So it chanced that the "Declaration" was inconveniently crowded on this particular morning. After the boat had got under way, the captain approached his roughest looking cabin passenger and inquired in a low tone of voice if he was really and truly the messenger from Oregon. "Thar's what I've got to show for it;" answered Meek, producing his papers. "Well, all I have to say is, Mr. Meek, that you are the best runner this boat ever had; and you are welcome to your passage ticket, and anything you desire besides," Finding that this bright thought had succeeded so well, Meek's spirits rose with the occasion, and the passengers had no reason to complain that he had not kept his word. Before he reached Wheeling his popularity was immense, notwithstanding the condition of his wardrobe. On the morning of his arrival in Wheeling it happened that the stage which then carried passengers to Cumberland, where they took the train for Washington, had already departed. Elated by his previous good fortune our ragged hero resolved not to be delayed by so trivial a circumstance; but walking pompously into the stage office inquired, with an air which must have smacked strongly of the mock-heroic, if he, "could have a stage for Cumberland?" The nicely-dressed, dignified, elderly gentleman who managed the business of the office, regarded the man who proffered this modest request for a moment in motion-less silence, then slowly raising the spectacles over his eyes to a position on his forehead, finished his survey with unassisted vision. Somewhat impressed by the manner in which Meek bore this scrutiny, he ended by demanding, "Who are you?" Amused by the absurdity of the tableau they were enacting, Meek straightened himself up to his six feet two, and replied with an air of superb self-assurance: "I am Envoy Extraordinary and Minister Plenipotentiary from the Republic of Oregon to the Court of the United States." After a pause in which the old gentleman seemed to be recovering from some great surprise, he requested to see the credentials of this extraordinary envoy. Still more sur-prised he seemed on discovering for himself that the personage before him was really a messenger from Oregon to the government of the United States. But the effect was magical. In a moment the bell-rope was pulled, and in an incre-dibly short space of time a coach stood at the door ready to convey the waiting messenger on his way to Washington. In the meantime in a conversation with the stage agent, Meek had explained more fully the circumstances of his mis-sion, and the agent had become much interested. On parting, Meek received a ticket to the relay house, with many expressions of regret from the agent that he could ticket him no farther. "But it is all the same," said he; "you are sure to go through." "Or run a train off the track," rejoined Meek, as he was bowed out of the office.

It happened that there were some other passengers waiting to take the first stage, and they crowded into this car glad for the unexpected opportu-nity, but wondering at the queer-looking passenger to whom the agent was so polite. This scarcely concealed curiosity was all that was needed to stimulate the mad-cap spirits of our so far "conquering hero." Putting his head out of the window just at the moment of starting, he electrified everybody, horses included, by the utterance of a war-whoop and yell that would have done credit to a wild Comanche. Satisfied with the speed to which this demoniac noise had excited the driver's prancing steeds, he ensconced himself in his corner of the coach and quietly waited for his fellow passengers to recover from their stunned sensations. When their complete recovery had been effected, there followed the usual questioning and explanations, which ended in the inevitable lionizing that was so much to the taste of this sensational individual. On the cars at Cumberland, and at the eating-houses, the messenger from Oregon kept up his sensational character, indulging in alternate fits of mountain manners, and again assuming a disproportionate amount of grandeur; but in either view proving himself very amusing. By the time the train reached the relay house, many of the passengers had become acquainted with Meek, and were prepared to understand and enjoy each new phase of his many-sided comicality. The ticket with which the stage agent presented him, deadheaded him only to this point. Here again he must make his poverty a jest, and joke himself through to Washington.

Accordingly, when the conductor came through the car in which he, with several of his new acquaintances were sitting, demanding tickets, he was obliged to tap his blanketed passenger on the shoulder to attract his attention to the "Ticket, sir." "Ha ko any me ca, hanch?" said Meek, starting up and addressing him in the Snake tongue. "Ticket, sir," repeated the conductor, staring. "Ka hum pa, hanch?" returned Meek, assuming a look which indicated that English was as puzzling to him, as Snake to the other people. Finding that his time would be wasted on this singular passenger, the conductor went on through the train; returning after a time with a fresh demand for his ticket. But Meek sustained his character admirably, and it was only through the excessive amusement of the passengers that the conductor suspected that he was being made the subject of a practical joke. At this stage of affairs it was privately explained to him, who and what his waggish customer was, and tickets were no more mentioned during the journey. On the arrival of the train at Washington, the heart of our hero became for a brief moment of time "very little;" He felt that the importance of his mission demanded some dignity of appearance, some conformity to established rules and precedents. But of the latter he knew absolutely nothing; and concerning the former, he realized the absurdity of a dignitary clothed in blankets and a wolfskin cap. "Joe Meek I must remain," said he to himself, as he stepped out of the train, and glanced along the platform at the crowd of porters with the names of their hotels on their hat-bands. Learning from inquiry that Coleman's was the most fashionable place, he decided that to Coleman's he would go, judging correctly that it was best to show no littleness of heart even in the matter of hotels.

When Meek arrived at Coleman's it was the dinner hour, and following the crowd to the dining-saloon, he took the first seat he came to, not without being very much stared at. He had taken his cue and the staring was not unexpected, consequently not so embarrassing as it might otherwise have been. A bill of fare was laid beside his plate. Turning to the colored waiter who placed it there, he startled him first by inquiring in a low growling voice—"What's that, boy?" "Bill of fare, sah," replied the boy, who recognized the Southerner in the use of that one word. "Read," growled Meek again, "the people in my country can't read." Though taken by surprise, the waiter, politely obedient, proceeded to enumerate the courses on the bill of fare. when it came to game—"Stop thar, boy," commanded Meek, "what kind of game?" "Small game, sah." "Fetch me a piece of antelope," leaning back in his chair with a look of satisfaction on his face. "Got none of that, sah; don't know what that ar', sah." "Don't know," with a look of pretended surprise. "In my country antelope and deer ar' small game; bear and buffalo ar' large game. I reckon if you haven't got one, you haven't got the other. In that case you may fetch me some beef." The waiter disappeared grinning, and soon returned with the customary thin and small cut, which Meek eyed at first contemptuously, and then accepting it in the light of a sample swallowed it at two mouthfuls, returning the plate to the waiter with an approving smile, and saying loud enough to be overheard by a score of people, "Boy, that will do. Fetch me about four pounds of the same kind."

By this time the blanketed beef-eater was the recipient of general attention, and the "boy" who served him comprehending with that quickness which dis-tinguishes servants, that he had no ordinary backwoodsman to deal with, was all the time on the alert to make himself useful. People stared, then smiled, then asked each other, who is it? loud enough for the stranger to hear. Meek looked neither to the right nor to the left, pretending not to hear the whispering. When he had finished his beef, he again addressed himself to the attentive "boy." "That's better meat than the old mule I eat in the mountains." Upon this remark the whispering became more general, and louder, and smiles more frequent. "What have you got to drink, boy?" continued Meek, still unconscious. "Isn't there a sort of wine called—some kind of pain?" "Champagne, sah?" "That's the stuff, I reckon; bring me some." While Meek was drinking his champagne, with an occasional aside to his faithful attendant, people laughed and wondered, "who the devil he was." At length having finished his wine, and overhearing many open inquiries as to his identity, the hero of many bear-fights slowly arose, and addressing the company through the before-mentioned "boy," said: "You want to know who I am?" "If you please, sah; yes, if you please, sah, for the sake of these gentlemen present," replied the "boy," answering for the company. "Wall then," proclaimed Meek with a grandiloquent air quite at variance with his blanket coat and unkempt hair, yet which displayed his fine person to advantage, "I am Envoy Extraordinary and Minister Plenipotentiary from the Republic of Oregon to the Court of the United States." With that he turned and strode from the room. He had not proceeded far, however, before he was overtaken by a party of gentlemen in pursuit. Senator Underwood of Kentucky immediately introduced himself, calling the envoy by name, for the despatch from St. Louis had prepared the president and the senate for Meek's appearance in Washington, though it had not advised them of his style of dress and address. Other gentlemen were introduced, and questions followed questions in rapid succession. When curiosity was somewhat abated, Meek expressed a wish to see the president without delay. To Underwood's question as to whether he did not wish to make his toilet before visiting the White House, his reply was, "Business first, and toilet afterwards." "But," said Underwood, "even, your business can wait long enough for that." "No, that's your mistake, Senator, and I'll tell you why; I can't dress, for two reasons—both good ones. I've not got a cent of money, nor a second suit of clothes." The generous Kentuckian offered to remove the first of the objections on the spot, but Meek declined. I'll see the President first, and hear what he has to say about my mission." Then calling a coach from the stand, he sprang into it, answering the driver's question of where he would be taken, with another inquiry: "What should a man of my style want to go? To the White House, of course," and so was driven away amid the general laughter of the gentlemen present, in the portico at Coleman's, who had rather doubted his intention to pay his respects to the president in his dirty blankets. He was admitted to the presidential mansion by a mulatto of about his own age, with whom he remembered playing when a lad, for it must be remembered that the Meeks and Polks were related, and this servant had grown up in the family. On inquiring to see the President, he was directed to the office of the private secretary, Knox Walker, also a relative of Meek, on his mother's side. On entering he found the room filled with gentlemen waiting to see the President. The secretary sat reading a paper, over the top of which he glanced but once at the new-comer, to ask him to be seated. But Meek was not in a humor for sittting, and said, "I should like to see the President immediately. Just tell him, if you please, that there is a gentleman from Oregon waiting to see him on very important business." At the word Oregon, the secretary sprang up, dashed his paper to the floor, and crying out "Uncle Joe" came forward with both hands extended to greet his long lost relative.

"Take care, Knox, don't come too close," said Meek, stepping back, "I'm ragged, dirty, and lousy." But Walker seized his cousin's hand, without seeming fear of the consequences, and for a few moments there was an animated exchange of questions and answers, which Meek at last interrupted to repeat his request to be admitted to the President without delay. When once the secretary got away he soon returned with a request from the President for the appearance of the Oregon messenger, all other visitors being dismissed for that day. Polk's reception proved as cordial as Walker's had been. He seized the hand of his newly found relative, and welcomed him in his own name, as well as that of messenger from the distant, much loved, and long neglected Oregon. The interview lasted for a couple of hours. Oregon and family affairs were talked over together; the President promising to do all for Oregon that he could. After this the President insisted on sending for Mrs. Polk and Mrs. Walker to make his acquaintance. "When I heard the silks rustling in the passage, I felt more frightened than if a hundred Blackfeet had whooped in my ear. A mist came over my eyes, and when Mrs. Polk spoke to me I could think of nothing to say in return."

But Meek was not the sort of man to be long in getting used to a situation, however novel or difficult. In a very short time he was *au fait* in the customs of the capital. His perfect frankness led people to laugh at his errors as eccentricities; his good looks and natural *bonhomie* procured him plenty of admirers; while his position at the White House caused him to be envied and lionized at once. On the day following his arrival the President sent a message to Congress accompanied by the memorial from the Oregon legislature and other documents appertaining to the Oregon cause. Meek was introduced to Benton, Oregon's indefatigable friend, and received from him the kindest treatment;

also to Dallas, president of the senate; Douglas, Fremont, Gen. Houston, and all the men who had identified themselves with the interests of the West.

In the meantime our hero was making the most of his opportunities, attending dinners and champagne suppers, besides giving an occasional one of the latter. At the presidential levees he made himself agreeable to witty and distinguished ladies, answering innumerable questions about Oregon and Indians. On the latter subject, where he had an interested and confiding audience, he was probably at his best, and some of his hearers no doubt were very nervous on going to bed, and often during the night felt to see if the brain covering was still intact.

Meek found his old comrade, Kit Carson, in Washington, staying with Fremont at the home of Senator Benton. Carson on leaving the mountains was as poor as the average mountain-man, and had no resources at this time except the pay furnished by Fremont for his services as guide and explorer in the California and Oregon expeditions, and in these discoveries Carson as much as Fremont deserves the name of pathfinder.

So long as Meek's purse was supplied, as it generally was, Carson could borrow from him, but one being quite as careless of money as the other, they were sometimes both out of pocket at the same time. In which case the conversation was likely to be as follows:

Carson: Meek, Id me have some money, can't you?

Meek: I haven't got any money, Kit.

Carson: Go and get some.

Meek: —it, what am I to get money from?

Carson: Try the "contingent fund," can't you?

Shortly after the arrival of Meek congress appropriated ten thousand dollars, to be expended under the direction of the president, in payment for services and expenses of such persons as had been engaged by the provisional government of Oregon in conveying communications to and from the United States; and for purchase of presents for such Indian tribes as the peace and quiet of the country required. Of this money Meek received seven thousand four hundred dollars, Mr. Thornton, who came by water from Oregon, two thousand six hundred, and the Indian tribes the whole of the remainder. His old employer, Wilkes, who was ill in Washington, sent for him to come and tell "some of those Oregon lies" for his amusement, and Meek, to humor him, stretched some of his good stories to the most wonderful dimensions. On one of his visits, Polk, detecting the restless state of his mind, asked laughingly, "Well, Meek, what do you want now?" "I want to be franked." "How long will five hundred dollars last you?" "About as many days as there ar' hundreds, I reckon," "You are shockingly extravagant, Meek. Where do you think all this money is to come from?" "It is not my business to know, Mr. President, but it is the business of these United States to pay the expenses of the messenger from Oregon, isn't it?" The following night he gave a champagne supper. Washington manners were in some respects too much like mountain manners for five hundred dollars to go a great ways.

On the fourth of July, Polk laid the corner-stone of the National Monument, the address was delivered by Winthrop, the military display, and the fireworks in the evening being unusually fine. In the procession General Scott and staff rode on one side of the President's carriage, Col. May and Meek on the other, Meek making a great display of horsemanship, in which as a mountain-man he excelled.

The bill before Congress, for the extension of the Government over that territory, was objected to by the Southern members, as they were against more free soil. The President was anxious that the bill should pass, Benton of Missouri also, Butler of South Carolina opposed it. Numerous were the skirmishes which these two Senators had over the Oregon question; and a duel would, in one instance, have resulted, had not the arrest of the parties put a termination to the affair.

The close of the session was at hand, Congress was to adjourn at noon Monday, August 14. At ten o'clock Saturday night, no adjournment having prevailed, Senator Foote, of Mississippi, arose and commenced to speak in a manner most dull and drawling; he intended to occupy the floor until the hour of adjournment on Monday. Commencing at the creation of Adam and Eve, he gave the Bible story; the fall of man; the history of the children of Israel; the stories of the prophets; ecclesiastical history, thus continuing to drawl through the time hour after hour. Sleepy senators betook themselves to the cloak-rooms to lunch, to drink, to talk to the waiting ones, and to sleep. Thus the night passed and the Sabbath morning's sun arose, and still Foote was in the midst of his Bible disquisition. At length, two hours after sunrise, a consultation was held between Butler, Mason, Calhoun, Davis, and Foote, which resulted in the announcement that no further opposition would be offered to taking the vote upon the final passage of the Oregon bill. A vote was then taken, and the bill passed.

The long suspense was at last ended and Meek prepared to return to Oregon, his life-long habits of unrestrained freedom began to revolt against the conventionalities in Washington, the novelty of which had long since disappeared. In appointing officers for the new territory he was made United States Marshal; no office could have suited him better. The governorship was offered to Mr. Shields who declined, General Joseph Lane of Indiana was then appointed and his commission given to Meek to deliver to him in the shortest time possible, and then to proceed at once to Oregon. The President's last words were, "Good bless you, Meek; tell Lane to have a territorial government organized during my administration."

While in St. Louis young Lane who accompanied his father, wanted a knife, and as they met a man on the street with a large number he began to beat down the price, whereupon Meek made an offer for the whole lot in order to prevent Lane from getting one at any price. Most satisfied with this investment, he next made a purchase of three whole pieces of silk, at one dollar and fifty cents a yard. At this stage of the transaction Gen. Lane interfered sufficiently to inquire "what he expected to do with that stuff?" "Can't tell," answered Meek, "but I reckon it is worth the money." "Better save your money," said the more prudent Lane.

At St. Louis they met Lieutenant Hawkins, who was to command the escort of twenty-five riflemen, also Doctor Hayden, surgeon of the company. On the tenth of September the government of Oregon was on its way, taking the southern route over the Santa Fe trail, to the latter place, thence down the Gila to Fort Yuma, Arizona, and San Pedro Bay in California, where they expected to find a vessel to carry them the remainder of the journey. The party which on leaving Leavenworth six months before numbered fifty-five, now numbered only seven. This was due to the many desertions on account of the gold excitement which had just broken out in California. They arrived weary, dusty, foot-sore, famished, and suffering, at Williams's ranch on the Santa Anna River, Cal, where they were kindly received, and their wants ministered to.

At this place our hero developed, in addition to his various accomplishments, a talent for speculation. While overhauling his baggage, the knives and the silk which had been purchased of the peddler in St. Louis were brought to light; no sooner did the senoras catch a glimpse of the shining fabrics than they went into raptures over them, after the fashion of their sex, and to the expense of their spouse. Seeing the state of mind to which these raptures, if unheeded, were likely to reduce the ladies of his house, Mr. Williams approached Meek delicately on the subject of purchase. But Meek, in the first flush of speculative shrewdness declared that he had bought the goods for his own wife, and he could not find it in his heart to sell them. However, as the senoras were likely to prove inconsolable, Mr. Williams again mentioned the desire of his family to be clad in silk, and the great difficulty, nay, impossibility, of obtaining the much coveted fabric in that part of the world, and accompanied his remarks with an offer of ten dollars a yard for the lot. At this magnificent offer our hero affected to be overcome by regard for the feelings of the senoras, and consented to sell his dollar and a half silk at ten dollars a yard. In the same manner, finding that knives were a desirable article in that country, very much wanted by miners and others, he sold out his few dozen at an ounce of gold dust each, netting the convenient little profit of about five hundred dollars.

When Gen. Lane was informed of the transaction, and reminded of his objection to the original purchase, he laughed heartily. "Well, Meek" he said, "you were drunk when you bought them, and by—I think you must have been drunk when you sold them; but drunk or sober, I will own that you can beat me at a bargain."

On the second of March the Oregon government arrived at its destination, and on the third put into operation the Territorial Government, one day before the expiration of President Polk's term of office.

CHAPTER 8

ADVENTURES OF ZENAS LEONARD
from *Narrative of the Adventures of Zenas Leonard*

By Himself

Oct. 22nd. The nights getting somewhat cold, and snow falling more or less every day, we began to make preparations to return to our winter quarters, at the mouth of Laramies river; and on the 25th commenced our tour down the river. On the 28th we arrived at the mountain, that we crossed going up, but found it impossible, owing to the enormous depth of the snow to pass over it. On the morning of the 30th we started a number of men up and down the valley, on search of a place to cross the mountain, who returned the next day and reported that they had found no passing place over the mountain; when under these circumstances a majority of the company decided in favor of encamping in this valley for the winter, and when the ice melted out of the river, in the spring, commence trapping until such times as the snow melted off the mountain; when we would return to the mouth of the river, where we had secreted our goods.

On the 1st day of November we commenced travelling up the valley, on search of a suitable place to pass the winter, and on the evening of the 4th, we arrived at a large grove of Cottonwood timber, which we deemed suitable for encamping in. Several weeks were spent in building houses, stables, &c, necessary for ourselves, and horses during the winter season. This being done, we commenced killing buffaloe, and hanging up the choice pieces to dry, so that if they should leave the valley we would have a sufficient quantity of meat to last us until spring. We also killed Deer, Bighorn Sheep, Elk, Antelope, &c., and dressed the hides to make moccasins.

About the 1st of December finding our horses getting very poor, we thought it necessary to commence feeding them on Cottonwood bark; for which purpose each man turned out and peeled and collected a quantity of this bark, from the grove in which we were encamped for his horses; but to our utter surprise and discomfiture, on presenting it to them they would not eat it, and upon examining it by tasting, we found we were deceived, men were dispatched up and down the valley, on search of Sweet Cottonwood, but returned without success. Several weeks were spent in fruitless exertion to obtain feed for our horses; finally we were compelled to give it up, & they commenced dying. It seldom happened during all our difficulties, that my sympathies were more sensibly touched, than on viewing these starving creatures. I would willingly have divided my provision with my horses, if they would have eat it.

On new-years day, notwithstanding our horses were nearly all dead, as being fully satisfied that the few that were yet living must die soon, we concluded to have a feast in our best style; for which purpose we made preparation by sending out four of our best hunters, to get a choice piece of meat for the occasion. These men killed ten Buffaloe, from which they selected one of the fattest humps they could find and brought in, and after roasting it handsomely before the fire, we all seated ourselves upon the ground, encircling, what we there called a splendid repast to dine upon. Feasting sumptuously, cracking a few jokes, taking a few rounds with our rifles, and wishing heartily for some liquor, having none at that place we spent the day.

The glorious 8th arrived, the recollection of the achievements of which, are calculated to gladden the hearts of the American people; but it was not so glorious to us. We found our horses on that day, like Pakenham's forces, well nigh defunct. Here we were in this valley, surrounded on either side by insurmountable barriers of snow, with all our merchandize and nothing to pack it upon, but two mules—all the rest of our horses being dead. For ourselves we had plenty to eat, and were growing fat and uneasy; but how we were to extricate ourselves from this perilous situation, was a question of deep and absorbing interest to each individual About the 10th we held a consultation. to decide what measures should be taken for our relief. Mr. Stephens, our pilot having been at Santafee, in New Mexico, some 8 or 10 years previous, informed the company that horses in that place, were very cheap; and that he was of the opinion he could take them to it, if they saw proper to follow him. It was finally agreed upon by the company, that a part of them should start for Santafee; but not, however, without a good deal of confusion; as many were of the opinion that the snow on the mountain in the direction of Santafee, would be found to be as insurmountable, as in the direction of their merchandize, and also that the distance was too great to attempt to travel on foot, at that season of the year. It appearing from the maps to be little short of 800 miles.

On the morning of the 14th, finding every thing in readiness for our Santafee trip, we set out, each man with his bedding, rifle and nine Beaver skins, packed upon his back; leaving four men only to take care of our merchandize, and the two mules. The beaver skins we took for the purpose of trading to the inhabitants of Santafee for horses, mules, &c. We appointed from the middle of April till the middle of May, as our time for returning; and if we did not return within that time, our four men were to wait no longer, but return to the mouth of the Laramies river, to meet the rest of the company, We continued in the direction of Santafee, without any extraordinary occurrence, for several days. Found game plenty and but little snow, until we arrived at the foot of a great mountain, which appeared to be totally covered with snow. Here we thought it advisable to kill and jirk some buflaloe meat, to eat while crossing this mountain, after which we continued our course; finding much difficulty in travelling, owing to the stormy weather & deep snow, so much so indeed, that had it not been for a path made by the buflaloe bulls it would have been impossible to travel.

The channel of the river where it passes through these mountains is quite narrow in places and the banks very steep. In such places the beaver build their dams from bank to bank; and when they become old the beaver leave them, and they break and overflow the ground, which then produces a kind of flag grass. In the fall of the year, the Buffaloe collect in such places to eat this grass, and when the snow falls too deep they retreat to the plains; and it was in these trails that we ascended the mountain.

We still continued our course along this buflaloe path, which led us to the top of the mountain; nothing occurring more than it continued to snow day and night. On the 25th we arrived on the top of the mountain, and wishing to take a view of the country, if it should cease snowing. In the morning it still continued to snow so rapidly that we were obliged to remain in the camp all day, and about the middle of the day, we eat the last of our jirk, and that evening we were obliged to go to bed supperless.

On the 29th it still continued to snow, and having nothing to eat, we thought it high time to be making some move, for our preservation, or we must perish in this lonely wilderness. The question then arose, shall we return to the valley from whence we came, or continue in the direction of Santafee, This question caused considerable disturbance. Those who were in favor of going ahead, argued that it was too far back to game, that it would be impossible to return before starving to death; while those who were for returning contented that it was the heighth of imprudence, to proceed in the direction of Santafee. Accordingly we made preparations, and started. We travelled across the summit of the mountain, where we found a plain about a mile wide, which with great difficulty, owing to the fierceness of the wind, we succeeded in crossing; but when we attempted to go into the timber, on the opposite side from the mountain, we found it impossible, in consequence of the depth of the snow, and were obliged to turn back and recross the plain. As we returned by the fire we had made going over the plain the first time, we halted for the purpose of mutually deciding what to do; when it was determined by the company, that we would, if possible, return to our four men & two mules. We then started on search of the buffaloe path which we had followed to the top of the mountain but owing to the strong wind that had blown for several days, and increased depth of the snow, it was invisible. We then attempted to travel in the snow without the path, but we found this equally as impossible, as in the direction of Santafee.

Here we were, in a desolate wilderness, uninhabited (at that season of the year) by even the hardy savage or wild beast, surrounded on either side by huge mountains, of snow, without one mouthful to eat, save a few beaver skins, our eyes almost destroyed by the piercing wind, and our bodies at times almost buried by the flakes of snow which were driven before it. Oh! how heartily I wished myself at home; but wishing, in such a case appeared useless; action alone could save us. We had not even leather to make snow shoes, but as good fortune would have it, some of the men had the front part of their pantaloons lined with deer skin, and others had great coats of different kinds of skin, which we collected together to make snow shoes of. This appeared, to present to us the only means of escape from starvation and death. After gathering up every thing of leather kind that could be found, we got to making snow shoes, and by morning each man was furnished with a pair. But what were we to subsist upon while crossing the mountain, was a painful question that agitated every bosom, and employed every tongue in company, Provision, we had none, of any description; having eaten every thing we had that could be eat with the exception of a few beaver skins, and, after having fasted several days, to attempt to travel the distance of the valley, without any thing to eat, appeared almost worse than useless. Thinking, however, that we might as well perish one place as another, and that it was the best to make an exertion to save ourselves; and after each man had selected two of the best beaver skins to eat as we travelled along, we hung the remainder upon a tree, and started to try our fortune with the snow shoes. Owing to the softness of the snow, and the poor construction of our snow shoes, we soon found this to be a difficult and laborious mode of travelling. The first day after we started with our snow shoes we travelled but three or four miles and encamped for the night, which, for want of a good fire, we passed in the most distressing manner. Wood was plenty but we were unable to get it, and it kept one or two of the men busy to keep what little fire we had from going out as it melted the snow and sunk down. On the morning (30th Jan.) after roasting and eating some of our beaver skins, we continued our journey through the snow. In this way we continued to travel until the first day of February, in the after noon, when we came to where the crust on the snow was sufficiently strong to carry us. Here we could travel somewhat faster, but at the best not much faster than a man could crawl on his hands and feet, as some of the men from hunger and cold were almost insensible of their situation, and so weak that they could scarcely stand on their feet, much less walk at speed. As we approached the foot of the mountain the snow became softer and would not carry us. This caused the most resolute despair, as it was obviously impossible, owing to extreme weakness, for us to wade much further through the snow. As we moved down the mountain plunging and falling through the snow, we approached a large spruce or cedar tree, the drooping branches of which had prevented the snow from falling to the ground about its trunk. Here we halted to rest while collected under the sheltering boughs of this tree, viewing, with horrified feelings, the way-worn, and despairing countenances of each, other, a Mr. Carter, a Virginian, who was probably the nighest exhausted of any of the company, burst into tears and said, "here i must die." This made a great impression upon the remainder of the company, and they all, with the exception of a Mr. Hockday and myself, despaired of going any further. Mr. Hockday, however, after some persuasion, telling their, that if they had the strength to follow us we would break the rod as far as possible, if not out to the valley, succeeded in getting them started once more. Mr. Hockday was a large muscular man, as hardy as a mule and as resolute as a lion; yet kind and affectionate. He was then decidedly the stoutest man in the company, and myself, probably, the next stoutest. As for our Captain, Mr. Stephens, he was amongst the weakest of the company.

We resumed our journey, and continued to crawl along through the deep snow slowly till the evening of the fourth, when we arrived in the plain, at the foot of the mountain. Here we found the snow so shallow that we could dispense with the use of our snow shoes; and while in the act of taking them off some of the men discovered, at the distance of 70 or 80 yards; two animals feeding in the brush, which they supposed to be buffaloe, but from blindness, caused by weakness and pine smoke, could not be positive. Mr. Hockday and I were selected to approach and kill one of the animals without regard to what they might prove to be, while the remainder of the company were to go to a neighboring grove of timber and kindle a fire. Having used our guns as walking canes in the snow, we found them much out of order, and were obliged to draw out the old loads and put in new ones, before attempting to shoot. After taking every precaution we deemed necessary to insure success, we started and crawled along on our hands and knees, until we approached within ten or fifteen steps of the animals, when Mr. Hockday prepared to shoot; but upon finding that he could not see the sight of the gun or hold it at arms length, forbore, and proposed to me to shoot. I accordingly fixed myself and pulled trigger. My gun missed fire? I never was so wrecked with agitation as at that moment. "There," said I, "our game is gone, and we are not able to follow it much further;" but as good fortune had it, the Buffaloe, (for such we had discovered them to be), did not see nor smell us, and after raising their heads out of the snow, and looking around for a few moments for the cause of the noise, again commenced feeding. I then picked the flint of my gun, fired and broke the back of one of the Buffaloe, my ball not taking effect within 18 inches of where I thought I aimed. The men in the grove of timber, on hearing the report of my rifle came staggering forth to learn the result, and when they received the heart-cheering intelligence of success they raised a shout of joy. It was amusing to witness *the* conduct of some of the men on this occasion Before we had caught the buffaloe they appeared scarcely able to speak-but a moment after that, were able to hollow like Indians at war. I will no describe the scene that followed, here the reader may imagine it, and account of it would be repulsive and offensive rather than agreeable. This was the ninth day since we had eaten anything but dried beaver skins. We remained at this place for four days feasting upon the carcass of this Buffaloe, during which time we recruited considerably in strength and spirits, and on the 8th we resumed our journey down the river in search of our four men and two mules, and soon landed in the valley where game was plenty, and but little snow to obstruct our march. We continued our journey, killing plenty of game and living well, without any strange occurrence until the 14th, when we halted within a short distance of our old camp, and sent two or three of our worst looking men ahead to see whether they would be recognized by the four men. They were not known immediately on arriving at the camp, but no sooner engaged in conversation that they were recognized by the four men, and heartily welcomed back.

Here we remained at our old station until the 14th of March, during which period, having plenty of good buffaloe meat to eat, we regained our usual health and appearance. Anxious to be doing something, eight of us made preparations to start again to Santafee for horses. We were to travel south, along the foot of the mountain till we came to a certain river which heads in the mountain near where we had hung the beaver skins on the pine tree; after finding this river we were to commence trapping, and also to endeavor to get the beaver fur off the mountain into the valley. The balance of the company, 13 in number, were to remain at the camp and secrete the merchandize, and then follow us to this river, where we were to meet; and if we had succeeded in getting the beaver skins off the mountain, we were to join together and proceed in the direction of Santafee. With this understanding we started, and, pursued our course slowly along the base of the mountain—found game plenty, met with no obstacle to impede our march, and on the 20th we arrived on the bank of the river. After remaining here a few days the ice melted out of the creeks and we commenced and continued to trap for beaver until the 28th during which time we caught a fine quantity of fur, and built ourselves a wigwam after the Indian fashion. The weather continuing warm and pleasant, and having a large quantity of dried meat on hand we concluded to hide our traps, beaver skins, baggage, &c., in our wigwam and pack a portion of the jirked meat on our backs and make an effort to get the beaver skins off the pine tree where we had left them in January. We started, and after travelling up the river along the side of the mountain for two or three days, we came in contact with huge mountains of snow and insurmountable icebergs, and were compelled to abandon our course & return back again to the plain. When we had arrived within a short distance of our wigwam, on our return, we discovered several trails of moccasin tracks in the snow. Some of the company became somewhat alarmed at these signs, supposing them to be the trails of hostile Indians, others appeared rejoiced, and said it was the remainder of our company. The dispute was soon decided, for on arriving at our wigwam, we found it completely robbed of everything we had left in it: traps, blankets, beaver skins and other utensils were all gone. Nothing remained but the naked frame of the little hut. We had now nothing left to sleep on save one old blanket for each man which we had with us on the mountain, and had nearly lost all our traps. Under these highly aggravating circumstances some of the men became desperate, declared they would retake their property or die in the attempt. For my part, I viewed the matter calmly and seriously and determined to abide the dictates of prudence only. Seeing from the trail of the Indians that they were not very numerous, and had a number of horses with them, we determined, after some controversy, to rob them of their horses, or other property commensurate to our loss. Accordingly we made preparations for our perilous adventure, we eat supper, prepared our fire arms, and a little after dark set out on search of the enemy, the night was calm and clear. We traversed the valley up and down for several hours without making any discoveries; we then ascended an adjacent hill, from the summit of which we discovered at a considerable distance a number of dim fires. A controversy here arose amongst the men as to the expediency of attacking the Indians. It was finally decided, however, by a majority of the company, that we should attack them at all hazards. We started in the direction of the fires, and after travelling some distance, and having lost sight of the fires, some of the men again became discouraged, and strongly urged the propriety of abandoning the project; but on calling a vote a majority again decided in favor of attacking the Indians and in a few minutes after we arrived on the top of a hill, within 50 or 60 yards of the enemy's camp. Here we halted for the purpose of reconnoitering. At this time the moon was just rising above the summit of the mountain, and casting its glimmering rays o'er the valley beneath, but did not shine on the Indian camp. There were five fires and the Indians appearing more numerous than we had expected to find them, we thought it advisable to be as careful and judicious about attacking them as possible. At the foot of this hill, near a large rock, we left our hats, coats and every thing that was unnecessary in action. We also designated this as a point of meeting, in case we should get separated in the skirmish; and had an understanding that but two should fire at a time, and that Capt Stephens was to command. Mr. Hockday and I were selected to shoot first. We then started & crawled silently along on our hands and knees until we got within eight or ten, steps of one of the fires, where we laid down in the brush, with our heads close together to consult as to the most proper mode of surprising the savages, whose dusky forms were then extended in sleep around the dying embers. While in this position, some eager for the conflict, others trembling with fear, a, large dog rose from one of the fires and commenced growling and barking in the most terrifying manner. The spell of silence was now broken, and an immediate and final skirmish with our enemy rendered unavoidable. Thinking ourselves rather too much exposed to the fire of the Indians we retreated fifteen or twenty steps down the bank. Some of the Indians then came to the top of the bank and commenced shooting arrows at us, and yelling at the extent of their lungs. At this moment Mr. Stephens was heard to say in a firm tone "now is the time my boys, we must fight or die;" upon this Mr. Hockday and I fired; one of the Indians on the bank was seen to fall, and the remainder ran back to the camp. On hearing the report of our rifles the Indians, to the number of two or three hundred, rose out of the bushes and literally covered the plain, while their terrific war whoop-mingled with an occasional crack of a rifle, rendered the aspect of things more threatening than the most timid had before anticipated. We ran to our appointed place to meet, but before we had time to gather our baggage, we found ourselves completely surrounded and hemmed in on every side by the savages. Finding that we could not escape by flight, but must fight, we ran to the top of the hill, and having sheltered ourselves as well as we could amongst the rocks, commenced yelling and firing in turn, (yelling is a very essential point in Indian warfare). This scene was kept up for near an hour without any damage to our company, and as we supposed, but little injury to the Indians, The savages seeing we were determined to defend ourselves to the last gave way on the opposite side of the hill from their camp, and we made our escape out of their circle, and were glad to get away with our lives, without any of our property or that of the Indians, The scenes of this night will ever be indelibly impressed upon my memory.

After travelling five or six miles we came to a deep ravine or hollow, we carefully descended the precipice to the flat below, where we encamped for the night; but from fright, fatigue, cold and hunger, I could not sleep, and lay contemplating on the striking contrast between a night in the villages of Pennsylvania and one on the Rocky Mountains.

In the latter, the plough-hoys whistle, the gambols of the children on the green, the lowing of the herds, and the deep tones of the evening bell, are unheard; not a sound strikes upon the ear, except perchance the distal howling of some wild beast, or war-whoop of the uncultivated savage. All was silent on this occasion save the muttering of a small brook as wound its way through the deep cavities of the gulph down, the mountain, and the gentle whispering of the breeze, as it crept through the dark pine or cedar forest, and sighed in melancholy accents; nor is it the retiring of the "god of day" to his couch in the western horizon that bring on this desolate scene. His rising in the east does not change the gloom aspect. Night and day are nearly the same in this respect.

About midnight we were alarmed by a shrill whistle on the rock above, & supposing it to be the Indians on pursuit of us we seized our gun and ran a few rods from our fires. After waiting for some time, without hearing any more noise, one of the men ascended the precipice, and discovered that the object of our fears was a large drove of Elk. In the morning we continued to travel down this ravine and I was struck with the rough and picturesque appearance of the adjacent hills. On our right and left, arose like two perpendicular ramparts, to the heighth of near two hundred feet, two chains of mountains. Not a blade of grass, bush or plains was to be seen on these hard slopes. Huge rocks, detached from the main body, supported by the recumbent weight of other unseen rocks, appear in the act of falling, and presented a frightful appearance, nothing met the eye but an inexhaustible avalanch of rocks, sombre, gray or black rocks. Dante had designed to picture in one of his circles, the Hell of Stones, had might have taken this scene for his model. This is one scenery in the vicinity of the Rocky Mountains; and perhaps an hour's travel would present another of a very different character, one that the artist who designed to depict a beautiful and enchanting landscape would, select for a model

After travelling some fifteen or twenty miles, we came to the track where the main body of the Indians with whom we had the skirmish the evening before, had passed along and. It was near half a mile wide, and the snow was literally trodden into the earth. I have since understood from whites who had been in the habit of trading with this nation, prior to their declaration of hostilities against the whites, that they numbered from seven to eight hundred warriors. Alarmed at this formidable appearance of the hostile Indians, we mutually declined the idea of going to Santa Fee, and turned and travelled in the direction of the main body of our company.

We continued to travel day after day, with all possible speed, occasionally killing a buffaloe, a goat, or a bighorn, as we passed over the plains and prairies which were literally covered with these animals; and on the morning of the 9th of April, we arrived safe at our old camp, & were gratified to find our thirteen men and two mules in the enjoyment of good health, with plenty to eat and drink. After exchanging civilities all around, by a hearty shake of the hand, and taking some refreshment, which was immediately prepared for us, I related to the company the dismal tidings of the near approach of the hostile Indians, and the circumstances of being robbed by them, and being defeated in the attempt to retake our property. All were now satisfied of the imprudence of attempting to go to Santa Fee by this route, as well as of the necessity of devising some other method of saving our merchandize, We finally concluded to conceal our merchandize, baggage, fur, and every thing that we could not pack on our backs or on the two mules, and return to our appointed winter quarters, at the mouth of the Laramies River, with the expectation of meeting Capt. Gant, and obtaining some assistance from him. On the morning of the 20th of April, having made every necessary preparation, we set out on our journey for the mouth of the Laramies river. After two days travel, we came to the foot of the mountain which we had endeavored in vain to cross in November, The snow was still deep on the top of it; but by aid of the buffaloe trails, we were enabled to scale it without much difficulty, except that our mules suffered with hunger, having had nothing to eat but pine brush. At the foot of the mountain we found an abundance of sweet cottonwood, and our mules being very fond of it, we detained two or three days to let them recruit from their suffering in crosing the mountains. This mountain and the one we left our fur on, are covered with the most splendid timber of different kinds such as fir, cedar, white pine, &c. On the margin of the rivers and creeks in the plains, the only timber is cottonwood, undergrowth, willow and rose bushes; out in the middle of the plains there is none of any description, In the month of June, a person by taking a view of the country east of this mountain with a spy glass, could see nothing but a level plain extending from the foot of the mountain as far as the eye can penetrate, covered with green grass, and beautiful flowers of various descriptions; and by turning to the northwest, the eye meets nothing but a rough and dismal looking mountain, covered with snow, and presenting all the appearance of dreary winter. These plains extend to the state of Missouri, with scarce a hill or a grove of timber to interrupt the sight, and literally covered with game of almost every kind.

On the 25th we again resumed our journey down the river, and continued ahead without any difficulty, passing over nearly the same ground that we had travelled over going up the fall before; killing plenty of game, buffaloe, deer, bear, bighorn, antelope, &c. and on the 20th May we landed at the mouth of the Laramies; but to our utter astonishment and discomfiture we discovered that not one of the parties had returned according to the agreement.

CHAPTER 9

GAME AND INHABITANTS OF THE NORTHERN MOUNTAINS

from *Journal of a Trapper*

By Osborne Russell

It has been my design whilst keeping a journal to note down the principal circumstances which came under my immediate observation as I passed along, and I have mostly deferred giving a general description of Indians and animals that inhabit the Rocky Mountains until the last end in order that I might be able to put the information I have collected in a more compact form. I have been very careful in gathering information from the most intelligent Indians and experienced white hunters, but have excluded from this journal such parts (with few exceptions) as I have not proved true by experience. I am fully aware of the numerous statements which have been given to travelers in a jocular manner by the hunters and traders among the Rocky Mountains, merely to hear themselves talk, or according to the mountaineers expression, give them a long yarn or "fish story" to put in their journals, and I have frequently seen those "fish stories" published with the original very much enlarged which had not at first the slightest ground for truth to rest upon. It is utterly impossible for a person who is merely traveling through or even residing one or two years in the Rocky Mountains to give an accurate description of the country or its inhabitants.

These are among the reasons for which I offer this to public view, hoping that it not only may be of interest to my self but the means of correcting some erroneous statements which have gone forth to the world, unintentionally perhaps by their authors.

THE WOLVERINE, CARCAJOU OR GLUTTON

This species of animal is very numerous in the Rocky Mountains and very mischievous and annoying to the hunters. They often get into the traps setting for beaver or search out the deposits of meat which the weary hunter has made during a toilsome day's hunt among mountains too rugged and remote for him to bear the reward of his labours to the place of encampment, and when finding these deposits the carcajou carries off all or as much of the contents as he is able, secreting it in different places among the snow, rock or bushes in such a manner that it is very difficult for man or beast to find it. The avaricious disposition of this animal has given rise to the name of glutton by naturalists, who suppose that it devours so much at a time as to render it stupid and incapable of moving or running about, but I have never seen an instance of this kind; on the contrary I have seen them quite expert and nimble immediately after having carried away four to five times their weight in meat. I have good reason to believe that the carcajou's appetite is easily satisfied upon meat freshly killed, but after it becomes putrid it may become more voracious, but I never saw one myself or a person who had seen one in a stupid, dormant state caused by glutting, although I have often wished it were the case.

The body is thick and long, the legs short, the feet and claws are longer in proportion than those of the black bear, which it very much resembles, with the exception of its tail, which is twelve inches long and bushy. Its body is about three feet long and stands fifteen inches high; its color is black excepting the sides, which are of a dirty white or light brown.

Its movements are somewhat quicker than those of the bear and it climbs trees with ease. I have never known, either by experience or information, the carcajou to prey upon animals of its own killing larger than very young fawns or lambs, although it has been described by naturalists and generally believed that it climbs trees and leaps down upon elk, deer and other large animals and clings to their back till it kills them in spite of their efforts to get rid of it by speed or resistance, but we need go no further than the formation of the animal to prove those statements erroneous. Its body, legs, feet and mouth are shaped similarly to the black bear, as has been already stated, but its claws are somewhat longer and stronger in proportion, and like the bear, its claws are somewhat blunted at the points, which would render it impossible for them to cling to the back of an elk or deer while running, I do not pretend to say, however, what may be its habits in other countries, I only write from experience. They do not den up like the bear in winter, but ramble about the streams among the high mountains, where they find springs open. Its hair is three inches long and in the summer is coarse like the bear, but winter it is near as fine as that of the red fox. The female brings forth its young in April and generally brings two at a birth.

THE WOLF

Of this species of animal there are several kinds, as the buffalo wolf, the big prairie wolf and the small prairie or medicine wolf. The buffalo wolf is from two to three feet high and from four to five feet long from the tip of his nose to the insertion of the tail. Its hair is long, coarse and shaggy. Its color varies from a dark grey to a snowy whiteness. They are not ferocious toward man and will run at the sight of him. The big prairie wolf is two feet high and three and a half feet long; its hair is long and shaggy, its color is a dirty grey, often inclining to a brown or brindle. The least known is little prairie or medicine wolf. Its size is somewhat larger than the red fox; its color is brownish grey and its species something between the big wolf and the fox. The Indians are very superstitious about this animal. When it comes near a village and barks they say there is people near. Some pretend to distinguish between its warning the approach of friends or enemies and in the latter case I have often seen them secure their horses and prepare themselves to fight. I have often seen this prophecy tolerably accurately fulfilled and again I have as often seen it fail, but a superstitious Indian will always account for the failure.

The habits of these three kinds of wolves are similar. Their rutting season is in March. The female brings forth from two to six at a birth.

THE PANTHER

This animal is rarely seen in the plains, but confines itself to the more woody and mountainous districts. Its color is light brown on the back and the belly is a sort of ash color; its length is five feet from the tip of the nose to the insertion of the tail, which is about one-half the length of the body. It is very destructive on sheep and other animals that live in the high mountains, but will run at the sight of a man and has a great antipathy to fire.

THE MARMOT

This animal inhabits the rocks and precipices of the highest mountains. Its color is a dark brown, its height less than the smallest rabbit; its ears and paws are shaped like those of the rat, and its cry resembles that of the bleating of the young lambs. During the summer it collects large quantities of hay and mud with which it secures its habitation from the cold during the winter. On my first acquaintance with this animal I was led to suppose that the hay which they accumulate in summer was calculated to supply them with food during the winter, but this I found to be erroneous by visiting their habitation in the early part of spring and finding their stock in nowise diminished. I have good reason to suppose that they lie dormant during the winter.

THE PORCUPINE

This species of animal is too well known to need a minute description in this place. They are, however, very numerous and their flesh is much esteemed by some of the Indian tribes for food, and their quills are held in the highest estimation by all for embroidering their dresses, and other functions, which is done with peculiar elegance and uncommon skill. It subsists chiefly on the bark of trees and other vegetables.

THE BADGER

This species of animal are numerous in the Rocky Mountains. Their skins are much used by the Snake and Bannock Indians for clothing, as well as their flesh for food. They make their habitation in the ground in the most extensive plains and are found ten miles from water.

THE GROUND HOG

These animals are also very numerous and their skins much used by the Indians for clothing in sections of country where deer and buffalo are not to be found. They are not so large as the ground hog of the United States, but are in all respects the same species. They live among the rocks near streams and feed upon grass and other vegetables. The shrill cry with which their sentinels give warning of danger resembles that of the United States species.

THE GRIZZLY BEAR

Much has been said by travelers in regard to this animal, yet while giving a description of animals that inhabit the Rocky Mountains, I do not feel justified in simply passing over in silence the most ferocious species without undertaking to contribute some little information respecting it which, although it may not be important, I hope *some* of it at least will be new. It lives chiefly upon roots and berries, being of too slow a nature to live much upon game of its own killing, and from May to September it never tastes flesh. The rutting season is in November and the female brings forth from one to three at a birth. I have not been able to ascertain the precise time that the female goes with young, but I suppose from experience and inquiry it is about fourteen weeks. The young are untameable and manifest a savage ferocity when scarcely old enough to crawl. Several experiments have been tried in the Rocky Mountains for taming them, but to no effect. They are possessed of great muscular strength. I have seen a female, which was wounded by a rifle ball in the loins so as to disable her, kill her young with one stroke of her forepaws as fast as they approached her. If a young cub is wounded and commences making a noise, the mother invariably springs upon it and kills it. When grown they never make a noise except a fearful growl. They get to be fatter than any other animals in the Rocky Mountains during the season when wild fruit is abundant. The flesh of the grizzly bear is preferable to pork. It lives in winter in caves in the rocks or holes dug in the ground on high ridges. It loses no flesh while confined to its den during the winter, but is equally as fat in the spring when it leaves the den as when it enters it at the beginning of the winter. There is seldom to be found more than one in a den excepting the female and her young. I have seen them measure seven feet from the tip of the nose to the insertion of the tail. It will generally run from the scent of a man, but when it does not get the scent it will often let him approach close enough to spring on him and when wounded it is a dangerous animal to trifle with. Its speed is comparatively slow down hill but much greater in ascending. It never climbs trees, as its claws are too straight for the purpose.

THE BLACK BEAR

The black bear of the mountains are much the same species as those of the states. In comparison with the grizzly it is entirely harmless. It is seldom found in the plains, but inhabits the timbered and mountainous districts. They are not very numerous and their habits are too well known to need a detailed description here.

THE MOUNTAIN SHEEP OR BIG HORN

These animals answer somewhat to the description given by naturalists of the musmon or wild sheep which are natives of Greece, Corsica and Tartary. The male and female very much resemble the domestic ram and ewe, but are much larger. The horns of the male are much larger in proportion to the body than the domestic rams, but those of the females are almost in the same proportion to the domestic ewe. In the month of May, after they have shed their old coat and the new one appears, their color is dark blue or mouse color, except the extremity of the rump and hinder parts of the thighs, which are white. As the season advances and the hair grows long it gradually turns or fades to a dirty brown. In the month of December the hair is about three inches long, thickly matted together, rendering it impenetrable to the cold. Its hair is similar in texture to that of the deer, and like the latter it is short and smooth upon its forehead and legs. They inhabit the highest and most craggy mountains and never descend to the plains unless compelled by necessity. In the winter season the snow drives them down to the low craggy mountains facing the south, but in the spring as the snow begins to recede they follow it, keeping close to where the grass is short and tender. Its speed on the smooth ground is slower than the deer, but in climbing steep rocks or precipices it is almost incredible, insomuch that the wolf, lynx and panther give up the chase whenever the sheep reach the rugged crags.

The fearful height from which it jumps and the small points on which it alights without slipping or missing its footing is astonishing to its pursuers, whether man or beast. Its hoofs are very hard and pointed and it reposes upon the most bleak points of rock both in summer and winter. The male is a noble looking animal as he stands upon an elevated point with his large horns curling around his ears like the coil of a serpent, and his head held proudly erect, disdaining the lower regions and its inhabitants. Its flesh has a similar taste to mutton, but its flavor is more agreeable and the meat more juicy. Their rutting season is in November, when the rams have furious battles with each other in the same manner as the domestic rams. The victor often knocks his opponent over a high precipice when he is dashed to pieces in the fall. The sound of their heads coming in contact is often heard a mile distant. The female produces from one to three at a birth. The lambs are of a whitish color, very innocent and playful. Hunting sheep is often attended with great danger, especially in the winter season, when the rocks and precipices are covered with snow and ice, but the excitement created by hunting them often enables the hunter to sur-mount obstacles which at other times would seem impossible. The skins, when dressed are finer, softer and far superior to those of the deer for clothing. It is of them that the squaws make their dresses which they embroider with beads and porcupine quills dyed with various colors, which are wrought into figures displaying a tolerable degree of taste and ingenuity.

THE GAZELLE OR MOUNTAIN ANTELOPE

This animal, for beauty and fleetness, surpasses all the ruminating animals of the Rocky Mountains. Its body is rather smaller than the common deer; its color on the back and upper part of the sides is light brown, the hinder part of the thighs and belly are white, the latter having a yellowish cast. The under part of the neck is white with several black stripes running across the throat down to the breast. Its legs are very slim, neat and small. Its ears are black on the inside and around the edges with the remainder brown. Its horns are also black and flattened; the horns of the males are much longer than those of the females, but formed in the same manner; they project up about eight inches on the males and then divide into two branches, the one inclining backward and the other forward with sometimes an additional branch coming out near the head inclining inward. The two upper branches are six inches long, the hindermost forming a sort of hook. The nose is black and a strip of the same color runs round under the eyes and terminates under the ears. It runs remarkably smooth and in the summer season the fleetest horses but rarely overtake it. Its natural walk is stately and elegant, but it is very timid and fearful and can see to a great distance, but with all its timidity and swiftness of foot its curiosity often leads it to destruction. If it discovers anything of a strange appearance (particularly anything red) it goes direct to it and will often approach within thirty paces. They are very numerous in the plains, but seldom found among timber. Their flesh is similar to venison. The female produces two at a birth and the young are suckled until a month old. They are easily domesticated.

THE BLACK-TAILED DEER

This animal is somewhat larger than the common deer of the United States. Its ears are very long, from which it has derived the appellation of mule deer. Its color in summer is red, but in the latter part of August its hair turns to a deep blue ground with about half an inch of white on each hair one-fourth inch from the outer ends, which presents a beautiful grey color. It lives among the mountains and seldom descends among the plains. Its flesh is similar in every respect to the common deer. The tail is about six inches long and the hair upon it smooth except upon the end, where there is a small tuft of black. The female goes six months with young and generally produces two at a birth. The young is brought forth in April and remains in an almost helpless state for one month. During its state of inability the mother secretes it in some secure place in the long grass and weeds, where it remains contented while she often wanders half a mile from it in search of food. The color of the fawn is red intermingled with white spots, and it is generally believed by Indians that so long as those spots remain (which is about two and one-half months) that no beast of prey can scent them. This I am inclined to believe, as I have often seen wolves pass very near the place where fawns were lying without stopping or altering their course, and were it not for some secret provision of nature, the total annihilation of this species of animal would be inevitable in those countries infested by wolves and other beasts of prey as in the Rocky Mountains. This safeguard is given by the Great Founder of Nature, not only to the black-tailed deer but all of the species, including elk and antelope, whose young are so spotted at their birth. I do not consider that the mere white spots are a remedy against their scent of wild beasts, but they mark the period of inability, for when these disappear the little animals are capable of eluding their pursuers by flight. The male, like the common deer, drops its horns in February. It then cannot be distinguished from the former except by its larger size.

THE RABBIT

This species of animal is very numerous and various in their sizes and colors. The large hares of the plains are very numerous, the common sized rabbits are equally or more numerous than the others, and there is also the small brown rabbit which does not change its color during the winter season as do the others; but the most singular kind is the black rabbit. It is a native of mountainous forests. Its color is coal black excepting two small white spots which are on the throat and lower part of the belly. In winter its color is milk white. Its body is about the size of the common rabbit with the exception of its ears, which are much longer. Another kind is the black-tailed rabbit of the plains. It is rather larger than the common rabbit and derives its name from the color of its tail, which never changes its color.

THE ELK

This animal is eight feet long from the tip of the nose to the insertion of the tail, and stands four and one-half feet high. Its proportions are similar to those of the deer, except the tail, which is four inches long and composed of a black gummy substance intermingled with fibers around the bone, the whole being clothed with skin and covered with hair like the body. Its color in summer is red but in winter is a brownish grey except the throat and belly, the former being dark brown and the latter white inclining to yellow, extending to the hind part of the thighs as far as the insertion of the tail. They are very timid and and harmless even when so disabled as to render escape impossible. Its speed is very swift when running single, but when running in large bands they soon become wearied by continual collision with each other, and if they are closely pressed by the hunter on horseback they soon commence dropping down flat on the ground to elude their pursuers and will suffer themselves to be killed with a knife in this position. When the band is first located the hunters keep at some distance behind to avoid dispersing them, and to frighten them the more a continual noise is kept up by halloing and shooting over them, which causes immediate confusion and collision of the band and the weakest elk soon begin to fall to the ground exhausted. Their rutting time is in September, when they collect in immense bands among the timber along the streams and among the mountains, It has been stated by naturalists that the male is a very formidable and dangerous animal when pursued, but I never saw it act on the offensive, neither have I ever known one to offer resistance in defense of itself against man otherwise than by involuntary motions of its head or feet when too much disabled to rise from the ground. I have often seen the female come about the hunter who has found where her young is secreted uttering the most pitiful and persuasive moans and pleading in the most earnest manner that a dumb brute is capable of for the life of her young. This mode or persuasion would, I think, excite sympathy in the breast of any human that was not entirely destitute of the passion.

The fawn has a peculiar cry after it is able to run which resembles the first scream of a child, by which it answers the dam, who calls it by a note similar to the scream of a woman in distress.

In the month of September the males have a peculiar shrill call which commences in a piercing whistle and ends in a coarse gurgling in the throat. By this they call the females to assemble and each other to the combat, in which by their long antlers they are rendered formidable to each other. The hair stands erect and the head is lowered to give or receive the attack, but the victor seldom pursues the vanquished.

THE BUFFALO OR BISON

This animal has been so minutely described by travelers that I have considered it of little importance to enter into the details of its shape and size, and shall therefore omit those descriptions with which I suppose the public to be already acquainted, and try to convey some idea of its peculiarities which probably are not so well known. The vast numbers of these animals which once traversed such an extensive region on North America are diminishing. The continued increasing demand for robes in the civilized world has already and is still contributing in no small degree to their destruction, whilst on the other hand the continued increase of wolves and other four-footed enemies far exceeds that of the buffaloes. When these combined efforts for their destruction are taken into consideration, it will not be doubted for a moment that this noble race of animals, so useful in supplying the wants of man, will at no far distant period become extinct in North America, The buffalo is already a stranger, although so numerous ten years ago, in that part of the country which is drained by the sources of the Colorado, Bear and Snake Rivers, and occupied by the Snake and Bannock Indians. The flesh of the buffalo cow is considered far superior to that of the domestic beef and it is so much impregnated with salt that it requires but little seasoning when cooked. All the time, trouble and care bestowed by man upon improving the breed and food of meat cattle seems to be entirely thrown away when we compare those animals in their original state which are reared upon the food supplied them by nature with the same species when domesticated and fed on cultivated grasses and grains, and the fact seems to justify the opinion that nature will not allow herself to be outdone by art, for it is fairly proven in this enlightened age that the rude and untaught savage feasts on better beef and mutton than the most learned and experienced agriculturists. Now if every effect is produced by a cause, perhaps I may stumble upon the cause which produces the effect in this instance. At any rate I shall attempt it:

In the *first* place, the rutting season of the buffaloes is regular, commencing about the 15th Of July when the males and females are fat, and ends about the 15th of August. Consequently the females bring forth their young in the latter part of April and the first of May, when the grass is most luxuriant and thereby enables the cow to afford the most nourishment for her calf and enables the young to quit the natural nourishment of its dam and feed upon the tender herbage sooner than it would at any other season of the year. Another proof is the fact that when the rutting season commences the strongest, healthiest and most vigorous bulls drive the weaker ones from the cows, hence the calves are from the best breed, which is thereby kept upon a regular basis. In the summer season they generally go to water and drink once in twenty-four hours, but in the winter they seldom get water at all. The cows are fattest in October and the bulls in July. The cows retain their flesh in a great measure throughout the winter until the spring opens and they get at water, from whence they become poor in a short time. So much for the regularity of their habits, and the next point is the food on which they subsist. The grass on which the buffaloes generally feed is short, firm and of the most nutritious kind. The salts with which the mountain regions are impregnated are imbibed in a great degree by the vegetation and as there is very little rain in summer, autumn or winter, the grass arrives at maturity and dries in the sun without being cut it is made like hay; in this state it remains throughout the winter and while the spring rains are divesting the old growth of its nutritive qualities they are in the meantime pushing forward the new. The buffaloes are very particular in their choice of grass, always

184

preferring the short of the uplands to that of the luxuriant growth of the fertile alluvial bottoms. Thus they are taught by nature to choose such food as is most palatable and she has also provided that such as is most palatable is the best suited to their condition and that condition the best calculated to supply the wants and necessities of her rude, untutored children for whom they were prepared. Thus nature looks with a smile of derision upon the magnified efforts of art to excel her works by a continual breach of her laws.

The most general mode practiced by Indians for killing buffalo is running upon horseback and shooting them with arrows, but it requires a degree of experience for both man and horse to kill them in this manner with any degree of safety, particularly in places where the ground is rocky and uneven. The horse that is well trained for this purpose not only watches the ground over which he is running and avoids the holes, ditches and rocks by shortening or extending his leaps, but also the animal which he is pursuing in order to prevent being "horned" when 'tis brought suddenly to bay, which is done instantaneously, and if the buffalo wheel to the right the horse passes as quick as thought to the left behind it and thereby avoids its horns; but if the horse in close pursuit wheels on the same side with the buffalo he comes directly in contact with its horns and with one stroke the horse's entrails are often torn out and his rider thrown headlong to the ground. After the buffalo is brought to bay the trained horse will immediately commence describing a circle about ten paces from the animal in which he moves continuously in a slow gallop or trot which prevents the raging animal from making a direct bound at him by keeping it continuously turning around until it is killed by the rider with arrows or bullets. If a hunter discovers a band of buffalo in a place too rough and broken for his horse to run with safety and there is smooth ground near by, he secretly rides on the leeward side as near as he can without being discovered. He then starts up suddenly without apparently noticing the buffalo and gallops in the direction he wishes the band to run. The buffalo, on seeing him run to the plain, start in the same direction in order to prevent themselves from being headed and kept from the smooth ground. The same course would be pursued if he wished to take them to any particular place in the mountains. One of the hunters' first instructions to an inexperienced hand is "run toward the place where you wish the buffalo to run but do not close on them behind until they get to that place." For instance, if the hunter is to the right, the leading buffaloes keep inclining to the right and if he should fall in behind and crowd upon the rear they would separate in different directions and it would be a mere chance if any took the direction he wished them. When he gets to the plain he gives his horse the rein and darts through the band, selects his victim, reins his horse alongside and shoots, and if he considers the wound mortal, he pulls up the rein, the horse, knowing his business, keeps along galloping with the band until the rider has reloaded when he darts forward upon another buffalo as at first. A cow seldom stops at bay after she is wounded, and therefore is not so dangerous-as a bull, who wheels soon after he is pushed from the band and becomes fatigued, whether he is wounded or not. When running over ground where there is rocks, holes or gullies, the horse must be reined up gradually if he is reined at all. There is more accidents happen in running buffalo by the riders getting frightened and suddenly checking their horses than any other way. If they come upon a coulee which the horse can leap by an extra exertion the best plan is to give him the rein and the whip or spur at the same time and fear not, for any ditch that a buffalo can leap can be cleared with safety by a horse and one too wide for a buffalo to clear an experienced rider will generally see in time to check his horse gradually before he gets to it. And now, as I have finished my description of the buffaloes and the manner or killing them, I wish to put a simple question for the reader's solution:

If kings, princes, nobles and gentlemen can derive so much sport and pleasure as they boast of in chasing a fox or simple hare all day, which when they have caught is of no use to them, what pleasure can the Rocky Mountain hunter be expected to derive in running with a well trained horse such a noble and stately animal as the bison, which when killed is of some service to him? There are men of noble birth, noble estates and noble minds who have attained to a tolerable degree of perfection in fox hunting in Europe and buffalo hunting in the Rocky Mountains, and I have heard some of them decide that the points would not bear a comparison if the word "fashion" could be stricken from the English language.

It also requires a considerable degree of practice to approach on foot and kill buffalo with a rifle. A person must be well acquainted with the shape and make of the animal and the manner in which it is standing in order to direct his aim with certainty. And it also requires experience to enable him to choose a fat animal. The best looking buffalo is not always the fattest and a hunter by constant practice may lay down rules for selecting the fattest when on foot which would be no guide to him when running upon horseback, for he is then placed in a different position and one *which* requires different rules for choosing.

THE BEAVER

The beaver, as almost every one knows, is an amphibious animal, but the instinct with which it is possessed surpasses the reason of a no small portion of the human race. Its average size is about two and one-half feet long from the point of the nose to the insertion of the tail, which is from ten to fifteen inches long and from five to nine broad, flat in the shape of a spade rounded at the corners and covered with a thick, rough skin resembling scales. The tail serves the double purpose of steering and assisting it through the water by a quick up and down motion. The hind feet are webbed and the toe next the outside on each has a double nail which serves the purpose of a toothpick to extract the splinters of wood from their teeth. As they are the only animals that cut large trees for subsistence, they are also the only animals known to be furnished with nails so peculiarly adapted to the purpose for which they are used. Its color is of a light brown generally, but I have seen them of a jet black frequently, and in one instance I saw one of a light cream color having the feet and tail white. The hair is of two sorts, the one longer and coarser, the other fine, short and silky. The teeth are like those of the rat but are longer and stronger in proportion to the size of the animals. To a superficial observer they have but one vent for their excrements and urine, but upon a closer examination without dissection separate openings will be seen, likewise four gland openings forward of the arms, two containing oil with which they oil their coats, the others containing the castorium, a collection of gummy substance of a yellow color which is extracted from the food of the animal and conveyed through small vessels into the glands. It is this deposit which causes the destruction of the beaver by the hunters. When a beaver, male or female, leaves the lodge to swim about their pond, they go to the bottom and fetch up some mud between their forepaws and breast, carry it on the bank and emit upon it a small quantity of castorium. Another beaver passing the place does the same, and should a hundred beaver pass within the scent of the place, they would each throw up mud covering up the old castorium and emit new upon that which they had thrown up. The trapper extracts this substance from the gland and carries it in a wooden box. He sets his trap in the water near the bank about six inches below the surface, throws a handful of mud upon the bank about one foot from it and puts a small portion of the castorium thereon. After night the beaver comes out of his lodge, smells the fatal bait 200 or 300 yards distant and steers his course directly for it. He hastens to ascend the bank, but the trap grasps his foot and soon drowns him in the struggle to escape, for the beaver, though termed an amphibious animal, cannot respire beneath the water.

The female brings forth her young in April and produces from two to six at a birth, but what is most singular, she seldom raises but two, a male and a female. This peculiarity of the beaver has often been a matter of discussion among the most experienced of hunters, whether the dam or father kills the young, but I have come to the conclusion that it is the mother for the following reasons:

First, the male is seldom found about the lodge for ten or fifteen days after the female brings forth; second, there is always a male and female saved alive; third, I have seen the dead kittens floating in the ponds freshly killed and at the same time have caught the male when he was living more than one-half mile from the lodge. I have found, where beaver are confined to a limited space, they kill nearly all the kittens, which is supposed to be done to keep them from becoming too numerous and destroying the timber and undergrowth too fast. I have caught fifty full grown beaver in a valley surrounded by mountains and cascades where they had not been disturbed for four years and with this number there were but five or six kittens and yearlings. The young ones pair off generally at three years of age to set up for themselves and proceed up or down a stream as instinct may suggest until they find the best place for wood and undergrowth connected with the most convenient place for building a dam, which is constructed by cutting small trees and brush, dragging them into the water on both sides of the stream, and attaching one end to each bank, while the other extends into the stream inclining upward against the current. Then mud, small stones and rubbish are dragged or pushed onto it to sink it to the bottom. They proceed in this manner till the two ends meet in the middle of the stream, the whole forming a sort of curved line across, but the water raising often forces the dam down the stream until it becomes nearly straight. In the meantime they have selected a spot for the lodge either upon the bank or upon a small island formed by the rising water, but it is generally constructed on an island in the middle of the pond with sticks and mud in such a manner that when the water is raised sufficiently high, which generally is from four to seven feet, it has the appearance of a potash kettle turned on the surface bottom upwards, standing from four to six feet above the water. There is no opening above the water, but generally two below. The floor on which they sleep and have their beds of straw or grass, is about twelve inches above the water level.

The room is arched over and kept neat and clean. When the leaves begin to fall, the beavers commence laying in their winter store. They often cut down trees from twelve to eighteen inches in diameter and cut off the branches covered with smooth bark into pieces from two to six feet long. These they drag into the water, float them to the lodge, sink them to the bottom of the pond, and there fasten them. In this manner they proceed until they have procured about half a cord of wood, solid measure, for each beaver's winter supply. By this time the dam freezes over and all is shut up with ice. The beaver has nothing to do but leap into the water through the subterranean passage and bring up a stick of wood which is to furnish him his meal. This he drags up by one end into the lodge, eats off the bark to a certain distance, then cuts off the part he has stripped and throws it into the water through another passage, and so proceeds until he has finished his meal. When the ice and snow disappears in the spring, they clear their pond of the stripped wood and stop the leaks which the frosts have occasioned in their dam. Their manner of enlarging their lodge is by cutting out the inside and adding more to the out. The covering of the lodge is generally about eighteen inches thick, formed by sticks and mud intermingled in such a manner that it is very difficult for man, beast or cold to penetrate through it.

THE SNAKE INDIANS

The appellation by which this nation is distinguished is derived from the Crows, but from what reason I have never been able to determine. They call themselves Sho-sho-nies, but during an acquaintance of nine years, during which time I made further progress in their language than any white man had done before me, I never saw one of the nation who could give me either the derivation or definition of the word "Sho-sho-nie." Their country comprises all the regions drained by the head branches of Green and Bear Rivers and the east and southern head branches of the Snake River. They are kind and hospitable to whites, thankful for favors, indignant at injuries and but little addicted to theft in their large villages. I have seldom heard them accused of inhospitality; on the contrary I have found it to be a general feature of their character to divide the last morsel of food with the hungry stranger, let their means be what it might for obtaining the next meal. The Snakes, and in fact most of the Rocky Mountain Indians, believe in a Supreme Deity who resides in the sun and in infernal deities residing in the moon and stars, but all subject to the supreme control of the one residing in the sun. They believe that the spirits of the departed are permitted to watch over the actions of the living and every warrior is protected by a guiding angel in all his actions so long as he obeys his rules, a violation of which subjects the offender to misfortunes and disasters during the displeasure of the offended deity. Their prophets, judges or medicine men are supposed to be guided by deities differing from the others, insomuch as he is continually attendant upon the devotee from birth, gradually instituting into his mind the mysteries of his profession, which cannot be transmitted from one mortal to another. The prophet or juggler converses freely with his supernatural director, who guides him up from childhood in his manner of eating, drinking and smoking, particularly the latter, for every prophet has a different mode of handling, filling, lighting and smoking the big pipe—such as profound silence in the circle while the piper is lighting the pipe, turned around three times in the direction of the sun by the next person on the right previous to giving it to him, or smoking with the feet uncovered. Some cannot smoke in the presence of a female or a dog, and a hundred other movements equally vague and superstitious which would he too tedious to mention here. A plurality of wives is very common among the Snakes and the marriage contract is dissolved only by the consent of the husband, after which the wife is at liberty to marry again. Prostitution among the women is very rare and fornication whilst living with the husband is punished with the utmost severity. The women perform all the labor about the lodge except the care of the horses. They are cheerful and affectionate to their husbands and remarkably fond and careful of their children.

The government is a democracy. Deeds of valor promote the chief to the highest points attained, from which he is at any time liable to fall for misdemeanor in office. Their population amounts to between 5,000 and 6,000, about half of which live in large villages and range among the buffaloes; the remainder live in small detached companies comprised of from two to ten families, who subsist upon roots, fish, seeds and berries; they have but few horses and are much addicted to thieving. From their manner of living they have received the appellation of "Root digger." they rove about in the mountains in order to seclude themselves from their warlike enemies, the Blackfeet. Their arrows are pointed with quartz or obsidian, which they dip in poison extracted from the fangs of the rattlesnake and prepared with antelope liver. These they use in hunting and war, and however slight the wound may be that is inflicted by one of them, death is almost inevitable, but the flesh of animals killed by these arrows is not injured for eating. The Snakes who live upon buffalo and live in large villages seldom use poison upon their arrows, either in hunting or war. They are well armed with fusees and well supplied with horses. They seldom stop more than eight or ten days in one place, which prevents the accumulation of filth which is so common among Indians that are stationary. Their lodges are spacious, made of dressed buffalo skins sewed together and set upon eleven or thirteen long smooth poles to each lodge, which are dragged along for that purpose. In the winter of 1842 the principal chief of the Snakes died in an apoplectic fit and in the following year his brother died, but front what disease I could not learn. These being the two principal pillars that upheld the nation, the loss of them was and is to this day deeply deplored. Immediately after the death of the latter the tribe scattered in smaller villages over the country in consequence of having no chief who could control and keep them together. Their ancient warlike spirit seems to be buried with their leaders and they are fast falling into degradation. Without a head the body is of little use.

THE CROW INDIANS

This once formidable tribe once lived on the north side of the Missouri, east of the mouth of the Yellowstone. About the year 1790 they crossed the Missouri and took the region of country which they now inhabit by conquest from the Snakes. It is bounded on the east and south by a low range of mountains called the "Black Hills," on the west by the Wind River mountains, and on the north by the Yellowstone River. The face of the country presents a diversity of rolling hills and valleys and includes several plains admirably adapted for grazing. The whole country abounds with coal and iron in great abundance and signs of lead and copper are not infrequently found, and gypsum exists in immense quarries. Timber is scarce except along the streams and on the mountains. Wild fruit such as cherries, service berries, currants, gooseberries and plums resembling the pomegranate are abundant. The latter grow on small trees generally six or eight feet high, ranging in color and flavor from the most acute acid to the mildest sweetness. Hops grow spontaneously and in great abundance along the streams.

When the Crows first conquered this country their numbers amounted to about 8,000 persons, but the ravages of war and smallpox combined have reduced their numbers to about 2,000, of which 1,200 are females. They are proud, treacherous, thievish, insolent and brave when they are possessed with a superior advantage, but when placed in the opposite situation they are equally humble, submissive and cowardly. Like the other tribes of Indians residing in the Rocky Mountains, they believe in a Supreme Deity who resides in the sun and lesser deities residing in the moon and stars. Their government is a kind of democracy. The chief who can enumerate the greatest number of valiant exploits is unanimously considered the supreme ruler. All the greatest warriors below him and above a certain grade are councillors and take their seats in the council according to their respective ranks—the voice of the lowest rank having but little weight in deciding matters of importance. When a measure is adopted by the council and approved by the head chief it is immediately put in force by the order of the military commander, who is appointed by the council to serve for an indefinite period. A standing company of soldiers is kept up continually for the purpose of maintaining order in the village. The captain can order any young man in the village to serve as a soldier in turn and the council only can increase or diminish the number of soldiers at pleasure. The greatest chiefs cannot violate the orders which the captain receives from the council. No office or station is hereditary, neither does wealth constitute dignity. The greatest chief may fall below the meanest citizen for misdemeanor in office and the lowest citizen may arise to the most exulted station by the performance of valiant deeds. The Crows, both male and female, are tall, well proportioned, handsome featured, with very light copper colored skins. Prostitution of their wives is very common but sexual intercourse between near relatives is strictly prohibited. When a young man is married he never after speaks to his mother-in-law nor the wife to the father-in-law, although they may all live in the same lodge. If the husband wishes to say anything to the mother-in-law, he speaks to the wife, who conveys it to the mother, and in the same way communication is conveyed between the wife and father-in-law. This custom is peculiar to the Crows. They never intermarry with other nations, but a stranger if he wishes can always be accommodated with a wife while he stops at the village but cannot take her from it when he leaves.

Their laws for killing buffalo are rigidly enforced. No person is allowed to hunt buffalo in the vicinity where the village is stationed without first obtaining leave of the council. For the first offense the offender's hunting apparatus are broken and destroyed, for the second his horses are killed and his property destroyed and he beaten with rods, the third is punished by death by shooting. When a decree is given by the council it is published by the head chief who rides to and fro through the village like a herald and proclaims it aloud to all. They generally kill their meat by surrounding a band of buffaloes, and when once enclosed but few escape. The first person who arrives at a dead buffalo is entitled to one-third of the meat and if the person who killed it is the fourth one on the spot, he only gets the hide and tongue, but in no case can he get more than one-third of the meat if a second and third person appear before it is placed on the horses for packing. A person whether male or female, poor or rich, gets the second or third division according to the time of arrival, each one knowing what parts they are allowed. This is also a custom peculiar to the Crows which has been handed down from time immemorial.

Their language is clear, distinct and not intermingled with guttural sounds, which renders it remarkably easy for a stranger to learn. It is a high crime for a mother or father to inflict corporal punishment on their male children, and if a warrior is struck by a stranger he is irretrievably disgraced unless he can kill the offender immediately.

Taking prisoners of war is never practiced with the exception of subjugating them to servile employment. Adult males are never returned as prisoners but generally killed on the spot, but young males are taken to the village and trained up in their mode of warfare until they imbibe the Crow customs and language, when they are eligible to the high station their deeds of valor permit. The Crows are remarkably fond of gaudy and glittering ornaments. The eye teeth of the elk are used as a circulating medium and are valued according to their size.

There exists among them many customs similar to those of the ancient Israelites. A woman after being delivered of a male child, cannot approach the lodge of her husband under forty days and for a female fifty is required, and seven days' separation for every natural menses. The distinction between clean and unclean animals bears a great degree of similarity to the Jewish law. They are remarkable for their cleanliness and variety of cooking, which exceeds that of any other tribe in the Rocky Mountains. They seldom use salt, but often season their cooking with herbs of various kinds and flavors.

Sickness is seldom found among them and they naturally live to a great age. There is no possibility of ascertaining the precise age of any mountain Indians, but an inference may be drawn with tolerable correctness from their outward appearance and such indefinite information from their own faint recollection of dates as may be collected by an intimate acquaintance with their habits, customs, traditions and manner of living. I have never known a mountain Indian to be troubled with the toothache or decayed teeth, neither have I ever known a case of insanity except from known and direct causes. I was upon one particular occasion invited to smoke in a circle comprising thirteen aged Crow warriors, the youngest of whom appeared to have seen upwards of 100 winters, and yet they were all in good health and fine spirits. They had long since left the battle ground and council room to younger aspirants of sixty and under. It is really diverting to hear those hoary headed veterans when they are collected together conversing upon the good old times of their forefathers and condemning the fashions of the present age. They have a tradition among them that their most powerful chief who died sometime since, commanded the sun and moon to stand still two days and nights in the valley of Wind River whilst they conquered the Snakes and that they obeyed him. They point out the place where the same chief changed the wild sage of the prairie into a band of antelope when the village was in a starving condition. I have also been shown a spring on the west side of the Big Horn River, below the upper mountain, which they say was once bitter, but through the medicine of this great chief the waters were made sweet.

They have a great aversion to distilled spirits of any kind, terming it the "white man's fool water," and say if a Crow drinks it he ceases to be a Crow and becomes a foolish animal so long as the senses are absorbed by its influence.

CHAPTER 10

TROUBLE IN THE FAMILY
from *The Life and Adventures of James P. Beckworth*

By Himself

*Great Battle with the Black Feet.—Departure of General Ashley.—His
Farewell Speech to the Mountaineers.—Removal of our Rendezvous.
—Peace between the Flat Heads and Black Feet.—Trading-post at
their Village.—I become Son-in-law to the Black Foot Chief.
—Trouble in the Family.—Wife punished for Disobedience.
—Troubled Waters finally stilled.*

Two days after the arrival of the general, the tocsin again sounded through our whole camp, "The Black Feet! the Black Feet!" On they came, making the very earth tremble with the tramp of their fiery war horses. In their advance they surprised three men and two women belonging to the Snakes, who were out some distance from camp, gathering roots. The whole five were instantly overtaken, killed, and scalped. As soon as the alarm was given, the old prophet came to our camp, and, addressing Mr. Sublet, said,

"Cut Face, three of my warriors and two women have just been killed by the Black Feet. You say that your warriors can fight—that they are great braves. Now let me see them fight, that I may know your words are true."

Sublet replied, "You shall see them fight, and then you will know that they are all braves—that I have no cowards among my men, and that we are all ready to die for our Snake friends."

"Now, men," added he, turning to us, "I want every brave man to go and fight these Black Feet, and whip them, so that the Snakes may see that we can fight, and let us do our best before them as a warning to them. Remember, I want none to join in this battle who are not brave. Let all cowards remain in camp."

Every man was impatient to take part; but, seeing that his camp would be deserted and his goods exposed, he detained quite a number, as well to guard the goods as to keep the general company, he not wishing to take part in the battle.

There were over three hundred trappers mounted in a few moments, who, with Captain Sublet at their head, charged instantly on the enemy. The Snake warriors were also on hand, thirsting to take vengeance on the Black Feet for the five scalps of their friends. After retreating before us about five miles, they formed in a place of great security, in a deep hollow on the border of the lake. At our arrival, the battle recommenced in good earnest. We and our allies fought them for about six hours, they certainly displaying great intrepidity, for they would repeatedly issue from their stronghold and make a bold sortie against us. When intrenched in their position, they had a great advantage over us, as it was difficult for a man to approach them without being shot, and to charge on them as they were situated would have occasioned us great loss of life. One Indian issuing from their position was shot through the back bone, thus depriving his legs of all power of motion. Seeing him fall, Sublet said to me, "Jim, let us go and haul him away, and get his scalp before the Indians draw him in."

We went, and, seizing each a leg, started toward our lines with him: the wounded Indian grasping the grass with both hands, we had to haul with all our strength. An Indian, suddenly springing over their breast-work, struck me a heavy blow in the back with his gun, causing me to loose hold of my leg and run. Both I and my companion were unarmed; and I, not knowing how many blows were to follow, deemed discretion on this particular occasion the better part of valor. Sublet made a strong demonstration against my assailant with his fists, at the same time calling me back and cursing me for running. I returned, and, together, we dragged the Indian to one of our men, also wounded, for him to dispatch. But the poor fellow had not strength sufficient to perforate the Indian's skin with his knife, and we were obliged to perform the job ourselves.

After six hours' fighting, during which time a number of the enemy were slain, we began to want nourishment. Sublet requested our allies "to rub out" all their foes while we went and procured refreshment; but on our leaving, they followed us, and we all arrived in camp together. On our return to the field of battle we found the Black Feet were gone, having departed precipitately, as they had left a number of their dead, a thing unusual with the Indians. The fruits of our victory were one hundred and seventy-three scalps, with numerous quivers of arrows, war-clubs, battle-axes, and lances. We also killed a number of their horses, which doubtless was the reason of their leaving so many of their dead on the field of battle. The trappers had seven or eight men wounded, but none killed. Our allies lost eleven killed in battle, besides the five slain before; but none of those killed in battle were scalped.

Had this battle been fought in the open plain, but few of our foes could have escaped; and even as it was, had we continued to fight, not a dozen could have got away. But, considering that we were fighting for our allies, we did not exert ourselves.

As usual on all such occasions, our victory was celebrated in camp, and the exercises lasted several days, conformably to Indian custom.

General Ashley, having disposed of all his goods and completed his final arrangements, departed for St.Louis, taking with him nearly two hundred packs of beaver. Previous to his departure, he summoned all the men into his presence, and addressed them, as nearly as I can recollect, in the following words:

"Mountaineers and friends! When I first came to the mountains, I came a poor man. You, by your indefatigable exertions, toils, and privations, have procured me an independent fortune. With ordinary prudence in the management of what I have accumulated, I shall never want for any thing. For this, my friends, I feel myself under great obligations to you. Many of you have served with me personally, and I shall always be proud to testify to the fidelity with which you have stood by me through all danger, and the friendly and brotherly feeling which you have ever, one and all, evinced toward me. For these faithful and devoted services I wish you to accept my thanks; the gratitude that I express to you springs from my heart, and will ever retain a lively hold on my feelings.

"My friends! I am now about to leave you, to take up my abode in St. Louis. Whenever any of you return thither, your first duty must be to call at my house, to talk over the scenes of peril we have encountered, and partake of the best cheer my table can afford you.

"I now wash my hands of the toils of the Rocky Mountains. Farewell, mountaineers and friends! May God bless you all!"

We were all sorry to part with the general. He was a man of untiring energy and perseverance, cheerfully enduring every toil and privation with his men. When they were short of food, he likewise hungered; he bore full share in their sufferings, and divided his last morsel with them. There was always something encouraging in his manner; no difficulty dejected him; kind and generous in his disposition, he was loved equally by all. If, which was seldom, he had any disagreement with them, if he discovered himself in fault, he would freely acknowledge his error, and ask forgiveness.

Before he left he had a word of advice for me. "James," he commenced, "since I have been here I have heard much of your exploits. I like brave men, but I fear you are reckless in your bravery. Caution is always commendable, and especially is it necessary in encounters with Indians. I wish you to be careful of yourself, and pay attention to your health, for, with the powerful constitution you possess, you have many valuable years before you. It is my hearty desire to have you do well, and live to a good old age; correct your fault of encountering risks for the mere ostentatious display of your courage. Whenever you return home, come and see me, James; you will be a thousand times welcome; and, should you ever be in need of assistance, call on me first. Good-by."

He left the camp amid deafening cheers from the whole crowd. I did not see him again until the year 1836.

At the general's departure, we broke up our camp and marched on to the country of the Flat Heads, on the Snake River. On our arrival at the new rendezvous, we were rejoiced to learn that peace existed between the two nations, the Flat Heads and Black Feet, and that they were in friendly intercourse together. This was very favorable for our purpose; for it is with Indian tribes as with civilized nations, when at war, various branches of business are impoverished, and it becomes inconvenient for those engaged in them to make more than trifling purchases, just for the supply of their immediate wants. Hostilities are still more destructive to Indian commerce than to that of civilized nations, for the reason, that the time and resources of the whole community are engaged in their prosecution. The "sinews of war" with the Indian mean, literally, himself and his horse.

We spent the summer months at our leisure, trading with the Indians, hunting, sporting, and preparing for the fall harvest of beaver. We made acquaintance with several of the Black Feet, who came to the post to trade. One of their chiefs invited Mr. Sublet to establish a branch post in their country, telling him that they had many people and horses, and plenty of beaver, and if his goods were to be obtained they would trade considerably; his being so far off prevented his people coming to Mr. Sublet's camp.

The Indian appearing sincere, and there being a prospect of opening a profitable trade, Sublet proposed to establish a post among the Black Feet if any of the men were willing to risk their scalps in attending it. I offered to go, although I was well aware the tribe knew that I had contributed to the destruction of a number of their braves; but, to the Indian, the greater the brave, the higher their respect for him, even though an enemy. So, taking my boy Baptiste and one man with me, we packed up and started for Beaver River, which is a branch of the Missouri, and in the heart of the Black Foot country.

On our arrival, the Indians manifested great appearance of friendship, and were highly pleased at having a trading-post so conveniently at hand. I soon rose to be a great man among them, and the chief offered me his daughter for a wife. Considering this an alliance that would guarantee my life as well as enlarge my trade, I accepted his offer, and, without any superfluous ceremony, became son-in-law to *As-as-to*, the head chief of the Black Feet. *As-as-to*, interpreted, means heavy shield. To me the alliance was more offensive than defensive, but thrift was my object more than hymeneal enjoyments. Trade prospered greatly. I purchased beaver and horses at my own price. Many times I bought a fine beaver-skin for a butcher-knife or a plug of tobacco.

After a residence among them of a few days, I had slight difficulty in my family affairs. A party of Indians came into camp one day, bringing with them three white men's scalps. The sight of them made my blood boil with rage; but there was no help for it, so I determined to wait with patience my day of revenge. In accordance with their custom, a scalp-dance was held, at which there was much additional rejoicing.

My wife came to me with the information that her people were rejoicing, and that she wished to join them in the dance.

I replied, "No; these scalps belonged to my people; my heart is crying for their death; you must not rejoice when my heart cries; you must not dance when I mourn."

She then went out, as I supposed, satisfied. My two white friends, having a great curiosity to witness the performance, were looking out upon the scene. I reproved them for wishing to witness the savage rejoicings over the fall of white men who had probably belonged to our own company.

One of them answered, "Well, your wife is the best dancer of the whole party; she out-dances them all."

This was a sting which pierced my very heart. Taking my battle-axe, and forcing myself into the ring, I watched my opportunity, and struck my diso-bedient wife a heavy blow in the head with the side of my battle-axe, which dropped her as if a ball had pierced her heart.

I dragged her through the crowd, and left her; I then went back to my tent.

This act was performed in such a bold manner, under the very noses of hundreds of them, that they were thunderstruck, and for a moment remained motionless with surprise. When I entered the tent, I said to my companions, "There, now, you had better prepare to hold on to your own scalps, since you take so much interest in a celebration over those of your murdered brethren." Their countenances turned ashy pale, expecting instant death.

By this time the whole Indian camp was in a blaze. "Kill him! kill him! burn him! burn him!" was shouted throughout the camp in their own language, which I plainly understood. I was collected, for I knew they could kill me but once.

Soon I heard the voice of my father-in-law crying, in a tone which sounded above all, "Stop! hold! hold! warriors! listen to your chief."

All was hushed in an instant, and he continued, "Warriors! I am the loser of a daughter, and her brothers have lost a sister; you have lost nothing. She was the wife of the trader; I gave her to him. When your wives disobey your commands, you kill them; that is your right. That thing disobeyed her husband; he told her not to dance; she disobeyed him; she had no ears; he killed her, and he did right. He did as you all would have done, and you shall neither kill nor harm him for it. I promised the white chief that, if he would send a trader to my people, I would protect him and return him unharmed; this I must do, and he shall not be hurt here. Warriors! wait till you meet him in battle, or, perhaps, in his own camp, then kill him; but here his life is sacred. What if we kill them all, and take what they have? It will last but a few suns; we shall then want more. Whom do we get sach-o-path (powder) from? We get it from the whites; and when we have expended what we have, we must do without, or go to them for more. When we have no powder, can we fight our enemies with plenty? If we kill these three men, whom I have given the word of a chief to protect, the white chief will send us no more, but his braves will revenge the death of their brothers. No, no; you shall not harm them here. They have eaten of our meat, and drunk of our water; they have also smoked with us. When they have sold their goods, let them return in peace."

At this time there were a great many Flat Heads at the Black Foot camp, as they were at peace with each other. After the speech of my father-in-law, a great brave of the Flat Heads, called Bad Hand, replied, "Hey! you are yourself again; you talk well; you talk like *As-as-to* again. We are now at peace; if you had killed these men, we should have made war on you again; we should have raised the battle-axe, never to have buried it. These whites are ours, and the Flat Heads would have revenged their deaths if they had been killed in your camp."

The chief then made a loud and long harangue, after which all became quiet. *As-as-to* next came to my camp and said, "My son, you have done right; that woman I gave you had no sense; her ears were stopped up; she would not hearken to you, and you had a right to kill her. But I have another daughter, who is younger than she was. She is more beautiful; she has good sense and good ears. You may have her in the place of the bad one; she will hearken to all you say to her."

"Well," thought I, "this is getting married again before I have even had time to *mourn*."

But I replied, "Very well, my father, I will accept of your kind offer," well knowing, at the same time, that to refuse him would be to offend, as he would suppose that I disdained his generosity.

My second wife was brought to me. I found her, as her father had represented, far more intelligent and far prettier than her other sister, and I was really proud of the change. I now possessed one that many a warrior had performed deeds of bloody valor to obtain; for it is a high honor to get the daughter of a great chief to wife, and many a bold warrior has sacrificed his life in seeking to attain such a prize.

During the night, while I and my wife were quietly reposing, some person crawled into our couch, sobbing most bitterly. Angry at the intrusion, I asked who was there.

"Me," answered a voice, which, although well-nigh stifled with bitter sobs, I recognized as that of my other wife, whom every one had supposed dead. After lying outside the lodge senseless for some hours, she had recovered and groped her way to my bed.

"Go away," I said, "you have no business here; I have a new wife now, one who has sense."

"I will not go away," she replied; "my ears are open now. I was a fool not to hearken to my husband's words when his heart was crying, but now I have good sense, and will always hearken to your words."

It did really seem as if her heart was broken, and she kept her position until morning. I thought myself now well supplied with wives, having *two* more than I cared to have; but I deemed it hardly worth while to complain, as I should soon leave the camp, wives and all.

It is a universal adage, "When you are among Romans, do as the Romans do." I conformed to the customs of a people really pagan, but who regarded them selves both enlightened and powerful. I was risking my life for gold, that I might return one day with plenty, to share with her I tenderly loved. My body was among the Indians, but my mind was far away from them and their bloody deeds. Experience has revealed to me that civilized man can accustom himself to any mode of life when pelf is the governing principle—that power which dominates through all the ramifications of social life, and gives expression to the universal instinct of self-interest. By living with the savages, and becoming familiar with their deeds of injustice and cruelty—witnessing friends and companions struck down without a moment's warning—if a man has feeling, in a short time it becomes callous toward the relentless savage, who can mock the dying struggles of the white man, and indulge his inhuman joy as he sees his warm life-blood saturate the earth, on which, a few moments since, his victim stood erect in seeming security. Many a companion have I seen fall in the wild prairie or the mountain forest, dying with some dear name upon his lips, his body left as food for the wild beasts, or his bones to whiten in the trackless wilderness.

It will be said, "He might have staid at home, and not have hazarded his life amid such dangers." So it might be said of the hardy mariner, whose compass guides him through all parts of the pathless ocean. The same motive impels them both on their perilous career—self-interest, which, while it gratifies their individual desires, at the same time enriches and advances society, by adding its acquisitions to the mart of commerce.

We left the Black Foot country after a stay of twenty days, having purchased thirty-nine packs of beaver and several splendid horses at a sum trifling in real value, but what they considered as far exceeding the worth of their exchanges. The chief lent us an escort of two hundred and fifty mounted warriors, in addition to which nearly one hundred Flat Heads returned with us to our camp, whom we met the second day on our road (they having become alarmed for our safety, and being on the way to revenge our deaths, in the event of the Black Feet having proved treacherous). On our arrival we were greeted with the liveliest expressions of joy. Presents were made to our escort, and Mr. Sublet sent my father-in-law a valuable gift for his kindness to me, and as the assurance of his most distinguished consideration. I also sent some dress patterns to my wives, in addition to the presents I had previously made them. The Black Feet, apparently well satisfied, returned to their homes.

CHAPTER 11

A MOUNTAIN HUNT

By Francis Parkman Jr.

The camp was full of the newly-cut lodge-poles; some, already prepared, were stacked together, white and glistening, to dry and harden in the sun; others were lying on the ground, and the squaws, the boys, and even some of the warriors were busily at work peeling off the bark and paring them with their knives to the proper dimensions. Most of the hides obtained at the last camp were dressed and scraped thin enough for use, and many of the squaws were engaged in fitting them together and sewing them with sinews, to form the coverings for

the lodges. Men were wandering among the bushes that lined the brook along the margin of the camp, cutting sticks of red willow, or shongsasha, the bark of which, mixed with tobacco, they use for smoking. Reynal's squaw was hard at work with her awl and buffalo sinews upon her lodge, while her proprietor, having just finished an enormous breakfast of meat, was smoking a social pipe along with Raymond and myself. He proposed at length that we should go out on a hunt. "Go to the Big Crow's lodge," said he, "and get your rifle. I'll bet the gray Wyandotte pony against your mare that we start an elk or a black-tailed deer, or likely as not, a bighorn, before we are two miles out of camp. I'll take my squaw's old yellow horse; you can't whip her more than four miles an hour, but she is as good for the mountains as a mule."

I mounted the black mule which Raymond usually rode. She was a very fine and powerful animal, gentle and manageable enough by nature; but of late her temper had been soured by misfortune. About a week before I had chanced to offend some one of the Indians, who out of revenge went secretly into the meadow and gave her a severe stab in the haunch with his knife. The wound, though partially healed, still galled her extremely, and made her even more perverse and obstinate than the rest of her species.

The morning was a glorious one, and I was in better health than I had been at any time for the last two months. Though a strong frame and well compacted sinews had borne me through hitherto, it was long since I had been in a condition to feel the exhilaration of the fresh mountain wind and the gay sunshine that brightened the crags and trees. We left the little valley and ascended a rocky hollow in the mountain. Very soon we were out of sight of the camp, and of every living thing, man, beast, bird, or insect. I had never before, except on foot, passed over such execrable ground, and I desire never to repeat the experiment. The black mule grew indignant, and even the redoubtable yellow horse stumbled every moment, and kept groaning to himself as he cut his feet and legs among the sharp rocks.

It was a scene of silence and desolation. Little was visible except beetling crags and the bare shingly sides of the mountains, relieved by scarcely a trace of vegetation. At length, however, we came upon a forest tract, and had no sooner done so than we heartily wished ourselves back among the rocks again; for we were on a steep descent, among trees so thick that we could see scarcely a rod in any direction.

If one is anxious to place himself in a situation where the hazardous and the ludicrous are combined in about equal proportions, let him get upon a vicious mule, with a snaffle bit, and try to drive her through the woods down a slope of 45 degrees. Let him have on a long rifle, a buckskin frock with long fringes, and a head of long hair. These latter appendages will be caught every moment and twitched away in small portions by the twigs, which will also whip him smartly across the face, while the large branches above thump him on the head. His mule, if she be a true one, will alternately stop short and dive violently forward, and his position upon her back will be somewhat diversified and extraordinary. At one time he will clasp her affectionately, to avoid the blow of a bough overhead; at another, he will throw himself back and fling his knee forward against the side of her neck, to keep it from being crushed between the rough bark of a tree and the equally unyielding ribs of the animal herself. Reynal was cursing incessantly during the whole way down. Neither of us had the remotest idea where we were going; and though I have seen rough riding, I shall always retain an evil recollection of that five minutes' scramble.

At last we left our troubles behind us, emerging into the channel of a brook that circled along the foot of the descent; and here, turning joyfully to the left, we rode in luxury and ease over the white pebbles and the rippling water, shaded from the glaring sun by an overarching green transparency. These halcyon moments were of short duration. The friendly brook, turning sharply to one side, went brawling and foaming down the rocky hill into an abyss, which, as far as we could discern, had no bottom; so once more we betook ourselves to the detested woods. When next we came forth from their dancing shadow and sunlight, we found ourselves standing in the broad glare of day, on a high jutting point of the mountain. Before us stretched a long, wide, desert valley, winding away far amid the mountains. No civilized eye but mine had ever looked upon that virgin waste. Reynal was gazing intently; he began to speak at last.

"Many a time, when I was with the Indians, I have been hunting for gold all through the Black Hills. There's plenty of it here; you may be certain of that. I have dreamed about it fifty times, and I never dreamed yet but what it came true. Look over yonder at those black rocks piled up against that other big rock. Don't it look as if there might be something there? It won't do for a white man to be rummaging too much about these mountains; the Indians say they are full of bad spirits; and I believe myself that it's no good luck to be hunting about here after gold. Well, for all that, I would like to have one of these fellows up here, from down below, to go about with his witch-hazel rod, and I'll guarantee that it would not be long before he would light on a gold mine. Never mind; we'll let the gold alone for to-day. Look at those trees down below us in the hollow; we'll go down there, and I reckon we'll get a black-tailed deer."

But Reynal's predictions were not verified. We passed mountain after mountain, and valley after valley; we explored deep ravines; yet still to my companion's vexation and evident surprise, no game could be found. So, in the absence of better, we resolved to go out on the plains and look for an antelope. With this view we began to pass down a narrow valley, the bottom of which was covered with the stiff wild-sage bushes and marked with deep paths, made by the buffalo, who, for some inexplicable reason, are accustomed to penetrate, in their long grave processions, deep among the gorges of these sterile mountains.

Reynal's eye was ranging incessantly among the rocks and along the edges of the black precipices, in hopes of discovering the mountain sheep peering down upon us in fancied security from that giddy elevation. Nothing was visible for some time. At length we both detected something in motion near the foot of one of the mountains, and in a moment afterward a black-tailed deer, with his spreading antlers, stood gazing at us from the top of a rock, and then, slowly turning away, disappeared behind it. In an instant Reynal was out of his saddle, and running toward the spot. I, being too weak to follow, sat holding his horse and waiting the result. I lost sight of him, then heard the report of his rifle, deadened among the rocks, and finally saw him reappear, with a surly look that plainly betrayed his ill success. Again we moved forward down the long valley, when soon after we came full upon what seemed a wide and very shallow ditch, incrusted at the bottom with white clay, dried and cracked in the sun. Under this fair outside, Reynal's eye detected the signs of lurking mischief. He called me to stop, and then alighting, picked up a stone and threw it into the ditch. To my utter amazement it fell with a dull splash, breaking at once through the thin crust, and spattering round the hole a yellowish creamy fluid, into which it sank and disappeared. A stick, five or six feet long lay on the ground, and with this we sounded the insidious abyss close to its edge. It was just possible to touch the bottom. Places like this are numerous among the Rocky Mountains. The buffalo, in his blind and heedless walk, often plunges into them unawares. Down he sinks; one snort of terror, one convulsive struggle, and the slime calmly flows above his shaggy head, the languid undulations of its sleek and placid surface alone betraying how the powerful monster writhes in his death-throes below.

We found after some trouble a point where we could pass the abyss, and now the valley began to open upon the plains which spread to the horizon before us. On one of their distant swells we discerned three or four black specks, which Reynal pronounced to be buffalo.

"Come," said he, "we must get one of them. My squaw wants more sinews to finish her lodge with, and I want some glue myself."

He immediately put the yellow horse at such a gallop as he was capable of executing, while I set spurs to the mule, who soon far outran her plebeian rival. When we had galloped a mile or more, a large rabbit, by ill luck, sprang up just under the feet of the mule, who bounded violently aside in full career. Weakened as I was, I was flung forcibly to the ground, and my rifle, falling close to my head, went off with a shock. Its sharp spiteful report rang for some moments in my ear. Being slightly stunned, I lay for an instant motionless, and Reynal, supposing me to be shot, rode up and began to curse the mule. Soon recovering myself, I rose, picked up the rifle and anxiously examined it. It was badly injured. The stock was cracked, and the main screw broken, so that the lock had to be tied in its place with a string; yet happily it was not rendered totally unserviceable. I wiped it out, reloaded it, and handing it to Reynal, who meanwhile had caught the mule and led her up to me, I mounted again. No sooner had I done so, than the brute began to rear and plunge with extreme violence; but being now well prepared for her, and free from incumbrance, I soon reduced her to submission. Then taking the rifle again from Reynal, we galloped forward as before.

We were now free of the mountain and riding far out on the broad prairie. The buffalo were still some two miles in advance of us. When we came near them, we stopped where a gentle swell of the plain concealed us from their view, and while I held his horse Reynal ran forward with his rifle, till I lost sight of him beyond the rising ground. A few minutes elapsed; I heard the report of his piece, and saw the buffalo running away at full speed on the right, and immediately after, the hunter himself unsuccessful as before, came up and mounted his horse in excessive ill-humor. He cursed the Black Hills and the buffalo, swore that he was a good hunter, which indeed was true, and that he had never been out before among those mountains without killing two or three deer at least.

We now turned toward the distant encampment. As we rode along, antelope in considerable numbers were flying lightly in all directions over the plain, but not one of them would stand and be shot at. When we reached the foot of the mountain ridge that lay between us and the village, we were too impatient to take the smooth and circuitous route; so turning short to the left, we drove our wearied animals directly upward among the rocks. Still more antelope were leaping about among these flinty hillsides. Each of us shot at one, though from a great distance, and each missed his mark. At length we reached the summit of the last ridge. Looking down, we saw the bustling camp in the valley at our feet, and ingloriously descended to it. As we rode among the lodges, the Indians looked in vain for the fresh meat that should have hung behind our saddles, and the squaws uttered various suppressed ejaculations, to the great indignation of Reynal. Our mortification was increased when we rode up to his lodge. Here we saw his young Indian relative, the Hail-Storm, his light graceful figure on the ground in an easy attitude, while with his friend the Rabbit, who sat by his side, he was making an abundant meal from a wooden bowl of wasna, which the squaw had placed between them. Near him lay the fresh skin of a female elk, which he had just killed among the mountains, only a mile or two from the camp. No doubt the boy's heart was elated with triumph, but he betrayed no sign of it. He even seemed totally unconscious of our approach, and his handsome face had all the tranquillity of Indian self-control; a self-control which prevents the exhibition of emotion, without restraining the emotion itself. It was about two months since I had known the Hail-Storm, and within that time his character had remarkably developed. When I first saw him, he was just emerging from the habits and feelings of the boy into the ambition of the hunter and warrior. He had lately killed his first deer, and this had excited his aspirations after distinction. Since that time he had been continually in search of game, and no young hunter in the village had been so active or so fortunate as he. It will perhaps be remembered how fearlessly he attacked the buffalo bull, as we were moving toward our camp at the Medicine-Bow Mountain. All this success had produced a marked change in his character. As I first remembered him he always shunned the society of the young squaws, and was extremely bashful and sheepish in their presence; but now, in the confidence of his own reputation, he began to assume the airs and the arts of a man of gallantry. He wore his red blanket dashingly over his left shoulder, painted his cheeks every day with vermilion, and hung pendants of shells in his ears. If I observed aright, he met with very good success in his new pursuits; still the Hail-Storm had much to accomplish before he attained the full standing of a warrior. Gallantly as he began to bear himself among the women and girls, he still was timid and abashed in the presence of the chiefs and old men; for he had never yet killed a man, or stricken the dead body of an enemy in battle. I have no doubt that the handsome smooth-faced boy burned with keen desire to flash his maiden scalping-knife, and I would not have encamped alone with him without watching his movements with a distrustful eye.

His elder brother, the Horse, was of a different character. He was nothing but a lazy dandy. He knew very well how to hunt, but preferred to live by the hunting of others. He had no appetite for distinction, and the Hail-Storm, though a few years younger than he, already surpassed him in reputation. He had a dark and ugly face, and he passed a great part of his time in adorning it with vermilion, and contemplating it by means of a little pocket looking-glass which I gave him. As for the rest of the day, he divided it between eating and sleeping, and sitting in the sun on the outside of a lodge. Here he would remain for hour after hour, arrayed in all his finery, with an old dragoon's sword in his hand, and evidently flattering himself that he was the center of attraction to the eyes of the surrounding squaws. Yet he sat looking straight forward with a face of the utmost gravity, as if wrapped in profound meditation, and it was only by the occasional sidelong glances which he shot at his supposed admirers that one could detect the true course of his thoughts.

Both he and his brother may represent a class in the Indian community; neither should the Hail-Storm's friend, the Rabbit, be passed by without notice. The Hail-Storm and he were inseparable; they ate, slept, and hunted together, and shared with one another almost all that they possessed. If there be anything that deserves to be called romantic in the Indian character, it is to be sought for in friendships such as this, which are quite common among many of the prairie tribes.

Slowly, hour after hour, that weary afternoon dragged away. I lay in Reynal's lodge, overcome by the listless torpor that pervaded the whole encampment. The day's work was finished, or if it were not, the inhabitants had resolved not to finish it at all, and all were dozing quietly within the shelter of the lodges. A profound lethargy, the very spirit of indolence, seemed to have sunk upon the village. Now and then I could hear the low laughter of some girl from within a neighboring lodge, or the small shrill voices of a few restless children, who alone were moving in the deserted area. The spirit of the place infected me; I could not even think consecutively; I was fit only for musing and reverie, when at last, like the rest, I fell asleep.

When evening came and the fires were lighted round the lodges, a select family circle convened in the neighborhood of Reynal's domicile. It was composed entirely of his squaw's relatives, a mean and ignoble clan, among whom none but the Hail-Storm held forth any promise of future distinction. Even his protests were rendered not a little dubious by the character of the family, less however from any principle of aristocratic distinction than from the want of powerful supporters to assist him in his undertakings, and help to avenge his quarrels. Raymond and I sat down along with them. There were eight or ten men gathered around the fire, together with about as many women, old and young, some of whom were tolerably good-looking. As the pipe passed round among the men, a lively conversation went forward, more merry than delicate, and at length two or three of the elder women (for the girls were somewhat diffident and bashful) began to assail Raymond with various pungent witticisms. Some of the men took part and an old squaw concluded by bestowing on him a ludicrous nick name, at which a general laugh followed at his expense. Raymond grinned and giggled, and made several futile attempts at repartee. Knowing the impolicy and even danger of suffering myself to be placed in a ludicrous light among the Indians, I maintained a rigid inflexible countenance, and wholly escaped their sallies.

In the morning I found, to my great disgust, that the camp was to retain its position for another day. I dreaded its languor and monotony, and to escape it, I set out to explore the surrounding mountains. I was accompanied by a faithful friend, my rifle, the only friend indeed on whose prompt assistance in time of trouble I could implicitly rely. Most of the Indians in the village, it is true, professed good-will toward the whites, but the experience of others and my own observation had taught me the extreme folly of confidence, and the utter impossibility of foreseeing to what sudden acts the strange unbridled impulses of an Indian may urge him. When among this people danger is never so near as when you are unprepared for it, never so remote as when you are armed and on the alert to meet it any moment. Nothing offers so strong a temptation to their ferocious instincts as the appearance of timidity, weakness, or security.

Many deep and gloomy gorges, choked with trees and bushes, opened from the sides of the hills, which were shaggy with forests wherever the rocks permitted vegetation to spring. A great number of Indians were stalking along the edges of the woods, and boys were whooping and laughing on the mountain-sides, practicing eye and hand, and indulging their destructive propensities by following birds and small animals and killing them with their little bows and arrows. There was one glen, stretching up between steep cliffs far into the bosom of the mountain. I began to ascend along its bottom, pushing my way onward among the rocks, trees, and bushes that obstructed it. A slender thread of water trickled along its center, which since issuing from the heart of its native rock could scarcely have been warmed or gladdened by a ray of sunshine. After advancing for some time, I conceived myself to be entirely alone; but coming to a part of the glen in a great measure free of trees and undergrowth, I saw at some distance the black head and red shoulders of an Indian among the bushes above. The reader need not prepare himself for a startling adventure, for I have none to relate. The head and shoulders belonged to Mene-Seela, my best friend in the village. As I had approached noiselessly with my moccasined feet, the old man was quite unconscious of my presence; and turning to a point where I could gain an unobstructed view of him, I saw him seated alone, immovable as a statue, among the rocks and trees. His face was turned upward, and his eyes seemed riveted on a pine tree springing from a cleft in the precipice above. The crest of the pine was swaying to and fro in the wind, and its long limbs waved slowly up and down, as if the tree had life. Looking for a while at the old man, I was satisfied that he was engaged in an act of worship or prayer, or communion of some kind with a supernatural being. I longed to penetrate his thoughts, but I could do nothing more than conjecture and speculate. I knew that though the intellect of an Indian can embrace the idea of an all-wise, all-powerful Spirit, the supreme Ruler of the universe, yet his mind will not always ascend into communion with a being that seems to him so vast, remote, and incomprehensible; and when danger threatens, when his hopes are broken, when the black wing of sorrow overshadows him, he is prone to turn for relief to some inferior agency, less removed from the ordinary scope of his faculties. He has a guardian spirit, on whom he relies for succor and guidance. To him all nature is instinct with mystic influence. Among those mountains not a wild beast was prowling, a bird singing, or a leaf fluttering, that might not tend to direct his destiny or give warning of what was in store for him; and he watches the world of nature around him as the astrologer watches the stars. So closely is he linked with it that his guardian spirit, no unsubstantial creation of the fancy, is usually embodied in the form of some living thing—a bear, a wolf, an eagle, or a serpent; and Mene-Seela, as he gazed intently on the old pine tree, might believe it to inshrine the fancied guide and protector of his life.

Whatever was passing in the mind of the old man, it was no part of sense or of delicacy to disturb him. Silently retracing my footsteps, I descended the glen until I came to a point where I could climb the steep precipices that shut it in, and gain the side of the mountain. Looking up, I saw a tall peak rising among the woods. Something impelled me to climb; I had not felt for many a day such strength and elasticity of limb. An hour and a half of slow and often intermittent labor brought me to the very summit; and emerging from the dark shadows of the rocks and pines, I stepped forth into the light, and walking along the sunny verge of a precipice, seated myself on its extreme point. Looking between the mountain peaks to the westward, the pale blue prairie was stretching to the farthest horizon like a serene and tranquil ocean. The surrounding mountains were in themselves sufficiently striking and impressive, but this contrast gave redoubled effect to their stern features.

* * *

When I took leave of Shaw at La Bonte's Camp, I promised that I would meet him at Fort Laramie on the 1st of August. That day, according to my reckoning, was now close at hand. It was impossible, at best, to fulfill my engagement exactly, and my meeting with him must have been postponed until many days after the appointed time, had not the plans of the Indians very well coincided with my own. They too, intended to pass the mountains and move toward the fort. To do so at this point was impossible, because there was no opening; and in order to find a passage we were obliged to go twelve or fourteen miles southward. Late in the afternoon the camp got in motion, defiling back through the mountains along the same narrow passage by which they had entered. I rode in company with three or four young Indians at the rear, and the moving swarm stretched before me, in the ruddy light of sunset, or in the deep shadow of the mountains far beyond my sight. It was an ill-omened spot they chose to encamp upon. When they were there just a year before, a war party of ten men, led by The Whirlwind's son, had gone out against the enemy, and not one had ever returned. This was the immediate cause of this season's warlike preparations. I was not a little astonished when I came to the camp, at the confusion of horrible sounds with which it was filled; howls, shrieks, and wailings were heard from all the women present, many of whom not content with this exhibition of grief for the loss of their friends and relatives, were gashing their legs deeply with knives. A warrior in the village, who had

lost a brother in the expedition; chose another mode of displaying his sorrow. The Indians, who, though often rapacious, are utterly devoid of avarice, are accustomed in times of mourning, or on other solemn occasions, to give away the whole of their possessions, and reduce themselves to nakedness and want. The warrior in question led his two best horses into the center of the village, and gave them away to his friends; upon which songs and acclamations in praise of his generosity mingled with the cries of the women.

On the next morning we entered once more among the mountains. There was nothing in their appearance either grand or picturesque, though they were desolate to the last degree, being mere piles of black and broken rocks, without trees or vegetation of any kind. As we passed among them along a wide valley, I noticed Raymond riding by the side of a younger squaw, to whom he was addressing various insinuating compliments. All the old squaws in the neighborhood watched his proceedings in great admiration, and the girl herself would turn aside her head and laugh. Just then the old mule thought proper to display her vicious pranks; she began to rear and plunge most furiously. Raymond was an excellent rider, and at first he stuck fast in his seat; but the moment after, I saw the mule's hind-legs flourishing in the air, and my unlucky follower pitching head foremost over her ears. There was a burst of screams and laughter from all the women, in which his mistress herself took part, and Raymond was instantly assailed by such a shower of witticisms, that he was glad to ride forward out of hearing.

Not long after, as I rode near him, I heard him shouting to me. He was pointing toward a detached rocky hill that stood in the middle of the valley before us, and from behind it a long file of elk came out at full speed and entered an opening in the side of the mountain. They had scarcely disappeared when whoops and exclamations came from fifty voices around me. The young men leaped from their horses, flung down their heavy buffalo robes, and ran at full speed toward the foot of the nearest mountain. Reynal also broke away at a gallop in the same direction, "Come on! come on!" he called to us. "Do you see that band of bighorn up yonder? If there's one of them, there's a hundred!"

In fact, near the summit of the mountain, I could see a large number of small white objects, moving rapidly upward among the precipices, while others were filing along its rocky profile. Anxious to see the sport, I galloped forward, and entering a passage in the side of the mountain, ascended the loose rocks as far as my horse could carry me. Here I fastened her to an old pine tree that stood alone, scorching in the sun. At that moment Raymond called to me from the right that another band of sheep was close at hand in that direction. I ran up to the top of the opening, which gave me a full view into the rocky gorge beyond; and here I plainly saw some fifty or sixty sheep, almost within rifle-shot, clattering upward among the rocks, and endeavoring, after their usual custom, to reach the highest point. The naked Indians bounded up lightly in pursuit. In a moment the game and hunters disappeared. Nothing could be seen or heard but the occasional report of a gun, more and more distant, reverberating among the rocks.

I turned to descend, and as I did so I could see the valley below alive with Indians passing rapidly through it, on horseback and on foot. A little farther on, all were stopping as they came up; the camp was preparing, and the lodges rising. I descended to this spot, and soon after Reynal and Raymond returned. They bore between them a sheep which they had pelted to death with stones from the edge of a ravine, along the bottom of which it was attempting to escape. One by one the hunters came dropping in; yet such is the activity of the Rocky Mountain sheep that, although sixty or seventy men were out in pursuit, not more than half a dozen animals were killed. Of these only one was a full-grown male. He had a pair of horns twisted like a ram's, the dimensions of which were almost beyond belief. I have seen among the Indians ladles with long handles, capable of containing more than a quart, cut from such horns.

There is something peculiarly interesting in the character and habits of the mountain sheep, whose chosen retreats are above the region of vegetation and storms, and who leap among the giddy precipices of their aerial home as actively as the antelope skims over the prairies below.

Through the whole of the next morning we were moving forward, among the hills. On the following day the heights gathered around us, and the passage of the mountains began in earnest. Before the village left its camping ground, I set forward in company with the Eagle-Feather, a man of powerful frame, but of bad and sinister face. His son, a light-limbed boy, rode with us, and another Indian, named the Panther, was also of the party. Leaving the village out of sight behind us, we rode together up a rocky defile. After a while, however, the Eagle-Feather discovered in the distance some appearance of game, and set off with his son in pursuit of it, while I went forward with the Panther. This was a mere *nom de guerre*; for, like many Indians, he concealed his real name out of some superstitious notion. He was a very noble looking fellow. As he suffered

217

his ornamented buffalo robe to fall into folds about his loins, his stately and graceful figure was fully displayed; and while he sat his horse in an easy attitude, the long feathers of the prairie cock fluttering from the crown of his head, he seemed the very model of a wild prairie-rider. He had not the same features as those of other Indians. Unless his handsome face greatly belied him, he was free from the jealousy, suspicion, and malignant cunning of his people. For the most part, a civilized white man can discover but very few points of sympathy between his own nature and that of an Indian. With every disposition to do justice to their good qualities, he must be conscious that an impassable gulf lies between him and his red brethren of the prairie. Nay, so alien to himself do they appear that, having breathed for a few months or a few weeks the air of this region, he begins to look upon them as a troublesome and dangerous species of wild beast, and, if expedient, he could shoot them with as little compunction as they themselves would experience after performing the same office upon him. Yet, in the countenance of the Panther, I gladly read that there were at least some points of sympathy between him and me. We were excellent friends, and as we rode forward together through rocky passages, deep dells, and little barren plains, he occupied himself very zealously in teaching me the Dakota language. After a while, we came to a little grassy recess, where some gooseberry bushes were growing at the foot of a rock; and these offered such temptation to my companion, that he gave over his instruction, and stopped so long to gather the fruit that before we were in motion again the van of the village came in view. An old woman appeared, leading down her pack horse among the rocks above. Savage after savage followed, and the little dell was soon crowded with the throng.

That morning's march was one not easily to be forgotten. It led us through a sublime waste, a wilderness of mountains and pine forests, over which the spirit of loneliness and silence seemed brooding. Above and below little could be seen but the same dark green foliage. It overspread the valleys, and the mountains were clothed with it from the black rocks that crowned their summits to the impetuous streams that circled round their base. Scenery like this, it might seem, could have no very cheering effect on the mind of a sick man (for to-day my disease had again assailed me) in the midst of a horde of savages; but if the reader has ever wandered, with a true hunter's spirit, among the forests of Maine, or the more picturesque solitudes of the Adirondack Mountains, he will understand how the somber woods and mountains around me might have awakened any other feelings than those of gloom. In truth they recalled gladdening recollections of similar scenes in a distant and far different land. After we had been advancing for several hours through passages always narrow, often obstructed and difficult, I saw at a little distance on our right a narrow opening between two high wooded precipices. All within seemed darkness and mystery. In the mood in which I found myself something strongly impelled me to enter. Passing over the intervening space I guided my horse through the rocky portal, and as I did so instinctively drew the covering from my rifle, half expecting that some unknown evil lay in ambush within those dreary recesses. The place was shut in among tall cliffs, and so deeply shadowed by a host of old pine trees that, though the sun shone bright on the side of the mountain, nothing but a dim twilight could penetrate within. As far as I could see it had no tenants except a few hawks and owls, who, dismayed at my intrusion, flapped hoarsely away among the shaggy branches. I moved forward, determined to explore the mystery to the bottom, and soon became involved among the pines. The genius of the place exercised a strange influence upon my mind. Its faculties were stimulated into extraordinary activity, and as I passed along many half-forgotten incidents, and the images of persons and things far distant, rose rapidly before me with surprising distinctness. In that perilous wilderness, eight hundred miles removed beyond the faintest vestige of civilization, the scenes of another hemisphere, the seat of ancient refinement, passed before me more like a succession of vivid paintings than any mere dreams of the fancy. I saw the church of St. Peter's illumined on the evening of Easter Day, the whole majestic pile, from the cross to the foundation stone, penciled in fire and shedding a radiance, like the serene light of the moon, on the sea of upturned faces below. I saw the peak of Mount Etna towering above its inky mantle of clouds and lightly curling its wreaths of milk-white smoke against the soft sky flushed with the Sicilian sunset. I saw also the gloomy vaulted passages and the narrow cells of the Passionist convent where I once had sojourned for a few days with the fanatical monks, its pale, stern inmates in their robes of black, and the grated window from whence I could look out, a forbidden indulgence, upon the melancholy Coliseum and the crumbling ruins of the Eternal City. The mighty glaciers of the Splugen too rose before me, gleaming in the sun like polished silver, and those terrible solitudes, the birthplace of the Rhine, where bursting from the bowels of its native mountains, it lashes and foams down the rocky abyss into the little valley of Andeer. These recollections, and many more, crowded upon me, until remembering that it was hardly wise to remain long in such a place, I mounted again and retraced my steps. Issuing from between the rocks I saw a few rods before me the men, women, and children, dogs and horses, still filing slowly across the little glen. A bare round hill rose directly above them. I rode to the top, and from this point I could look down on the savage procession as it passed just beneath my feet, and far on the left I could see its thin and broken line, visible only at intervals, stretching away for miles among the mountains. On the farthest ridge horsemen were still descending like mere specks in the distance.

I remained on the hill until all had passed, and then, descending, followed after them. A little farther on I found a very small meadow, set deeply among steep mountains; and here the whole village had encamped. The little spot was crowded with the confused and disorderly host. Some of the lodges were already completely prepared, or the squaws perhaps were busy in drawing the heavy coverings of skin over the bare poles. Others were as yet mere skeletons, while others still—poles, covering, and all—lay scattered in complete disorder on the ground among buffalo robes, bales of meat, domestic utensils, harness, and weapons. Squaws were screaming to one another, horses rearing and plunging, dogs yelping, eager to be disburdened of their loads, while the fluttering of feathers and the gleam of barbaric ornaments added liveliness to the scene. The small children ran about amid the crowd, while many of the boys were scrambling among the overhanging rocks, and standing, with their little bows in their hands, looking down upon a restless throng. In contrast with the general confusion, a circle of old men and warriors sat in the midst, smoking in profound indifference and tranquillity. The disorder at length subsided. The horses were driven away to feed along the adjacent valley, and the camp assumed an air of listless repose. It was scarcely past noon; a vast white canopy of smoke from a burning forest to the eastward overhung the place, and partially obscured the sun; yet the heat was almost insupportable. The lodges stood crowded together without order in the narrow space. Each was a perfect hothouse, within which the lazy proprietor lay sleeping. The camp was silent as death. Nothing stirred except now and then an old woman passing from lodge to lodge. The girls and young men sat together in groups under the pine trees upon the surrounding heights. The dogs lay panting on the ground, too lazy even to growl at the white man. At the entrance of the meadow there was a cold spring among the rocks, completely overshadowed by tall trees and dense undergrowth. In this cold and shady retreat a number of girls were assembled, sitting together on rocks and fallen logs, discussing the latest gossip of the village, or laughing and throwing water with their hands at the intruding Meneaska. The minutes seemed lengthened into hours. I lay for a long time under a tree, studying the Ogallalla tongue, with the zealous instructions of my friend the Panther. When we were both tired of this I went and lay down by the side of a deep, clear pool formed by the water of the spring. A shoal of little fishes of about a pin's length were playing in it, sporting together, as it seemed, very amicably; but on closer observation, I saw that they were engaged in a cannibal warfare among themselves. Now and then a small one would fall a victim, and immediately disappear down the maw of his voracious conqueror. Every moment, however, the tyrant of the pool, a monster about three inches long, with staring goggle eyes, would slowly issue forth with quivering fins and tail from under the shelving bank. The small fry at this would suspend their hostilities, and scatter in a panic at the appearance of overwhelming force.

"Soft-hearted philanthropists," thought I, "may sigh long for their peaceful millennium; for from minnows up to men, life is an incessant battle."

Evening approached at last, the tall mountain-tops around were still gay and bright in sunshine, while our deep glen was completely shadowed. I left the camp and ascended a neighboring hill, whose rocky summit commanded a wide view over the surrounding wilderness. The sun was still glaring through the stiff pines on the ridge of the western mountain. In a moment he was gone, and as the landscape rapidly darkened, I turned again toward the village. As I descended the hill, the howling of wolves and the barking of foxes came up out of the dim woods from far and near. The camp was glowing with a multitude of fires, and alive with dusky naked figures, whose tall shadows flitted among the surroundings crags.

I found a circle of smokers seated in their usual place; that is, on the ground before the lodge of a certain warrior, who seemed to be generally known for his social qualities. I sat down to smoke a parting pipe with my savage friends. That day was the 1st of August, on which I had promised to meet Shaw at Fort Laramie. The Fort was less than two days' journey distant, and that my friend need not suffer anxiety on my account, I resolved to push forward as rapidly as possible to the place of meeting. I went to look after the Hail-Storm, and having found him, I offered him a handful of hawks'-bells and a paper of vermilion, on condition that he would guide me in the morning through the mountains within sight of Laramie Creek.

The Hail-Storm ejaculated "How!" and accepted the gift. Nothing more was said on either side; the matter was settled, and I lay down to sleep in Kongra-Tonga's lodge.

Long before daylight Raymond shook me by the shoulder.

"Everything is ready," he said.

I went out. The morning was chill, damp, and dark; and the whole camp seemed asleep. The Hail-Storm sat on horseback before the lodge, and my mare Pauline and the mule which Raymond rode were picketed near it. We saddled and made our other arrangements for the journey, but before these were completed the camp began to stir, and the lodge-coverings fluttered and rustled as the squaws pulled them down in preparation for departure. Just as the light began to appear we left the ground, passing up through a narrow opening among the rocks which led eastward out of the meadow. Gaining the top of this passage, I turned round and sat looking back upon the camp, dimly visible in the gray light of the morning. All was alive with the bustle of preparation. I turned away, half unwilling to take a final leave of my savage associates. We turned to the right, passing among the rocks and pine trees so dark that for a while we could scarcely see our way. The country in front was wild and broken, half hill, half plain, partly open and partly covered with woods of pine and oak. Barriers of lofty mountains encompassed it; the woods were fresh and cool in the early morning; the peaks of the mountains were wreathed with mist, and sluggish vapors were entangled among the forests upon their sides. At length the black pinnacle of the tallest mountain was tipped with gold by the rising sun. About that time the Hail-Storm, who rode in front gave a low exclamation. Some large animal leaped up from among the bushes, and an elk, as I thought, his horns thrown back over his neck, darted past us across the open space, and bounded like a mad thing away among the adjoining pines. Raymond was soon out of his saddle, but before he could fire, the animal was full two hundred yards distant. The ball struck its mark, though much too low for mortal effect. The elk, however, wheeled in its flight, and ran at full speed among the trees, nearly at right angles to his former course. I fired and broke his shoulder; still he moved on, limping down into the neighboring woody hollow, whither the young Indian followed and killed him. When we reached the spot we discovered him to be no elk, but a black-tailed deer, an animal nearly twice the size of the common deer, and quite unknown to the East. We began to cut him up; the reports of the rifles had reached the ears of the Indians, and before our task was finished several of them came to the spot. Leaving the hide of the deer to the Hail-Storm, we hung as much of the meat as we wanted behind our saddles, left the rest to the Indians, and resumed our journey. Meanwhile the village was on its way, and had gone so far that to get in advance of it was impossible. Therefore we directed our course so as to strike its line of march at the nearest point. In a short time, through the dark trunks of the pines, we could see the figures of the Indians as they passed. Once more we were among them. They were moving with even more than their usual precipitation, crowded close together in a narrow pass between rocks and old pine trees. We were on the eastern descent of the mountain, and soon came to a rough and difficult defile, leading down a very steep declivity. The whole swarm poured down together, filling the rocky passageway like some turbulent mountain stream. The mountains before us were on fire, and had been so for weeks. The view in front was obscured by a vast dim sea of smoke and vapor, while on either hand the tall cliffs, bearing aloft their crest of pines, thrust their heads boldly through it, and the sharp pinnacles and broken ridges of the mountains beyond them were faintly traceable as through a veil. The scene in itself was most grand and imposing, but with the savage multitude, the armed warriors, the naked children, the gayly appareled girls, pouring impetuously down the heights, it would have formed a noble subject for a painter, and only the pen of a Scott could have done it justice in description.

We passed over a burnt tract where the ground was hot beneath the horses' feet, and between the blazing sides of two mountains. Before long we had descended to a softer region, where we found a succession of little valleys watered by a stream, along the borders of which grew abundance of wild gooseberries and currants, and the children and many of the men straggled from the line of march to gather them as we passed along. Descending still farther, the view changed rapidly. The burning mountains were behind us, and through the open valleys in front we could see the ocean-like prairie, stretching beyond the sight. After passing through a line of trees that skirted the brook, the Indians filed out upon the plains. I was thirsty and knelt down by the little stream to drink. As I mounted again I very carelessly left my rifle among the grass, and my thoughts being otherwise absorbed, I rode for some distance before discovering its absence. As the reader may conceive, I lost no time in turning about and galloping back in search of it. Passing the line of Indians, I watched every warrior as he rode by me at a canter, and at length discovered my rifle in the hands of one of them, who, on my approaching to claim it, immediately gave it up. Having no other means of acknowledging the obligation, I took off one of my spurs and gave it to him. He was greatly delighted, looking upon it as a distinguished mark of favor, and immediately held out his foot for me to buckle it on. As soon as I had done so, he struck it with force into the side of his horse, who gave a violent leap. The Indian laughed and spurred harder than before. At this the horse shot away like an arrow, amid the screams and laughter of the squaws, and the ejaculations of the men, who exclaimed: "Washtay!—Good!" at the potent effect of my gift. The Indian had no saddle, and nothing in place of a bridle except a leather string tied round the horse's jaw. The animal was of course wholly uncontrollable, and stretched away at full speed over the prairie, till he and his rider vanished behind a distant swell. I never saw the man again, but I presume no harm came to him. An Indian on horseback has more lives than a cat.

The village encamped on a scorching prairie, close to the foot of the mountains. The heat was most intense and penetrating. The coverings of the lodges were raised a foot or more from the ground, in order to procure some circulation of air; and Reynal thought proper to lay aside his trapper's dress of buckskin and assume the very scanty costume of an Indian. Thus elegantly attired, he stretched himself in his lodge on a buffalo robe, alternately cursing the heat and puffing at the pipe which he and I passed between us. There was present also a select circle of Indian friends and relatives. A small boiled puppy was served up as a parting feast, to which was added, by way of dessert, a wooden bowl of gooseberries, from the mountains.

"Look there," said Reynal, pointing out of the opening of his lodge; "do you see that line of buttes about fifteen miles off? Well, now, do you see that farthest one, with the white speck on the face of it? Do you think you ever saw it before?"

"It looks to me," said I, "like the hill that we were camped under when we were on Laramie Creek, six or eight weeks ago."

"You've hit it," answered Reynal.

"Go and bring in the animals, Raymond," said I: "we'll camp there to-night, and start for the Fort in the morning."

The mare and the mule were soon before the lodge. We saddled them, and in the meantime a number of Indians collected about us. The virtues of Pauline, my strong, fleet, and hardy little mare, were well known in camp, and several of the visitors were mounted upon good horses which they had brought me as presents. I promptly declined their offers, since accepting them would have involved the necessity of transferring poor Pauline into their barbarous hands. We took leave of Reynal, but not of the Indians, who are accustomed to dispense with such superfluous ceremonies. Leaving the camp we rode straight over the prairie toward the white-faced bluff, whose pale ridges swelled gently against the horizon, like a cloud. An Indian went with us, whose name I forget, though the ugliness of his face and the ghastly width of his mouth dwell vividly in my recollection. The antelope were numerous, but we did not heed them. We rode directly toward our destination, over the arid plains and barren hills, until, late in the afternoon, half spent with heat, thirst, and fatigue, we saw a gladdening sight; the long line of trees and the deep gulf that mark the course of Laramie Creek. Passing through the growth of huge dilapidated old cotton-wood trees that bordered the creek, we rode across to the other side.

The rapid and foaming waters were filled with fish playing and splashing in the shallows. As we gained the farther bank, our horses turned eagerly to drink, and we, kneeling on the sand, followed their example. We had not gone far before the scene began to grow familiar.

"We are getting near home, Raymond," said I.

There stood the Big Tree under which we had encamped so long; there were the white cliffs that used to look down upon our tent when it stood at the bend of the creek; there was the meadow in which our horses had grazed for weeks, and a little farther on, the prairie-dog village where I had beguiled many a languid hour in persecuting the unfortunate inhabitants.

"We are going to catch it now," said Raymond, turning his broad, vacant face up toward the sky.

In truth, the landscape, the cliffs and the meadow, the stream and the groves were darkening fast. Black masses of cloud were swelling up in the south, and the thunder was growling ominously.

"We will camp here," I said, pointing to a dense grove of trees lower down the stream. Raymond and I turned toward it, but the Indian stopped and called earnestly after us. When we demanded what was the matter, he said that the ghosts of two warriors were always among those trees, and that if we slept there, they would scream and throw stones at us all night, and perhaps steal our horses before morning. Thinking it as well to humor him, we left behind us the haunt of these extraordinary ghosts, and passed on toward Chugwater, riding at full gallop, for the big drops began to patter down. Soon we came in sight of the poplar saplings that grew about the mouth of the little stream. We leaped to the ground, threw off our saddles, turned our horses loose, and drawing our knives, began to slash among the bushes to cut twigs and branches for making a shelter against the rain. Bending down the taller saplings as they grew, we piled the young shoots upon them; and thus made a convenient penthouse, but all our labor was useless. The storm scarcely touched us. Half a mile on our right the rain was pouring down like a cataract, and the thunder roared over the prairie like a battery of cannon; while we by good fortune received only a few heavy drops from the skirt of the passing cloud. The weather cleared and the sun set gloriously. Sitting close under our leafy canopy, we proceeded to discuss a substantial meal of wasna which Weah-Washtay had given me. The Indian had brought with him his pipe and a bag of shongsasha; so before lying down to sleep, we sat for some time smoking together. Previously, however, our wide-mouthed friend had taken the precaution of carefully examining the neighborhood. He reported that eight men, counting them on his fingers, had been encamped there not long before. Bisonette, Paul Dorion, Antoine Le Rouge, Richardson, and four others, whose names he could not tell. All this proved strictly correct. By what instinct he had arrived at such accurate conclusions, I am utterly at a loss to divine.

It was still quite dark when I awoke and called Raymond. The Indian was already gone, having chosen to go on before us to the Fort. Setting out after him, we rode for some time in complete darkness, and when the sun at length rose, glowing like a fiery ball of copper, we were ten miles distant from the Fort. At length, from the broken summit of a tall sandy bluff we could see Fort Laramie, miles before us, standing by the side of the stream like a little gray speck in the midst of the bounding desolation. I stopped my horse, and sat for a moment looking down upon it. It seemed to me the very center of comfort and civilization. We were not long in approaching it, for we rode at speed the greater part of the way. Laramie Creek still intervened between us and the friendly walls. Entering the water at the point where we had struck upon the bank, we raised our feet to the saddle behind us, and thus, kneeling as it were on horseback, passed dry-shod through the swift current. As we rode up the bank, a number of men appeared in the gateway. Three of them came forward to meet us. In a moment I distinguished Shaw; Henry Chatillon followed with his face of manly simplicity and frankness; and Delorier came last, with a broad grin of welcome. The meeting was not on either side one of mere ceremony. For my own part, the change was a most agreeable one from the society of savages and men little better than savages, to that of my gallant and high-minded companion and our noble-hearted guide. My appearance was equally gratifying to Shaw, who was beginning to entertain some very uncomfortable surmises concerning me.

Bordeaux greeted me very cordially, and shouted to the cook. This functionary was a new acquisition, having lately come from Fort Pierre with the trading wagons. Whatever skill he might have boasted, he had not the most promising materials to exercise it upon. He set before me, however, a breakfast of biscuit, coffee, and salt pork. It seemed like a new phase of existence, to be seated once more on a bench, with a knife and fork, a plate and teacup, and something resembling a table before me. The coffee seemed delicious, and the bread was a most welcome novelty, since for three weeks I had eaten scarcely anything but meat, and that for the most part without salt. The meal also had the relish of good company, for opposite to me sat Shaw in elegant dishabille. If one is anxious thoroughly to appreciate the value of a congenial companion, he has only to spend a few weeks by himself in an Ogallalla village. And if he can contrive to add to his seclusion a debilitating and somewhat critical illness, his perceptions upon this subject will be rendered considerably more vivid.

Shaw had been upward of two weeks at the Fort. I found him established in his old quarters, a large apartment usually occupied by the absent bourgeois. In one corner was a soft and luxuriant pile of excellent buffalo robes, and here I lay down. Shaw brought me three books.

"Here," said he, "is your Shakespeare and Byron, and here is the Old Testament, which has as much poetry in it as the other two put together."

I chose the worst of the three, and for the greater part of that day lay on the buffalo robes, fairly reveling in the creations of that resplendent genius which has achieved no more signal triumph than that of half beguiling us to forget the pitiful and unmanly character of its possessor.

CHAPTER 12

JAMES "JIM" BRIDGER

from *Biographical Sketch of James Bridger*

By Grenville M. Dodge

At this late day it is a very difficult undertaking to attempt to write a connected history of a man who spent a long life on the plains and in the mountains, performing deeds and rendering services of inestimable value to this country, but who, withal, was so modest that he has not bequeathed to his descendants one written word concerning the stirring events which filled his active and useful life.

It is both a duty and a pleasure to make public such information as I possess and have been able to gather concerning James Bridger, and it is eminently proper and appropriate that this information should be published at the time when his remains are removed to the beautiful spot where they will forever rest, and a simple monument erected that posterity may know something of the remarkable man whose body lies beside it.

James Bridger was born in Richmond, Virginia, March 17, 1804. He was the son of James and Schloe Bridger. The father at one time kept a hotel in Richmond, and also had a large farm in Virginia. In 1812 he emigrated to St. Louis and settled on Six Mile Prairie. He was a surveyor, working in St. Louis and Illinois. His business kept him continually from home, and when his wife died in 1816 he was away from home at the time, and three little children were left alone. One, a son, soon died, the second—a daughter, and the third—the subject of this sketch. The father had a sister, who took charge of the children and farm. In the fall of 1817 the father died, leaving the two children entirely alone with their aunt on the farm. They were of Scotch descent. Their father's sister married John Tyler, who was afterwards President of the United States, and was, therefore, uncle by marriage to James Bridger.

After the death of his father and mother, Bridger had to support himself and sister. He got together money enough to buy a flatboat ferry, and when ten years of age made a living by running that ferry to St. Louis. When he was thirteen years old he was apprenticed to Phil Cromer to learn the blacksmith's trade. Becoming tired of this, in 1822 he hired out to a party of trappers under General Ashley, who were en route to the mountains. As a boy he was shrewd, had keen faculties of observation, and said when he went with the trappers that the money he earned would go to his sister.

The Rocky Mountain Fur Company was organized by General W. H. Ashley in 1822 and commanded by Andrew Henry. It left St. Louis in April, 1822, and it was with this party that Bridger enlisted.

Andrew Henry moved to the mouth of the Yellowstone, going by the Missouri River. They lost one of their boats which was loaded with goods worth $10,000, and while his land force was moving up parallel with his boats the Indians, under the guise of friendship, obtained his horses. This forced him to halt and build a fort for the winter at the mouth of the Yellowstone, and they trapped and explored in this locality until the spring of 1823.

Ashley, having returned to St. Louis in the fall of 1822, arrived with his second expedition in front of the Aricara villages on May 10, 1823, where he was defeated in battle by the Indians, losing one-half his men, his horses and baggage. He then sent a courier across country to Henry, who went down the Missouri River with his force, and joined Ashley near the mouth of the

Cheyenne. The United States forces under General Atkinson were then coming up the Missouri Valley to quell the Indian troubles, and Ashley and Henry expected to remain and meet them, and their party joined this force under Colonel Leavenworth.

After this campaign was over, Henry, with eighty men, including Bridger, moved in August, 1823, to his fort at the mouth of Yellowstone, and in crossing the country lost two men in a fight with the Indians. He arrived at the fort August 23, 1823, and found that twenty-two of his horses had been stolen by the Indians. He abandoned the fort, and moved by the Yellowstone to near the mouth of the Powder River. Meeting a band of Crows, he purchased forty-seven horses. He then divided his party, placing one part under Etienne Prevost, a noted trapper and trader. In the autumn of 1823 they moved by the Big Horn and Wind rivers to Green River. With this party was Bridger, and no doubt it was this party that late in the fall of 1823 discovered the South Pass. The South Pass is the southern end of the Wind River mountains, and all the country there gives down into a level valley until the Medicine Bow range is reached, some one hundred and fifty miles southeast. It forms a natural depression in the divide of the continent, and it is through this depression that the Union Pacific Railroad was built. This depression is a basin, smaller than Salt Lake, but has no water in it. It is known as the Red Desert, and extends about one hundred miles east and west, and sixty or seventy miles north and south. The east and west rims of this basin make two divides of the continent. In those days the South Pass was known to the trappers in the Wind River valley as the southern route.

This party trapped on Wind, Green and other rivers, and in 1823–1824 wintered in Cache valley on Bear River. So far as we have any proof, Bridger was the first man positively known to see Salt Lake. It is claimed that a Spanish missionary, Friar Escalante, of Santa Fe, visited the lake in 1776. To settle a wager as to the course of Bear River, Bridger followed the stream to Great Salt Lake and found the water salt. He returned to this party and reported what he had learned, and they concluded it was an arm of the Pacific Ocean. In the spring of 1825 four men in skin boats explored the shore line, and found it had no outlet.

Andrew Henry was in charge of the Rocky Mountain Fur Company until the fall of 1824, when Jedediah S. Smith took his place, and remained Ashley's partner until 1826. Ashley sold the Rocky Mountain Fur Company to Smith, Jackson and Sublette in July 1826. Bridger trapped in the interest of these men until 1829, Christopher Carson being with him this year. The winter of 1829–1830 Bridger spent on Powder River with Smith and Jackson, and in April 1830, went with Smith by the way of Yellowstone to the upper Missouri and to the Juditi basin, and then to yearly rendezvous on Wind River, near the mouth of the Porporgie.

Sublette left St. Louis April 10, 1830, with eighty-one men and ten wagons, with five mules to each wagon, and these were the first wagons to be used over what was known as the Oregon trail. They reached the Wind River rendezvous on July 16.

On August 4, 1830, Smith, Jackson and Sublette sold out the company to Milton G. Sublette, Henry Fraeb, John B. Gervais and James Bridger. The new firm was called the Rocky Mountain Fur Company, and under these people was the only time the company operated under its own name. The trappers divided and occupied different sections of the country. Bridger, with Fitzpatrick and Sublette, took two hundred men, went into the Big Horn basin, crossed the Yellowstone, then north to the great falls of the Missouri, ascended the Missouri to the three forks, went by the Jefferson to the divide, then south several hundred miles to Salt Lake. Here they obtained the furs collected by Peter Skene Ogden, of the Hudson Bay Company. They then covered the country to the eastward, and reached the valley of Powder River by the first of winter, traveling in all about twelve hundred miles. Here they spent the winter. It is probable that during this trip Bridger first saw Yellowstone Lake and geysers, and he was probably the first fur trader to make known the wonders of Yellowstone Park. He talked to me a great deal about it in the fifties, and his description of it was of such a nature that it was considered to be a great exaggeration, but the development of the park in later years shows that he did not exaggerate its beauties and wonders. Bridger was evidently well acquainted with its wonderful features. Captain Chittenden, in his "The Yellowstone National Park," quotes from Gunnison's "History of the Mormons," giving Bridger's descrption of the park as follows: "A lake, sixty miles long, cold and pellucid, lies embosomed among high precipitous mountains. On the west side is a sloping plain several miles wide, with clumps of trees and groves of pines. The ground resounds with the tread of horses. Geysers spout up seventy feet high, with a terrific, hissing noise, at regular intervals. Water falls are sparkling, leaping and thundering down the precipices, and collect in the pools below. The river issues from this lake, and for fifteen miles roars through the perpendicular canyon at the outlet. In this section are the 'Great Springs' so hot that meat is readily cooked in them, and, as they descend on the successive terraces, afford at length delightful baths. On the other side is an acid spring, which gushes out in a river torrent; and below is a cave, which supplies vermillion for the savages in abundance. In this admirable summary we readily discover the Yellowstone Lake, the Grand Canyon, the falls, the geyser basins, the mammoth springs and Cinnehar mountain."

Bridger talked about the Yellowstone Lake and its surroundings to everyone he met, and it was not his fault that the country was not explored and better known until in the sixties.

A small lake near the headwaters of the Yellowstone has been named Bridger Lake.

In the spring of 1831 Bridger and Sublette started for the Blackfoot country, where they met a band of the Crows who stole all their horses. Bridger led a party of this men in pursuit and recaptured all these horses as well as taking all the ponies of the Crows.

Fitzpatrick had gone to St. Louis to bring out the winter supplies. Bridger and Sublette followed nearly their previous year's route in their hunting, and in the fall reached the rendezvous on Green River, where they met Gervais and Frack, who were at the head of another party of the Rocky Mountain Fur Company.

After leaving St. Louis, Fitzpatrick came out with his supplies by the way of Santa Fe, and was so long in reaching the rendezvous on Green River that Sublette and Bridger returned to the Powder River to winter, and here they first met the competition of the American Fur Company, which finally drove the Rocky Mountain Fur Company out of the business. Fitzpatrick and Frack joined Bridger here on Powder River, but becoming disgusted with the movements of the American Fur Company, under Vandenburg and Dripps, Fitzpatrick and Bridger, with their entire outfit, moved west some four hundred miles to Pierre's Hole, near the forks of the Snake River. In the spring of 1832 they moved up Snake to Salt, up that stream and across to John Day River, up that river to its head, and across to Bear River in the Great Salt Lake Basin. Here they again met the American Fur Company, with Vandenburg and Dripps. They struck off into a different country, and finally rendezvoused again at Pierre's Hole, waiting for the supplies from the states being brought out by William L. Sublette. At their rendezvous concentrated this summer the Rocky Mountain Fur Company, the American Fur Company, under Vanderburg and Dripps; Arthur Nathaniel J. Wyeth with a new party coming mostly from the New England States, a large number of free traders and trappers and numerous bands of Indians, and here occurred the celebrated battle of Pierre's Hole, with the Gros Ventre Indians a Blackfoot tribe, which was one of the hardest battles fought in an early day on the plains, the losses being very heavy.

The battle of Pierre's Hole, or the Teton basin, was fought July 13, 1832. Of the different fur companies and free traders there were present some three hundred men and several hundred Indians of the Nez Perces and Flathead tribes. The Gros Ventres, about one hundred and fifty strong, always hostile to the whites, were returning from a visit to their kindred, the Arapahoes. They carried a British flag captured from Hudson Bay Company trappers.

When the Indians saw the band of trappers, who were some eight miles from the main rendezvous at Pierre's Hole, the Indians made signs of peace, but they were known to be so treacherous that no confidence was placed in their signs. However, Antoine Godin, whose father had been killed by this tribe, and a Flathead chief, whose nation had suffered untold wrongs from them, advanced to meet them. The Gros Ventre chief came forward, and when Godin grasped his hand in friendship the Flathead shot him dead. The Gros Ventres immediately retired to a grove of timber, and commenced piling up logs and entrenching. The trappers sent word to the rendezvous, and when Sublette and Campbell brought reinforcements the battle opened, the trappers charging the Indians and finally tried to burn them out, but did not succeed. The Gros Ventres, through their interpreter, made the trappers believe that a large portion of their tribe, some eight hundred, were attacking their rendezvous. Upon learning this. the trappers immediately left for its defense and found the story was a lie, but by this ruse the Indians were able to escape. The whites lost five killed and six wounded. The loss of the Gros Ventres was never fully known. They left nine killed, with twenty-five horses and all their baggage, and admitted a loss of twenty-six warriors. The Indians escaped during the night and effected a junction with their tribe.

In 1832 the American Fur Company, operated by Vandenburg and Dripps, came into the territory of the Rocky Mountain Fur Company, which was under Fitzpatrick and Bridger, and undertook to follow their parties, knowing that their trapping grounds yielded a great many furs. They followed them to the headwaters of the Missouri and down the Jefferson. Frack, Fitzpatrick and Bridger thought they would get rid of them by going right into the Blackfoot nation, which was very hostile. Finally Vandenburg and Dripps located on the Madison Fork on October 14, 1832, and near this place the Blackfeet killed Vandenburg and two of his men, and drove his party out. The Blackfeet also attacked Bridger and his party, and in his "American Fur Trade" Chittenden gives this account of the wounding of Bridger:

"One day they saw a body of Blackfeet in the open plain, though near some rocks which could be resorted to in case of need. They made pacific overtures, which were reciprocated by the whites. A few men advanced from each party, a circle was formed and the pipe of peace was smoked. It is related by Irving that while the ceremony was going on a young Mexican named Loretto, a free trapper accompanying Bridger's band, who had previously ransomed from the Crows a beautiful Blackfoot girl, and made her his wife, was then present looking on. The girl recognized her brother among the Indians. Instantly leaving her infant with Loretto she rushed into her brother's arms, and was recognized with the greatest warmth and affection.

"Bridger now rode forward to where the peace ceremonies were enacting. His rifle lay across his saddle. The Blackfoot chief came forward to meet him. Through some apparent distrust Bridger cocked his rifle as if about to fire. The chief seized the barrel and pushed it downward so that its contents were discharged into the ground. This precipitated a melee. Bridger received two arrow shots in the back, and the chief felled him to the earth with a blow from the gun, which he had wrenched from Bridger's hand. The chief then leaped into Bridger's saddle, and the whole party made for the cover of the rocks, where a desultory fire was kept up for some time. The Indian girl had been carried along with her people, and in spite of her pitiful entreaties was not allowed to return. Loretto, witnessing her grief, seized the child and ran to her, greatly to the amazement of the Indians. He was cautioned to depart if he wanted to save his life, and at his wife's earnest insistence he did so. Some time afterwards he closed his account with the Rocky Mountain Fur Company and rejoined his wife among her own people. It is said that he was later employed as an interpreter at the fort below the falls of the Missouri.

"One of the arrowheads which Bridger received in his back on this occasion remained there for nearly three years, or until the middle of August, 1835.

"At that time Dr. Marcus Whitman was at the rendezvous on Green River en route to Oregon. Bridger was also there, and Dr. Whitman extracted the arrow from his back. The operation was a difficult one, because the arrow was hooked at the point by striking a large bone, and a cartilaginous substance had grown around it. The doctor pursued the operation with great self-possession and perseverance, and his patient manifested equal firmness. The Indians looked on meantime with countenances indicating wonder, and in their own peculiar manner expressed great astonishment when it was extracted. The arrow was of iron and about three inches long."

In the early thirties Bridger discovered "Two Oceans Pass," the most remarkable pass, probably, in the world. It is eight thousand one hundred and fifty feet above the level of the sea. Its length is about one mile and width nearly the same. From the north a stream comes from the cañon and divides in the pass, part following to the Atlantic waters by the Yellowstone and part to the Pacific by the Snake River, the two minor streams bearing the names of Atlantic and Pacific creeks. A stream also comes from the south and makes the same divergence. Fish by these streams pass from one water to the other. Bridger used to tell the story of this river and fish passing through it, but no one believed it until in later years it was discovered to be true, and it is now one of the curiosities of Yellowstone Park.

The first great highway across the plains was no doubt developed by Bridger, and his trappers and traders, in their travels, as the most feasible route to obtain wood, water and grass. Its avoidance of mountains and difficult streams to cross was soon made patent to them. It was known in an early day as the Overland trail, and later on as the Oregon Trail. It was established by the natural forma-tion of the country. It was first used by the wild animals, who followed the present trail very closely in their wanderings, especially the buffalo. Next came the Indians, who in their travels followed it as being the most feasible method of crossing from the Missouri River to the mountains. Following them came the trappers and hunters, then their supply trains, first by pack and later by wagons. The first wheeled vehicle known to have passed over the trail was a six pound cannon taken out by General Ashley to his posts on Utah Lake in the summer of 1826, and the first carts to pass over it were those taken out by Bonneville. Then came the immigration to Oregon, which gave the route the name of the Oregon Trail. Next came the Mormons, and following them the great immigra-tion to California from 1849 on.

In his "American Fur Trade," Captain Chittenden gives this description of the Overland trail:

"As a highway of travel the Oregon Trail is the most remarkable known to history. Considering that it originated with the spontaneous use of the travelers; that no transit ever located a foot of it; that no level established its grades; that no engineer sought out the fords or built any bridges, or surveyed the mountain passes; that there was no grading to speak of, nor any attempt at metalling the roadbed, and the general good quality of this two thousand miles of highway will seem most extraordinary. Father De Smet, who was born in Belgium, the home of good roads, pronounced the Oregon Trail one of the finest highways in the wrorld. At the proper season of the year this was undoubtedly true. Before the prairies became too dry, the natural turf formed the best roadway for horses to travel on that has probably ever been known. It was amply hard to sustain traffic, yet soft enough to be easier to the feet even than the most perfect asphalt pavement Over such a road, winding ribbon-like through the verdant prairies amid the profusion of spring flowers, with grass so plentiful that the animals reveled on its abundance, and game everywhere greeted the hunter's rifle, and, finally, with pure water in the streams, the traveler sped his way with a feeling of joy and exhilaration. But not so when the prairies became dry and parched, the road filled with stifling dust, the stream beds mere dry ravines, or carrying only alkaline waters which could not be used, the game all gone to more hospitable sections, and the summer sun pouring down its heat with torrid intensity. It was then that the trail became a highway of desolation, strewn and abandoned property, the skeletons of horses, mules and oxen, and, alas! too often, with freshly made mounds and headboards that told the pitiful tale of sufferings too great to be endured. If the trail was the scene of romance, adventure, pleasure and excitement, so it was marked in every mile of its course by human misery, tragedy and death."

The immense travel which in later years passed over the Trail carved it into a deep furrow, often with several wide parallel tracks, making a total width of a hundred feet or more. It was an astonishing spectacle even to white men when seen for the first time.

Captain Raynolds, of the Corps of Engineers, United States Army, tells a good story on himself in this connection.

In the fall of 1859 he came south from the Yellowstone River along the eastern base of the Bighorn mountains and struck the Trail somewhere above the first ford of the North Platte. Before reaching it he innocently asked his guide, Bridger, if there was any danger of their crossing the Trail "without seeing it." Bridger answered him only with a look of contemptuous amazement.

It may be easily imagined how great an impression the sight of this road must have made upon the minds of the Indians.

Father De Smet has recorded some interesting observations upon this point.

In 1851 he traveled in company with a large number of Indians from the Missouri and Yellowstone rivers to Fort Laramie, where a great council was held in that year to form treaties with the several tribes. Most of these Indians had not been in that section before, and were quite unprepared for what they saw. "Our Indian companions," says Father DeSmet, "who had never seen but the narrow hunting paths by which they transport themselves and their lodges, were filled with admiration on seeing this noble highway, which is as smooth as a bare floor swept by the winds, and not a blade of grass can shoot up on it on account of the continual passing. They conceived a high idea of the 'Countless White Nation,' as they express it. They fancied that all had gone over that road, and that an immense void must exist in the land of the rising sun. Their countenances testified evident incredulity when I told them that their exit was in no wise perceived in the land of the whites. They styled the route the "Great Medicine Road of the Whites."

From 1833 to 1840 Bridger conducted trapping parties in the interest of the American Fur Company through the country west of the Rig Horn River, reaching to the Snake, and had many fights with and hairbreadth escapes from hostile Indians.

In 1840 he was associated with Benito Yasquez in charge of an extensive outfit, which they conducted in person until 1843, when Bridger and Yasquez built Fort Bridger, which seems to have terminated Bridger's individual trapping, and his experience as the head of trapping outfits.

In 1842 the Cheyennes and other Indians attacked the Shoshones near the site of Bridger's Fort and got away with the stock. Bridger at the head of the trappers and Snakes followed them, killing many of the Indians, and recapturing part of the stock. However, the Indians got away with several of the horses. On July 8, Mr. Preuss, of Fremont's expedition, met Bridger's party on the

North Platte, near the mouth of the Medicine Bow. Writing of this meet, he says:

"July 8. Our road today wras a solitary one. No game made its appearance—not even a buffalo or stray antelope; and nothing occurred to break the monotony until about five o'clock, when the caravan made a sudden halt. There was a galloping in of scouts and horsemen from every side—a hurrying to and fro in noisy confusion; rifles were taken from their cover; bullet-pouches examined; in short, there was a cry of 'Indians' heard again. I had become so accustomed to these alarms that now they made but little impression on me; and before I had time to become excited the newcomers were ascertained to be whites. It was a large party of traders and trappers, conducted by Mr. Bridger, a man well known in the history of the country. As the sun was low, and there was a fine grass patch not far ahead, they turned back and encamped for the night with us.

"Mr. Bridger was invited to supper, and, after the tablecloth was removed, we listened with eager interest to an account of their adventures. What they had met we would be likely to encounter; the chances which had befallen them would likely happen to us; and we looked upon their life as a picture of our own. He informed us that the condition of the country had become exceedingly dangerous. The Sioux, who had been badly disposed, had broken out into open hostility, and in the preceding autumn his party had encountered them in a severe engagement, in which a number of lives had been lost on both sides. United with the Cheyenne and Gros Ventre Indians, they were scouring the upper country in war parties of great force, and were at this time in the neighborhood of the Red Buttes, a famous landmark, which was directly in our path. They had declared war on every living thing which should be found westward of that point, though their main object was to attack a large camp of whites and Snake Indians who had a rendezvous in the Sweetwater valley. Availing himself of his intimate knowledge of the country, he had reached Laramie by an unusual route through the Black Hills, and avoided coming in contact with any of the scattered parties.

"This gentleman offered his services to accompany us so far as the head of the Sweetwater, but in the absence of our leader, which was deeply regretted by us all, it was impossible for us to enter upon such an arrangement."

Fort Bridger, located in latitude 41 degrees 18 minutes 12 seconds and longitude 110 degrees 18 minutes 38 seconds, is 1,070 miles west of the Missouri River by wagon road, and 886 miles by railroad. Bridger selected this spot on account of its being on the overland emigrant and Mormon trails, whether by the North or South Platte routes, as both come together at or near Bridger.

The land on which Fort Bridger is located was obtained by Bridger from the Mexican government before any of the country was ceded by Mexico to the United States. He lived there in undisputed possession until he leased the property in 1857 to the United States by formal written lease signed by Gen. Albert Sidney Johnston's quartermaster. The rental value was $600 per year, which was never paid by the government. After thirty years the government finally paid Bridger $6,000 for the improvements on the land, but nothing for the land. A bill is now pending in Congress to pay his estate for the value of the land. The improvements were worth a great deal more money, but after the government took possession it seemed to have virtually ignored the rights of Bridger, building a military post known as Fort Bridger on the leased ground.

Bridger's fort occupied a space of perhaps two acres surrounded by a stockade. Timbers were set in the ground and elevated eight or ten feet above the surface. Inside this stockade Bridger had his residence on one side, and his trading post on the corner directly across from it. It had swinging gates in the center of the front, through which teams and cattle could be driven safe from Indians and renegade white thieves. He owned a large number of cattle, horses and mules, and his place was so situated that he enjoyed a large trade with the Mormons, gold hunters, mountaineers and Indians.

In a letter Bridger wrote to Pierre Choutau, of St. Louis, on December 10, 1843, he says: "I have established a small fort, with blacksmith shop and a supply of iron, in the road of the immigrants on Black Fork and Green River, which promises fairly. In coming out here they are generally well supplied with money, but by the time they get here they are in need of all kinds of supplies, horses, provisions, smith-work, etc. They bring ready cash from the states, and should I receive the goods ordered will have considerable business in that way with them, and establish trade with the Indians in the neighborhood, who have a good number of beaver among them. The fort is a beautiful location on the Black Fork of Green River, receiving fine, fresh water from the snow on the Uintah range. The streams are alive with mountain trout. It passes the fork in several channels, each lined with trees, kept alive by the moisture of the soil."

It was a veritable oasis in the desert, and its selection showed good judgment on the part of the founder.

In 1856 Bridger had trouble with the Mormons. They threatened him with death and the confiscation of all his property at Fort Bridger, and he was robbed of all his stock, merchandise, and, in fact, of everything he possessed, which he claimed was worth $100,000. The buildings at the fort were destroyed by fire, and Bridger barely escaped with his life. This brought on what was known as the Utah expedition, under Gen. Albert Sidney Johnston. Bridger piloted the army out there, taking it through by what is known as the southern route, which he had discovered, which runs by the South Platte, up the Lodge Pole, over Cheyenne Pass, by old Fort Halleck, and across the continental divide at Bridger's Pass at the head of the Muddy, follows down Bitter Creek to Green River, crosses that river, and then up Black Fork to Fort Bridger.

As the troops had made no arrangements for winter, and shelter for the stock was not to be found in the vicinity of Salt Lake, Bridger tendered to them the use of Fort Bridger and the adjoining property, which offer was accepted by Johnston, who wintered his army there. It was at this time that the government purchased from Bridger his Mexican grant of Fort Bridger, but, as heretofore mentioned, never paid him for the property, merely agreeing to pay the rental, and claiming that Bridger's title was not perfect. This was a great injustice to Bridger. His title was one of possession. He had established here a trading post that had been of great benefit to the government and the overland immigration and he was entitled to all he claimed. The fort was the rendezvous of all the trade and travel, of the Indians, trappers and voyagers of all that section of the country.

Concerning his claim against the government, under date of October 27, 1873, Bridger wrote to Gen. B. F. Butler, United States Senator, as follows:

"...You are probably aware that I am one of the earliest and oldest explorers and trappers of the Great West now alive. Many years prior to the Mexican War, the time Fort Bridger and adjoining territories became the property of the United States, and for ten years thereafter (1857) I was in peaceful possession of my trading post, Fort Bridger, occupied it as such, and resided thereat a fact well known to the government, as well as the public in general.

"Shortly before the so-called Utah expedition, and before the government troops under Gen. A. S. Johnston arrived near Salt Lake City, I was robbed and threatened with death by the Mormons, by the direction of Brigham Young, of all my merchandise, stock—in fact everything I possessed, amounting to more than $100,000 worth—the buildings in the fort practically destroyed by fire, and I barely escaped with my life.

"I was with and piloted the army under said General Johnston out there, and since the approach of winter no convenient shelter for the troops and stock could be found in the vicinity of Salt Lake, I tendered to them my so-called fort (Fort Bridger), with the adjoining shelter, affording rally for winter quarters. My offer being accepted, a written contract was entered into between myself and Captain Dickerson, of the quartermaster's Department, in behalf of the United States, approved by Gen. A. S. Johnston, and more, so signed by various officers on the general's staff such as Major Fitz-John Porter, Doctors Madison, Mills and Bailey, Lieutenant Rich, Colonel Weigh, and others, a copy of which is now on file in the War Department at Washington. I also was furnished with a copy thereof, which was unfortunately destroyed during the war.

* * *

"I am now getting old and feeble and am a poor man, and consequently unable to prosecute my claim as it probably should be done. For that reason I respectfully apply to you with the desire of entrusting the matter into your hands, authorizing you, for me, to use such means as you may deem proper for the successful prosecution of this claim. I would further state that I have been strictly loyal during the late rebellion, and during the most of the time in the war in the employ of the government.

"Trusting confidently that you will do me the favor of taking the matter in hand or furnish me with your advice in the matter, I have the honor, etc."

On July 4, 1849, Bridger's second wife, a Ute, died. He had been for some time considering the movement of his family to the states, where his children could be educated, intending to devote his own time to the trading post at Fort Bridger. He went to the states in 1850, taking with him his third wife, a Snake woman, and settled upon a little farm near Little Santa Fe, Jackson County, Mo. Bridger usually spent the summers on the plains and went home winters.

In the spring of 1862, Bridger was at his home in Little Santa Fe, when the government called him onto the plains to guide the troops in the Indian campaigns. I found him there when I took command of that country in January, 1865, and placed him as guide of the Eleventh Ohio Cavalry in its march from Fort Riley to Fort Laramie. Bridger remained with them at Fort Laramie as their guide, and took part with them in the many encounters they had with the Indians, and his services to them were invaluable.

In the Indian campaign of 1865-1866, Bridger guided General Connor's column that marched from Fort Laramie to Tongue River, and took part in the battle on Tongue River.

Capt. H. E. Palmer, Eleventh Kansas Cavalry, acting assistant adjutant general to Gen. P. E. Connor, gives this description of the Indian camp on Tongue River August 26, 1865.

"Left Piney Fork at 6:45 a. m. Traveled north over a beautiful country until about 8 a. m., when our advance reached the top of the ridge dividing the waters of the Powder from that of the Tongue River. I was riding in the extreme advance in company with Major Bridger. We were two thousand yards at least ahead of the general and his staff; our Pawnee scouts were on each flank and a little in advance; at that time there was no advance guard immediately in front. As the major and myself reached the top of the hill we voluntarily halted our steeds. I raised my field glass to my eyes and took in the grandest view that I had ever seen. I could see the north end of the Big Horn range, and away beyond the faint outline of the mountains beyond the Yellowstone. Away to the northeast the Wolf mountain range was distinctly visible. Immediately before us lay the valley of Peneau Creek, now called Prairie Dog Creek, and beyond the Little Goose, Big Goose and Tongue River valleys, and many other tributary streams. The morning was clear and bright, with not a breath of air stirring. The old major, sitting upon his horse with his eyes shaded with his hands, had been telling me for an hour or more about his Indian life—his forty years' experience on the plains, telling me how to trail Indians and distinguish the tracks of different tribes; how every spear of grass, every tree and shrub and stone was a compass to the experienced trapper and hunter—a subject that I had discussed with him nearly every day. During the winter of 1863 I had contributed to help Mrs. Bridger and the rest of the family, all of which facts the major had been acquainted with, which induced him to treat me as an old-time friend.

"As I lowered my glass the major said: 'Do you see those ere columns of smoke over yonder?' I replied': 'Where, Major?' to which he answered; 'Over there by that ere saddle,' meaning a depression in the hills not unlike the shape of a saddle, pointing at the same time to a point nearly fifty miles away. I again raised my glasses to my eyes and took a long, earnest look, and for the life of me could not see any column of smoke, even with a strong field glass. The major was looking without any artificial help. The atmosphere seemed to be slightly hazy in the long distance like smoke, but there was no distinct columns of smoke in sight. As soon as the general and his staff arrived I called his attention to Major Bridger's discovery. The general raised his field glass and scanned the horizon closely. After a long look he remarked that there were no columns of smoke to be seen.

"The major quietly mounted his horse and rode on. I asked the general to look again as the major was very confident that he could see columns of smoke, which, of course, indicated an Indian village. The general made another examination and again asserted that there was no column of smoke. However, to satisfy curiosity and to give our guides no chance to claim that they had shown us an Indian village and we would not attack it, he suggested to Capt Frank North, who was riding with his staff, that he go with seven of his Indians in the direction indicated to reconnoiter and report to us at Peneau Creek on Tongue River, down which we were to march. I galloped on and overtook the major and as I came up to him overheard him remark about 'these damn paper collar soldiers telling him there was no columns of smoke.' The old man was very indignant at our doubting his ability to outsee us, with the aid of field glasses even. Just after sunset on August 27 two of the Pawnees who went out with Captain North towards Bridger's column of smoke two days previous came into camp with the information that Captain North had discovered an Indian village."

It was this village that Connor captured the next day the fight being known as the Battle of Tongue River.

In May 1869, Captain Raynolds was assigned to the exploration of the country surrounding Yellowstone Park, and I have no doubt it was from hearing of Bridger's knowledge of that park and its surroundings that caused him to engage Bridger for his guide. Bridger was with him about a year and a half, but they failed on this trip to enter the park, being stopped by the heavy snows in the passes, but they explored and mapped the country surrounding the park.

In 1860 Ned Buntline, the great short story romance writer, hunted up Bridger at his home in Weston, and Bridger gave him enough adventures to keep him writing the balance of his life. Bridger took a liking to Buntline, and took him across the plains with him on a scouting trip. After a while Buntline returned to the East, and not long afterwards the Jim Bridger stories commenced to be published. One of these was printed every week and Bridger's companions used to save them up and read them to him. Buntline made Bridger famous, and carried him through more hairbreadth escapes than any man ever had.

Bridger's first wife was the daughter of a Flathead chief. She died in 1846. Her children were Felix and Josephine, both of whom were sent to school at St Louis. Felix enlisted in the spring of 1863 in Company L, Second Missouri Artillery, under General Totten. He served throughout the Civil War, and later was with Custer in his Indian campaigns in Texas and Indian Territory. He died in 1876 on the farm near little Sante Fe, Mo., having returned there from Dallas, Texas.

Bridger's second wife was a Ute, who died July 4, 1849, at the birth of her first child, now Mrs. Virginia K. Waschman. Bridger brought this child up on buffalo's milk. When she was five years old she was sent to Robert Campbell in St. Louis, and two years later joined her sister Josephine in the convent.

When Virginia was about ten years old she obtained from Mrs. Robert Campbell a daguerreotype of her father which was taken in 1843. She colored or painted this picture, and in 1902 presented it to me, saying: "I am most sure you will be pleased with it as a gift from me, and it will remind you of the great old times that you and father had when you were out in the mountains among the wild Indians. I have often heard my father speak of you, and have wanted to see you and tell you a great many things that happened when I was a child at Fort Bridger. Before my father's death he was very anxious to see you regarding old Fort Bridger, but could not find you."

In 1850 Bridger took as his third wife a Snake woman. He bought a little farm near Santa Fe, Mo., and moved his family there from Fort Bridger that year. Mary was born in 1853. She married and now lives in the Indian Territory. William was born in 1857, and died from consumption in 1892. In 1858 his wife died and was buried in Boone cemetery, near Waldo Station, Mo. Bridger was on the plains at the time of her death, but returned to Missouri in the spring of 1859, soon after he heard of her death, and remained on the farm until 1862. This year he rented the farm to a man named Brooks, and bought the Col. A. G. Boone house in Westport. He left his family there in charge of a Mr. London and his wife, and on the call of the government in the spring of 1862 he left for the mountains to guide the troops on the plains. He remained on the plains until late in 1869 or 1870. In the spring of 1871 he moved back to his farm near the little Santa Fe.

Of this life from this time until his death, his daughter, Mrs. Waschman, writes me the following:

"In 1873 father's health began to fail him, and his eyes were very bad, so that he could not see good, and the only way that father could distinguish any person was by the sound of their voices, but all who had the privilege of knowing him were aware of his wonderful state of health at that time, but later, in 1874, father's eyesight was leaving him very fast, and this worried him so much. He has oftentimes wished that he could see you. At times father would get very nervous, and wanted to be on the go. I had to watch after him and lead him around to please him, never still one moment.

"I got father a good old gentle horse, so that he could ride around and to have something to pass away time, so one day he named his old horse 'Ruff.' We also had a dog that went with father; he named this old, faithful dog 'Sultan.' Sometimes father would call me and say: 'I wish you would go and saddle old Ruff for me; I feel like riding around the farm,' and the faithful old dog would go along. Father could not see very well, but the old faithful horse would guide him along, but at times father would draw the lines wrong, and the horse would go wrong, and then they would get lost in the woods. The strange part of it was the old faithful dog, Sultan, would come home and let us know that father was lost. The dog would bark and whine until I would go out and look for him, and lead him and the old horse home on the main road. Sometimes father wanted to take a walk out to the fields with old Sultan by his side, and cane in hand to guide his way out to the wheat field, would want to know how high the wheat was, and then father would go down on his knees and reach out his hands to feel for the wheat, and that was the way he passed away his time.

"Father at times wished that he could see, and only have his eyesight back again, so that he could go back out to see the mountains. I know he at times would feel lonesome, and long to see some of his old mountain friends to have a good chat of olden times away back in the fifties.

"Father often spoke of you, and would say, 'I wonder if General Dodge is alive or not; I would give anything in the world if I could see some of the old army officers once more to have a talk with them of olden times, but I know I will not be able to see any of my old-time mountain friends any more. I know that my time is near. I feel that my health is failing me very fast, and see that I am not the same man I used to be.'"

Bridger was seventy-seven years old when he died, and was buried on the Stubbins Watts farm, a mile north of Dallas, not far south of Westport. His two sons, William and Felix, were buried beside him.

On Bridger's gravestone is the following:

> "James Bridger, born March 17, 1804; died July 17, 1881.
> We miss thee in the circle around the fireside,
> We miss thee in devotion at peaceful eventide,
> The memory of your nature, so full of truth and love,
> Shall lead our thoughts to seek thee among the blest above."

At the time of his death, Bridger's home was a long, two-story house, not far from where he is buried, with big chimneys at each end. It is now abandoned and dilapidated, with windows all broken. It is about one mile south of Dallas. He had 160 acres of land. No one has lived in the house for years. The neighbors say it is haunted, and will not go near it.

One of his wives is buried in a graveyard several miles east of his grave.

I found Bridger a very companionable man. In person he was over six feet tall, spare, straight as an arrow, agile, rawboned and of powerful frame, eyes gray, hair brown and abundant even in old age, expression mild and manners agreeable. He was hospitable and generous, and was always trusted and respected. He possessed in a high degree the confidence of the Indians. He was one of the most noted hunters and trappers on the plains. Naturally shrewd, and possessing keen faculties of observation, he carefully studied the habits of all the animals, especially the beaver, and, profiting from the knowledge obtained from the Indians, with whom he chiefly associated, and with whom he became a great favorite, he soon became one of the most expert hunters and trappers in the mountains. The beaver at first abounded in every mountain stream in the country, but, at length, by being constantly pursued, they began to grow more wary and diminish in numbers, until it became necessary for trappers to extend their researches to more distant streams. Eager to gratify his curiosity, and with a natural fondness for mountain scenery, he traversed the country in every direction, sometimes accompanied by an Indian, but oftener alone. He familiarized himself with every mountain peak, every deep gorge, every hill and every landmark in the country. Having arrived upon the banks of some before undiscovered stream, and finding signs of his favorite game, he would immediately proceed to his traps, and then take his gun and wander over the hills in quest of game, the meat of which formed the only diet of the trapper at that early day. When a stream afforded game it wras trapped to its source, and never left as long as beaver could be caught.

While engaged in this thorough system of trapping, no object of interest escaped his scrutiny, and when once known it was ever after remembered. He could describe with the minutest accuracy places that perhaps he had visited but once, and that many years before, and he could travel in almost a direct line from one point to another in the greatest distances, with certainty of always making his goal. He pursued his trapping expeditions north to the British possessions, south far into New Mexico and west to the Pacific Ocean, and in this way became acquainted with all the Indian tribes in the country, and by long intercourse with them learned their languages, and became familiar with all their signs. He adopted their habits, conformed to their customs, became imbued with all their superstitions, and at length excelled them in strategy.

He was a great favorite with the Crow nation, and was at one time elected and became their chief.

Bridger was also a great Indian fighter, and I have heard two things said of him by the best plainsmen of this time; that he did not know what fear was, and that he never once lost his bearings, either on the plains or in the mountains.

In those days Bridger was rich. He was at the head of great trapping parties, and two great fur companies—the Rocky Mountain Fur Company and North-western Fur Company. When he became older he spent his winters in Westport, and in the summer was a scout and guide for government troops, getting ten dollars a day in gold.

Unquestionably Bridger's claims to remembrance rest upon the extraordinary part he bore in the explorations of the West. As a guide he was without an equal, and this is the testimony of every one who ever employed him. He was a born topographer; the whole West was mapped out in his mind, and such was his instinctive sense of locality and direction that it used to be said of him that he could smell his way where he could not see it. He was a complete master of plains and woodcraft, equal to any emergency, full of resources to overcome any obstacle, and I came to learn gradually how it was that for months such men could live without food except what the country afforded in that wild region. In a few hours they would put together a bull-boat and put us across any stream. Nothing escaped their vision, the dropping of a stick or breaking of a twig, the turning of the growing grass, all brought knowledge to them, and they could tell who or what had done it. A single horse or Indian could not cross the trail but that they discovered it, and could tell how long since they passed. Their methods of hunting game were perfect, and we were never out of meat, herbs, roots, berries, bark of trees and everything that was edible they knew. They could minister to the sick, dress wounds—in fact, in all my experience I never saw Bridger or the other voyagers of the plains and mountains meet any obstacle they could not overcome.

While Bridger was not an educated man, still any country that he had ever seen he could fully and intelligently describe, and could make a very correct estimate of the country surrounding it. He could make a map of any country he had ever traveled over, mark out its streams and mountains and the obstacles in it correctly, so that there was no trouble in following it and fully understanding it. He never claimed knowledge that he did not have of the country, or its history and surroundings, and was positive in his statements in relation to it. He was a good judge of human nature. His comments upon people that he had met and been with were always intelligent and seldom critical. He always spoke of their good parts, and was universally respected by the mountain men, and looked upon as a leader, also by all the Indians. He was careful to never give his word without fulfilling it. He understood thoroughly the Indian character, their peculiarities and superstitions. He felt very keenly any loss of confidence in him or his judgment, especially when acting as guide, and when he struck a country or trail he was not familiar with he would frankly say so, but would often say he could take our party up to the point we wanted to reach. As a guide I do not think he had his equal upon the plains.

CHAPTER 13

FOLLOWING THE SHEEP

from *The Life and Letters of John Muir*

By William Frederic Badè

THE Nebraska arrived at San Francisco, March 27th, and Muir lost no time there after he set foot on land. To his friends he was accustomed to relate, with touches of humor, how he met on the street, the morning after debarkation, a man with a kit of carpenter's tools on his shoulders. When he inquired of him "the nearest way out of town to the wild part of the State," the man set down his tools in evident astonishment and asked, "Where do you wish to go?" "Anywhere that's wild," was Muir's reply, and he was directed to the Oakland Ferry with the remark that that would be as good a way out of town as any.

On shipboard Muir had made the acquaintanceship of a young Englishman by the name of Chilwell, "a most amusing and faithful companion," who eagerly embraced the opportunity to visit Yosemite Valley with him. In those days the usual route to Yosemite was by river steamer to Stockton, thence by stage to Coulterville or Mariposa, and the remainder of the way over the mountains on horseback. But Muir disdained this "orthodox route," for "we had plenty of time," he said, "and proposed drifting leisurely mountainward by the Santa Clara Valley, Pacheco Pass, and the San Joaquin Valley, and thence to Yosemite by any road that we chanced to find; enjoying the flowers and light; 'camping out' in our blankets wherever overtaken by night and paying very little compliance to roads or times."

In his autobiographical manuscript Muir passes in a few sentences over the first part of this trip, intending according to his penciled directions to fill in from a description already written. This must refer to the detailed narrative published in "Old and New" in 1872, from which we excerpt the paragraphs descriptive of his walk as far as the top of the Pacheco Pass.

> We crossed the bay by the Oakland Ferry and proceeded up the Santa Clara valley to San José. This is one of the most fertile of the many small valleys of the coast; its rich bottoms are filled with wheat-fields, and orchards, and vineyards, and alfalfa meadows.
>
> It was now spring-time, and the weather was the best we ever enjoyed. Larks and streams sang everywhere; the sky was cloudless, and the whole valley was a lake of light. The atmosphere was spicy and exhilarating, my companion acknowledging over his national prejudices that it was the best he ever breathed—more deliciously fragrant than that which streamed over the hawthorn hedges of England. This San José sky was not simply pure and bright, and mixed with plenty of well-tempered sunshine, but it possessed a positive flavor, a *taste* that thrilled throughout every tissue of the body. Every inspiration yielded a well-defined piece of pleasure that awakened thousands of new palates everywhere. Both my companion and myself had lived on common air for nearly thirty years, and never before this discovered that our bodies contained such multitudes of palates, or

that this mortal flesh, so little valued by philosophers and teachers, was possessed of so vast a capacity for happiness.

We were new creatures, born again; and truly not until this time were we fairly conscious that we were born at all. Never more, thought I as we strode forward at faster speed, never more shall I sentimentalize about getting free from the flesh, for it is steeped like a sponge in immortal pleasure.

The foothills of the valley are in near view all the way to Gilroy, those of the Monte Diablo range on our left, those of Santa Cruz on our right; they are smooth and flowing, and come down to the bottom levels in curves of most surpassing beauty. They are covered with flowers growing close together in cloud-shaped companies, acres and hillsides in size, white, purple, and yellow, separate, yet blending like the hills upon which they grow....

The Pacheco Pass was scarcely less enchanting than the valley. It resounded with crystal waters, and the loud shouts of thousands of quails. The California quail is a little larger than the Bob White; not quite so plump in form. The male has a tall, slender crest, wider at top than bottom, which he can hold straight up, or droop backward on his neck, or forward over his bill, at pleasure; and, instead of "Bob White," he shouts "pe-check-a," bearing down with a stiff, obstinate emphasis on "check." Through a considerable portion of the pass the road bends and mazes along the groves of a stream, or down in its pebbly bed, leading one now deep in the shadows of dogwoods and alders, then out in the light, through dry chaparral, over green carex meadows banked with violets and ferns, and dry, plantless flood-beds of gravel and sand.

We found ferns in abundance in the pass. . . . Also in this rich garden pass we gathered many fine grasses and carices, and brilliant penstemons, azure and scarlet, and mints and lilies, and scores of others, strangers to us, but beautiful and pure as ever enjoyed the sun or shade of a mountain home.

At this point Muir's unpublished memoirs resume the thread of the narrative as follows:

At the top of the Pass I obtained my first view of the San Joaquin plain and the glorious Sierra Nevada. Looking down from a height of fifteen hundred feet, there, extending north and south as far as I could see lay a vast level flower garden, smooth and level like a lake of gold—the floweriest part of the world I had yet seen. From the eastern margin of the golden plain arose the white Sierra. At the base ran a belt of gently sloping purplish foothills lightly dotted with oaks, above that a broad dark zone of coniferous forests, and above this forest zone arose the lofty mountain peaks, clad in snow. The atmosphere was so clear that although the nearest of the mountain peaks on the axis of the range were at a distance of more than one hundred and fifty miles, they seemed to be at just the right distance to be seen broadly in their relationship to one another, marshaled in glorious ranks and groups, their snowy robes so smooth and bright that it seemed impossible for a man to walk across the open folds without being seen, even at this distance. Perhaps more than three hundred miles of the range was comprehended in this one view.

Descending the pass and wading out into the bed of golden composite five hundred miles long by forty or fifty wide, I found that the average depth of the vegetation was over knee-deep, and the flowers were so crowded together that in walking through the midst of them and over them more than a hundred were pressed down beneath the foot at every step. The yellow of these composite, both of the ray and disc flowers, is extremely deep and rich and bossy, and exceeds the purple of all the others in superficial quantity forty or fifty times their whole amount. But to an observer who first looks downward, then takes a wider and wider view, the yellow gradually fades, and purple predominates, because nearly all of the purple flowers are taller. In depth, the purple stratum is about ten or twelve inches, the yellow seven or eight, and down in the shade, out of sight, is another stratum of purple, one inch in depth, for the ground forests of mosses are there, with purple stems, and purple cups. The color-beauty of these mosses, at least in the mass, was not made for human eyes, nor for the wild horses that inhabit these plains, nor the antelopes, but perhaps the little creatures enjoy their own beauty, and perhaps the insects that dwell in these forests and climb their shining columns enjoy it. But we know that however faint, and however shaded, no part of it is lost, for all color is received into the eyes of God,

Crossing this greatest of flower gardens and the San Joaquin River at Hill's Ferry, we followed the Merced River, which I knew drained Yosemite Valley, and ascended the foothills from Snelling by way of Coulterville, We had several accidents and adventures. At the little mining town of Coulterville we bought flour and tea and made inquiries about roads and trails, and the forests we would have to pass through. The storekeeper, an Italian, took kindly pains to tell the pair of wandering wayfarers, new arrived in California, that the winter had been a very severe one, that in some places the Yosemite trail was still buried in snow eight or ten feet deep, and therefore we would have to wait at least a month before we could possibly get into the great valley, for we would surely get lost should we attempt to go on. As to the forests, the trees, he said, were very large; some of the pines eight or ten feet in diameter.

In reply I told him that it would be delightful to see snow ten feet deep and trees ten feet thick, even if lost, but I never got lost in wild woods. "Well," said he, "go, if you must, but I have warned you; and anyhow you must have a gun, for there are bears in the mountains, but you must not shoot at them unless they come for you and are very, very close up." So at last, at Mr. Chilwell's anxious suggestion, we bought an old army musket, with a few pounds of quail shot and large buckshot, good, as the merchant assured us, for either birds or bears.

Our bill of fare in camps was simple—tea and cakes, the latter made from flour without leaven and toasted on the coals—and of course we shunned hotels in the valley, seldom indulging even in crackers, as being too expensive. Chilwell, being an Englishman, loudly lamented being compelled to live on so light a diet, flour and water, as he expressed it, and hungered for flesh; therefore he made desperate efforts to shoot something to eat, particularly quails and grouse, but he was invariably unsuccessful and declared the gun was worthless. I told him I thought that it was good enough if properly loaded and aimed, though perhaps sighted too high, and promised to show him at the first opportunity how to load and shoot.

Many of the herbaceous plants of the flowing foothills were the same as those of the plain and had already gone to seed and withered. But at a height of one thousand feet or so we found many of the lily family blooming in all their glory, the Caloehortus especially, a charming genus like European tulips, but finer, and many species of two new shrubs especially, Ceanothus and Adenostoma. The oaks, beautiful trees with blue foliage and white bark, forming open groves, gave a fine park effect. Higher, we met the first of the pines, with long gray foliage, large stout cones, and wide-spreading heads like palms. Then yellow pines, growing gradually more abundant as we ascended. At Bower Gave on the north fork of the Merced the streams were fringed with willows and azalea, ferns, flowering dogwood, etc. Here, too, we enjoyed the strange beauty of the Cave in a limestone hill.

At Deer Flat the wagon-road ended in a trail which we traced up the side of the dividing ridge parallel to the Merced and Tuolumne to Crane Flat, lying at a height of six thousand feet, where we found a noble forest of sugar pine, silver fir, libocedrus, Douglas spruce, the first of the noble Sierra forests, the noblest coniferous forests in the world, towering in all their unspoiled beauty and grandeur around a sunny, gently sloping meadow. Here, too, we got into the heavy winter snow—a fine change from the burning foothills and plains.

Some mountaineer had tried to establish a claim to the Flat by building a little cabin of sugar pine shakes, and though we had arrived early in the afternoon I decided to camp here for the night as the trail was buried in the snow which was about six feet deep, and I wanted to examine the topography and plan our course. Chilwell cleared away the snow from the door and floor of the cabin, and made a bed in it of boughs of fernlike silver fir, though I urged the same sort of bed made under the trees on the snow. But he had the house habit.

After camp arrangements were made he reminded me of my promise about the gun, hoping eagerly for improvement of our bill of fare, however slight. Accordingly I loaded the gun, paced off thirty yards from the cabin, or shanty, and told Mr. Chilwell to pin a piece of paper on the wall and see if I could not put shot into it and prove the gun's worth. So he pinned a piece of an envelope on the shanty wall and vanished around the corner, calling out, Fire away."

I supposed that he had gone some distance back of the cabin, but instead he went inside of it and stood up against the mark that he had himself placed on the wall, and as the shake wall of soft sugar pine was only about half an inch thick, the shot passed through it and into his shoulder. He came rushing out, with his hand on his shoulder, crying in great concern, "You've shot *me*, you've shot *me*, Scottie." The weather being cold, he fortunately had on three coats and as many shirts. One of the coats was a heavy English overcoat. I discovered that the shot had passed through all this clothing and into his shoulder, and the embedded pellets had to be picked out with the point of a penknife. I asked him how he could be so foolish as to stand opposite the mark. "Because," he replied, "I never imagined the blank gun would shoot through the side of the 'ouse."

We found our way easily enough over the deep snow, guided by the topography, and discovered the trail on the brow of the valley just as the Bridal

Veil came in sight. I didn't know that it was one of the famous falls I had read about, and calling Chilwell's attention to it I said, " See that dainty little fall over there. I should like to camp at the foot of it to see the ferns and lilies that may be there. It looks small from here, only about fifteen or twenty feet, but it may be sixty or seventy." So little did we then know of Yosemite magnitudes!

After spending eight or ten days in visiting the falls and the high points of view around the walls, making sketches, collecting flowers and ferns, etc., we decided to make the return trip by way of Wawona, then owned by Galen Clark, the Yosemite pioneer. The night before the start was made on the return trip we camped near the Bridal Veil Meadows, where, as we lay eating our suppers by the light of the camp-fire, we were visited by a brown bear. We heard him approaching by the heavy crackling of twigs. Chilwell, in alarm, after listening a while, said, " I see it! I see it! It's a bear, a grizzly! Where is the gun? You take the gun and shoot him—you can shoot best." But the gun had only a charge of birdshot in it; therefore, while the bear stood on the opposite side of the fire, at a distance of probably twenty-five or thirty feet, I hastily loaded in a lot of buckshot. The buckshot was too large to chamber and therefore it made a zigzag charge on top of the birdshot charge, the two charges occupying about half of the barrel. Thus armed, the gun held at rest pointed at the bear, we sat hushed and motionless, according to instructions from the man who sold the gun, solemnly waiting and watching, as full of fear as the musket of shot. Finally, after sniffing and whining for his supper what seemed to us a long time, the young inexperienced beast walked off. We were much afraid of his return to attack us. We did not then know that bears never attack sleeping campers, and dreading another visit we kept awake on guard most of the night.

Like the Coulterville trail all the high-lying part of the Mariposa trail was deeply snow-buried, but we found our way without the slightest trouble, steering by the topography in a general way along the brow of the canyon of the south fork of the Merced River, and in a day or two reached Wawona. Here we replenished our little flour sack and Mr. Clark gave us a piece of bear meat.

We then pushed eagerly on up the Wawona ridge through a magnificent sugar pine forest and into the far-famed Mariposa Sequoia Grove. The sun was down when we entered the Grove, but we soon had a good fire and at supper that night we tasted bear meat for the first time. My flesh-hungry companion ate it eagerly, though to me it seemed so rank and oily that I was unable to swallow a single morsel.

After supper we replenished the fire and gazed enchanted at the vividly illumined brown boles of the giants towering about us, while the stars sparkled in wonderful beauty above their huge domed heads. We camped here long uncounted days, wandering about from tree to tree, taking no note of time. The longer we gazed the more we admired not only their colossal size, but their majestic beauty and dignity. Greatest of trees, greatest of living things, their noble domes poised in unchanging repose seemed to belong to the sky, while the great firs and pines about them looked like mere latter-day saplings.

While we camped in the Mariposa Grove, the abundance of bear tracks caused Mr. Chilwell no little alarm, and he proposed that we load the gun properly with buckshot and without any useless birdshot; but there was no means of drawing the charge—it had to be shot off. The recoil was so great that it bruised his shoulder and sent him spinning like a top. Casting down the miserable, kicking, bad luck musket among the Sequoia cones and branches that littered the ground, he stripped and examined his unfortunate shoulder and, in painful indignation and wrath, found it black and blue and more seriously hurt by the bruising recoil blow than it was by the shot at Crane Flat.

When we got down to the hot San Joaquin plain at Snelling the grain fields were nearly ready for the reaper, and we began to inquire for a job to replenish our remaining stock of money which was now very small, though we had not spent much; the grand royal trip of more than a month in the Yosemite region having cost us only about three dollars each. At our last camp, in a bed of cobble-stones on the Merced River bottom, Mr. Chilwell was more and more eagerly hungering for meat. He tried to shoot one of the jack-rabbits cantering around us, but was unable to hit any of them. I told him, when he begged me to take the gun, that I would shoot one for him if he would drive it up to the camp. He ran and shooed and threw cobble-stones without getting any of them up within shooting distance as I took good care to warn the poor beasts by making myself and the gun conspicuous. At last discovering the humor of the thing he shouted: "I say, Scottie, this makes me think of a picture I once saw in Punch—game-keepers driving partridges to be shot by a simpleton Cockney."

Then one of those curious burrowing owls alighted on the top of a fence-post beside us, and I said, " If you are so hungry for flesh why don't you shoot one of those owls?" "Howls," he said in disgust, "are only vermin." I argued that that was mere prejudice and custom, and that if stewed in a pot it would make good soup, and the flesh, too, that he hungered for, might also be found to be fairly good, but that if he didn't care for it, I didn't.

I finally pictured the flavor of the soup so temptingly that with watering lips he consented to try it, and the poor owl was shot. When he came to dress it the pitiful little red carcass seemed so worthless a morsel that he was tempted to throw it away, but I said, "No; now that you have it ready for the pot, boil it and at least enjoy the soup." So it was boiled in the teapot and bravely devoured, though he insisted that he did not like the flavor of either the soup or the meat. He charged me, saying: "Now, Scottie, if you go to England with me to see my folks, after our fortunes are made, don't you tell them as 'ow we' ad a howl for supper." He was always trying to persuade me to go to England with him.

Next day we got a job in a harvest field at Hopeton and were seated at a table once more. Mr. Chilwell never tired of describing the meanness and misery of so pure a vegetable diet as was ours on the Yosemite trip. "Just think of it," said he, "we lived a whole month on flour and water!" He ate so many hot biscuits at that table, and so much beans and boiled pork, that he was sick for three or four days afterwards, a trick the despised Yosemite diet never played him.

This Yosemite trip only made me hungry for another far longer and farther reaching, and I determined to set out again as soon as I had earned a little money to get near views of the mountains in all their snowy grandeur, and study the wonderful forests, the noblest of their kind I had ever seen—sugar pines eight and nine feet in diameter, with cones nearly two feet long, silver firs more than two hundred feet in height, Douglas spruce and libocedrus, and the kingly Sequoias.

After the harvest was over Mr. Chilwell left me, but I remained with Mr. Egleston several months to break mustang horses; then ran a ferry boat at Merced Falls for travel between Stockton and Mariposa, That same fall I made a lot of money sheep-shearing, and after the shearing was over one of the sheep-men of the neighborhood, Mr. John Connel, nicknamed Smoky Jack, begged me to take care of one of his bands of sheep, because the then present shepherd was about to quit. He offered thirty dollars a month and board and assured me that it would be a "foin aisy job."

I said that I didn't know anything about sheep, except the shearing of them, didn't know the range, and that his flock would probably be scattered over the plains and lost; but he said he would risk me, that "the sheep would show me the range, and all would go smooth and aisy." At length, considering that, being out every day, a fine opportunity would be offered to watch the growth of the flowery vegetation, and to study the birds and beasts, insects, weather, etc., I dared the job, and sure enough, as my employer said, the sheep soon showed me their range, leading me a wild chase in their search for grass over the dry sun-beaten plains.

Smoky Jack was known far and wide, and I soon learned that he was a queer character. Unmarried, living alone, playing the game of money making, he had already become sheep-rich—the owner of three or four bands, as the flocks are called. He had commenced his career as a sheep-man when he was poor, with only a score or two of coarse-wooled ewes, which he herded himself and faithfully followed and improved until they had multiplied into thousands.

He lived mostly on beans. In the morning after his bean breakfast he filled his pockets from the pot with dripping beans for luncheon, which he ate in handfuls as he followed the flock. His overalls and boots soon, of course, became thoroughly saturated, and instead of wearing thin, wore thicker and stouter, and by sitting down to rest from time to time, parts of all the vegetation, leaves, petals, etc., were embedded in them, together with wool fibers, butterfly wings, mica crystals, fragments of nearly everything that part of the world contained—rubbed in, embedded and coarsely stratified, so that these wonderful garments grew to have a rich geological and biological significance, like those of Mr. Delaney's shepherd.

Replying to my inquiry where the sheep were, he directed me to follow the road between French Bar and Snelling four or five miles, and "when you see a cabin on a little hill, that's the place." I found the place, and a queer place it proved to be. The shepherd whom I was to relieve hailed me with delight and within a few minutes of my arrival set off, exulting in his freedom. I begged him to stay until morning and show me the range, but this he refused, saying that it was quite unnecessary for him to show me the range; all I had to do was simply to let down the corral bars and the starving sheep would soon explain and explore the range.

Left alone, I examined the dismal little hut with dismay. A Dutch oven, frying-pan, and a few tin cups lay on the floor; a rickety stool and a bedstead, with a tick made of a wool sack, stuffed with straw and castoff overalls left by shearers, constituted the furniture. I went outside, looking for a piece of clean ground to lie down on, but no such ground was to be found. Every yard of it was strewn with some sort of sheep camp detritus, bits of shriveled woolly skin, bacon rinds, bones, horns and skulls mixed with all sorts of mysterious compound unclean rubbish! I therefore had to go back into the shanty and spread my blankets on the dirt floor as the least dangerous part of the establishment.

Next morning, by the time I had fried some pancakes and made a cup of tea, the sunbeams were streaming through the wide vertical seams of the shanty wall, and I made haste to open the corral. The sheep were crowding around the gate, and as soon as it was opened, poured forth like a boisterous uncontrollable flood, and soon the whole flock was so widely outspread and scattered over the plain, it seemed impossible that the mad starving creatures could ever be got together again. I ran around from side to side, headed the leaders off again and again, and did my best to confine the size of the flock to an area of a square mile or so.

About noon, to my delight and surprise, they lay down to rest and allowed me to do the same for an hour or so. Then they again scattered, but not so far nor so wildly, and I was still more surprised about half an hour before sundown, while I was wondering how I could ever get them driven back into the corral, to see them gather of their own accord into long parallel files, across Dry Creek on the bank of which the corral stood, and pour back into the corral and quietly lie down. This ended my first day of sheep-herding.

After the winter rains had set in, and the grass had grown to a height of three or four inches, herding became easy, for they quietly filled themselves; but at this time, just before the rain, when not a green leaf is to be seen, when the dead summer vegetation is parched and crumpled into dust and fragments of stems, the sheep are always hungry and unmanageable; but when full of green grass the entire flock moves as one mild, bland, contented animal This year the winter rains did not set in until the middle of December. Then Dry Creek became a full, deep, stately flowing river; every hollow in the hills was flooded, every channel so long dry carried a rushing, gurgling, happy stream.

Being out every day I had the advantage of watching the coming of every species of plant. Mosses and liverworts, no trace of which could be seen when dry and crumpled, now suddenly covered the entire plain with a soft velvet robe of living green. Then, at first one by one, the different species of flowering plants appeared, pushing up with marvelous rapidity and bursting into bloom, until all the ground was covered with golden composite, interrupted and enriched here and there with charming beds of violets, mints, clover, mariposa tulips, etc.

It was very interesting, too, to watch the awakening and coming to light and life of the many species of ants and other insects after their deathlike sleep during the cold rainy season; and the ground squirrels coming out of their burrows to sun themselves and feed on the fresh vegetation; and to watch the nesting birds and hear them sing—especially the meadow-larks which were in great abundance and sang as if every note was transformed sunshine.

Plovers in great numbers and of several species came to feed with snipes and geese and swans.

It was interesting, too, to watch the long-eared hares, or jack-rabbits as they are called, as they cantered over the flowery plain, or confidingly mingled with the flock. Several times I saw inquisitive sheep interviewing the rabbits as they sat erect, even touching noses and indulging apparently in interesting gossip. My dog was fond of chasing the hares, but they bounded along carelessly, and never were so closely pressed as to be compelled to dive into a burrow. They apparently trusted entirely to their speed of foot; but as soon as a golden eagle came in sight they made for the nearest burrow in terrified haste. Then, feeling safe, they would turn around and look out the door to watch the movements of their enemy.

Occasionally I have seen an eagle alight within a yard or two of the door of a burrow into which a hare had been chased, and observed their gestures while the hare and eagle looked each other in the face for an hour at a time, the eagle apparently hoping that the hare might venture forth. When, however, a hare was surprised at any considerable distance from a burrow, the eagle, in swift pursuit, rapidly overtakes it and strikes it down with his elbow, then wheels around, picks it up and carries it to some bare hilltop to feast at leisure.

By the end of May nearly all of the marvelous vegetation of the plains has gone to seed and is so scorched and sun-dried, it crumbles under foot as though it had literally been cast into an oven. Then most of the flocks are driven into the green pastures of the Sierra. A camp is made on the first favorable spot commanding a considerable range, and when it is eaten out the camp is moved to higher and higher pastures in succession, following the upward sweep of grassy, flowery summer towards the summit of the Range.

Ever since I had visited Yosemite the previous year I had longed to get back into the Sierra. When the heavy snows were melting in the spring sunshine, opening the way to the summits of the Range, and I was trying to plan a summer's excursion into their midst, wondering how I could possibly carry food to last a whole summer, Mr. Delaney, a neighbor of Smoky Jack's, noticing my love of plants and seeing some of the drawings I had made in my note-books, urged me to go to the mountains with his flock—not to herd the sheep, for the regular shepherd was to take care of them, but simply to see that the shepherd did his duties. He offered to carry my plant press and blankets, allow me to make his mountain camps my headquarters while I was studying the adjacent mountains, and perfect freedom to pursue my studies, and offering to pay me besides, simply to see that the shepherd did not neglect his flock,

Mr. Delaney was an Irishman who was educated at Maynooth College for a Catholic priest, a striking contrast to his so-called " Smoky " neighbor. He was lean and tall, and I naturally nicknamed him Don Quixote. I told him that I did not think I could be of any practical use to him because I did not know the mountains, knew nothing about the habits of sheep in the mountains, and that I feared that in pushing through brush, fording torrents, and in attacks of bears and wolves, the sheep would be scattered and not half of them ever see the plains again. But he encouraged me by saying that he himself would go to the mountains with the flock, to the first camp, and visit each camp in succession from time to time, bringing letters and fresh provisions, and seeing for himself how his flock was prospering; that the shepherd would do all the herding and that I would be just as free to pursue my studies as if there were no sheep in the question, to sketch and collect plants, and observe the wild animals; but as he could not depend upon his shepherd his fear was that the flock might be neglected, and scattered by bears, and that my services would only be required in cases of accidents of that sort.

I therefore concluded to accept his generous offer, The sheep were counted, the morning the start for the mountains was made, as they passed out of the corral one by one. They numbered two thousand and fifty, and were headed for the mountains. The leaders of the flock had not gone a mile from the home camp before they seemed to understand that they were on their way up to the high green pastures where they had been the year before, and eagerly ran ahead, while Don Quixote, with a rifle on his shoulder, led two pack animals, and the shepherd and an Indian and Chinaman to assist in driving through the foothills, and myself, marched in the rear.

Our first camp after crossing the dusty, brushy foothills, which were scarcely less sunburned than the plains, was made on a tributary of the North Fork the Merced River at an elevation of about three thousand feet above the sea. Here there were no extensive grassy meadows, but the hills and hollows and recesses of the mountain divide between the Merced and the Tuolumne waters were richly clothed with grass and lupines, while clover of different species and ceanothus bushes furnished pasture in fair abundance for several weeks, while the many waterfalls on the upper branches of the river, the charming lily gardens at the foot of them, and many new plants and animals to sketch and study, afforded endless work according to my own heart.

The sheep were kept here too long; the pasture within two or three miles of the camp was eaten bare, while we waited day after day, more and more anxiously, for the coming of the Don with provisions, and to assist and direct the moving of the camp to higher fresh pasturage. Our own pasturage was also exhausted. We got out of flour, and strange to say, although we had abundance of mutton and tea and sugar, we began to suffer. After going without bread for about a week it was difficult to swallow mutton, and our stomachs became more and more restless. The shepherd tried to calm his rebellious stomach by chewing great quantities of tobacco and swallowing most of the juice, and by making his tea very strong, using a handful for each cup. Strange that in so fertile a wilderness we should suffer distress for the want of a cracker, or a slice of bread, while the Indians of the neighborhood sustained their merry, free lives on clover, pine bark, lupines, fern roots, et cetera, with only now and then a squirrel, deer or bear, badger or coon.

At length the Don came down the long glen, and all our bread woes were ended. He brought with him not only an abundance of provisions, but two men to assist in driving the flock higher.

APPENDIX

MISCELLANEOUS IRON TOOLS AND WEAPONS THAT WENT INTO THE WEST

Mr. Astor's Inventory—The Basic Tools
from *Firearms, Traps, and Tools of the Mountain Men*

By Carl P. Russell

The volume of existing material pertaining to the frontiersman's implements and tools is actually large enough to embarrass the student who undertakes their identification, classification, interpretation, and publication. The three-dimensional objects are accumulating in numerous collections, and the documentary sources are abundant and replete with evidences of the origin, sale price, and distribution of these pieces; less is recorded regarding their practical use in the hands of frontier craftsmen. Meriwether Lewis provides us with a good starting point for our study; his 1803 requisitions for equipment and supplies to be used by the Lewis and Clark Expedition are preserved in the National Archives, and the Lewis and Clark Journals contain a number of testimonials regarding the use of tools in the field.[1] Enough of this extraordinary information is available to make a book on the historic objects of Lewis and Clark provenance; a few of the pieces are treated in the pages that follow.

---

[1] The original requisitions are preserved in the National Archives, and they appear in R G. Thwaites, ed.: *Original Journals of the Lewis and Clark Expedition* (8 vols.; New York: Dodd, Mead & Co.; 1904-5), VII, 231-46, Donald Jackson, ed.: *Letters of the Lewis and Clark Expedition* (Urbana: Univ. of Illinois Press; 1962), pp. 69-99, reprints them with related documents and adds his own valuable interpretive notes. An illustrated account of the three dimensional properties of Lewis and Clark is given in the manuscript report by C. P. Russell: "Preliminary Exhibit Plan for Lewis and Clark Memorial" (Nat'l Park Serv., Fort Clatsop, Ore., 1959), pp. 67—127.

A second highly important source of information regarding early iron tools in the Far West is John Jacob Astor's inventory of his properties seized by the British North West Company at Astoria on the Columbia River in October 1813. Surprisingly, this great body of information has not been republished by scholars who have in recent years concerned themselves with the history of trade and merchandising in the early West. The inventory is much too extensive (forty-three pages printed in eight-point type) to be presented here in its entirety, but sections of it that pertain most directly to the subject matter of the present chapter are given in Appendix D (pages 402-7). The prices indicated in the inventory represent the values as appraised by the North West Company buyers. In a very few categories of goods, 100 percent was added to the total cost of an item; in more instances, however, 75 percent was deducted from the appraised worth. The total Astoria inventory, exclusive of furs on hand, amounted to $13,256.00. Mr. Astor testified to the United States Congress that this was one fifth of the true worth (see appendix for the partial Astor inventory).

Entirely similar but smaller lots of merchandise were turned over to the North West Company at Mr. Astor's outposts eastward from Astoria. The inventory for Okunaakan [Okanogan] was $2,333.5825; at Spokane House, $1,715.1725; and John Reed's party and the "Freemen" with him on the Snake were allowed $1,907.57, from which amount 50 per cent was deducted immediately. A final scraping of the bottom of the barrel swelled the merchandise accounted for to the extent of $853,805, and the final inventory at Astoria proper totaled $13,256.0075. Furs sold to the North West Company at Astoria amounted to $39,173,665, thus making the gross purchase price for the establishments and the furs $58,291.0175.

Alleged indebtedness assumed by some of Mr. Astor's representatives then at Astoria reduced the net proceeds of the sale to $42,281.50. The bill of sale but not the inventories has been published in B. C. Payette's Oregon Country.[2] The shipping of cargoes from New York to the Pacific shore was costly and fraught with catastrophe, as witness the Tonquin disaster. Mr. Astor's allegation that he was robbed by the North West Company of 80 percent of the true worth of his properties on the Columbia (he declared the total value to be $200,000) seems to be fairly substantiated by the Columbia inventories and the bill of sale.

---

[2] Payette, comp.; *The Oregon Country under the Union Jack: [Alexander] Henry's Astoria Journal* (Montreal, 1961), pp. xiv-xix.

Extant records of early merchandising in the Western fur trade are rich in detail. Contemporary with the above-described Astoria business are the accounts of Colonel John Johnston's United States Indian Agency at Fort Wayne.[3] These accounts are representative of the government's Indian factory system of trade. The invoices, inventories, and memoranda included in the account books present an excellent picture of the variety and quantity of merchandise handled, and they reveal the prevailing prices of the day. Generally these government prices are lower than those charged by the commercial companies of the same period. Rather complete information on the Indian trade goods distributed by the government from 1801 to 1822 is found in the account books—Day Books, Stock Books, Memoranda Books, and Letter Books—representative of the business conducted at the Indian Trade headquarters offices in Philadelphia and George Town, D.C. The westernmost Indian factory was Fort Osage on the Missouri. A summary report on these significant fur-trade papers was prepared by Dr. Alfred F. Hopkins in 1941-2.[4] It is in the library of the director's office of the National Park Service, Washington, D.C.

Data regarding merchandise for distribution as gifts to Western Indians by William Clark's St. Louis Indian Office, 1823, are found in the Forsyth Papers[5] owned by the Wisconsin Historical Society. Prices here compare favorably with prices charged by the commercial companies.

Mr. Astor's agents engaged in a phenomenally successful fur trade after the fiasco on the Columbia. Until 1818 the Astor men concentrated on the Great Lakes trade with extensions into the Ohio-Mississippi region. In 1818, however, Russell Farnham of the Astor company was sent into the Missouri country to trade, and by the fall of 1821 Samuel Abbott, Astor's trusted agent, had established an American Fur Company Western Department with headquarters in St. Louis. Thereafter, the company linked with the Prattes and the Chouteaus proceeded slowly but surely on its march to monopoly in the West. Many of the letters and business records of the American Fur Company are available for study. The company's account books for the early business in Missouri have

3   Bert J, Griswold, ed.: *Fort Wayne, Gateway of the West, 1802-1813* (Indianapolis: Indian Library and Historical Dept.; 1927).

4   Dr. Alfred F. Hopkins, comp.: "Report on Indian. Trade Objects Purchased by the U. S. Government through its several Superintendents of Indian Trade at Philadelphia, Penn., and George Town, D.C., from 1801-22, inclusive" (MSS), 56 typed pages.

5   "Invoice of merchandise purchased and received as presents for Indians, 1823,. . . Apr. 28, 1823. Sundries received of Genl. William Clark for presents for Indians," in Forsyth Papers, Vol. 2, Draper Collection, Item 2, Wisconsin Historical Society. See also 17th Cong., 1st sess., Sen. Doc. 60, February 11, 1822, pp. 1-62, for detailed statements regarding trade goods and the firms that supplied the U. S. Indian Office.

not been searched, but the manuscript "Invoice Book No. 1," owned by the Chicago Historical Society, provides some 300 pages of descriptive accounts, with prices, of all manner of merchandise shipped by the company from Michilimackinac to twenty or more outposts in Michigan, Wisconsin, Illinois, and Indiana in 1821 and 1822. A survey of the tools and ironworks in these inventories reveals that the items are much the same as those which Mr. Astor shipped to the Columbia, but generally the Michilimackinac prices of 1821-2 were 100 to 500 per cent more than the prices paid to the Astorians by the North West Company on the Columbia in 1813.

There are several additional important collections of American Fur Company manuscripts in the Public Archives of Canada, Detroit Public Library, Missouri Historical Society, State Historical Society of Wisconsin, Minnesota Historical Society, Chicago Historical Society, and The New York Historical Society.[6] All shed light on the tools of the fur traders, but the "Orders Outward," "Orders Inward," "Ledgers," "Invoices," and "Inventories" contained in the massive assembly of American Fur Company Papers, 1831-49, owned by The New York Historical Society are especially pertinent to our present account of tools in the West. Furthermore, the Papers are most workable because of the two-volume *Calendar*[7] and the remarkable national distribution of the 37-reel microfilm copy of practically all the manuscripts. Ramsay Crooks, Astorian, was made president of the company when Astor with drew in 1834. Therefore the great body of the Papers are the expression of Crooks and his agents and portray very fully their way of life. West of the Mississippi, Pratte, Chouteau and Company (after 1838 Pierre Chouteau, Jr., and Company) constituted an affiliated firm. Its outposts and agencies were distributed from the Canadian border to Texas and westward across the Rockies. The Pratte-Chouteau business records are preserved in St. Louis and New York, where they served the present writer as one of the keys to the Western "tools" story. The tools themselves, as pictured in the illustrations that follow, are preserved in some forty museums and private collections, as indicated.

Needles and Awls

---

6 See the American Fur Company sources in the bibliography.

7 Calendar of the American fur Company Papers *1831-49* Grace Lee Nute, ed.: (Annual Report of the American Historical Association, 1944). (Washington, D.C.: U. S. Govt. Printing Office; 1945).

Figure 83a shows the rush matting needle that quickly replaced the aboriginal bone and wood versions of this simple tool so necessary to the primitive weaver. This flat "needle," or shuttle, served to interlace the horizontal strips of flattened rush (weft) with the vertical strips of the same material (warp) to make a fairly pliable, hard fabric—matting. The weaving was entirely a hand operation. No loom was required. The Indians of the Columbia River and parts of the Pacific Coast regions were especially noted for mats used as floor covering in their rectangular lodges, for side walls, doors, sun shades, windbreaks, coverings for piles of foodstuffs, for beds and bedding, for seats, and even for platters upon which to serve their food. The weaving of rush matting was not limited to Indians of the Far West; it was quite commonly practiced wherever the raw materials were abundant. For aboriginal matting needles recovered at a Fox Indian site, 1680-1730, see Wittry's paper.[8] The matting needle represented in figure 83a is No. A-80 in the Minnesota Historical Society collections and is

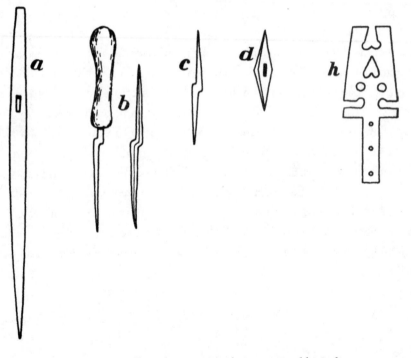

FIG. 83. *Some Small Implements Much Appreciated by Indians.*

---

8 W. L. Wittry: "The Bell Site; Early Historic Fox Village," *Wisconsin Archeologist*, XLIV: 1 (March 1963), p. 15.

Certain small iron tools were inexpensive but of prime importance in the Indian's daily work. Such were the various needles and awls supplied by the white man. Often the trader carried a generous supply of these easily transported items in order that he might win favor through the presentation of simple valued gifts that had cost him little more than the trouble of packing them. Drawing by William Macy, Jefferson National Expansion Memorial, St. Louis.

attributed to H. M. Rice, a trader of the 1840's and 1850's at Sauk Rapids, Lake Prairie, middle-upper Mississippi River section.

Figure 83b shows an iron "moccasin" awl with a handle. This specimen is No. D48 in the American Museum, and is attributed to the Iroquois. Because rawhide, dressed skins, gut, bark—even thin panels of wood—entered into so many of the Indian's everyday procedures of manufacture and repair, he found it necessary to incessantly sew, lace, and bind with sinew or rawhide thongs. To facilitate pushing the needle through exceedingly resistant materials, awls were used to break the way. Originally awls were polished, sharpened splinters of bone, antler, or wood. The white man brought to America the same iron awls that served Europe since the dawn of the Iron Age. The Indian seized upon the better implement. Seemingly, iron awls appear upon any and all invoices and inventories representative of the Indian trade, east or west, and through all the years. Maxwell publishes evidences that the earliest awls at Michilimackinac were tapered, cylindrical spikes of iron, pointed at both ends.[9] Charles E. Brown illustrates somewhat similar awls from Carcajou site, Wisconsin, and tells of the distribution of awls in Wisconsin by the explorer Nicholas Perot in 1965-6.[10] Of the fifty-two awls recovered at Fort Michilimackinac, nine were made with an offset at the middle, just as the specimen shown in figure 83b. "The provenance of these offset awls indicates a late arrival of this form at the fort. All nine were found above levels tentatively ascribed to the early 1760s."[11] The British regime at Fort Michilimackinac began with the arrival of British troops in September 1761 and it may be inferred that British interests thereafter introduced the offset pattern. Whether or not French traders anywhere ever supplied the offset awls has not been determined in the present study, but all evidence points to the fact that any and all organized trading companies after the late eighteenth century ordinarily featured the offset pattern. There were

---

[9] Moreau S. Maxwell: *Excavations at Fort Michilimackinac, 1959 Season* (East Lansing: Michigan State Univ.; 1961), pp. 88, 124.

[10] C. E, Brown: "Indian Trade Implements and Ornaments," *Wisconsin Archaeologist*, XVII: 3 (1918), p. 62.

[11] Maxwell: *Excavations,* pp. 88 and 124, Pl VIII.

exceptions, but they were extraordinary. Lewis and Clark, while en route home in the spring of 1806, stopped with the Nez Perce at Camp Chopunnish. The Nez Perce begged for iron awls, none of which remained in the skimpy stock of merchandise carried by the explorers at this juncture. Lewis wrote: "4 of our party pased the river and visited the lodge of the broken Arm for the purpose of traiding some awls which they had made of the links of a small chain belonging to one of their steel traps, for some roots. They returned in the evening having been very successful, they had obtained a good supply of roots and bread of cows."[12] It is unlikely that awls with an offset were improvised on this occasion. No forge was carried by the returning explorers. Such bending, straightening, and sharpening of the cold iron links as could be effected on a makeshift anvil with a hammer, pincers, and a file probably yielded nothing more than a fairly straight, sharp spike.

Figure 83c shows a "moccasin" awl, No. E-193 in the Minnesota Historical Society. The specimen is from the Sauk Rapids locality, Minnesota. Awls were shipped by the manufacturer and distributed by the trader without handles. A shaped and smooth section of deer antler usually was affixed by the Indian owner. British supply houses furnished many awls to the American trade. The American Fur Company Papers contain copies of many orders addressed to Hiram Cutler, Sheffield. "Our Indian awls are to be put up in papers of 50 each. They can be packed with fire steels and needles." Fifty gross was a usual complement, and, consistently, year after year the price paid to Cutler was about forty cents per gross. In the United States the book value was a dollar and a half per gross, or one cent each; in the field, "Indian" awls brought two to five cents each, if sold, but often they were handed out freely as good-will offerings. This was generally true of all companies all through the mountain-man period. Larger awls, termed "canoe awls," were inventoried at twenty-five cents each[13] and sold in the field at a mark-up as big as circumstances might dictate.

Figure 83d is described as a "snowshoe needle"; it is No. E-191 in the Minnesota Historical Society collection. Most northern tribes of Indians were adept in the ancient art of stringing strips of rawhide, usually deerskin, upon their own particular form of ashwood frame to produce the very necessary raquette. Usually, the stringing and spacing of the thongs was facilitated by the use of a short length of antler, deer, or caribou. The white man adopted the snowshoe enthusiastically and introduced the iron snowshoe needle as

12 *Journals*, Lewis's entry for May 24, 1806; Allen, ed,: *History of the Expedition*, II, 299.
13 American Fur Company Papers, 1821-2, (Invoice Book) "Illinois 1821."

an "improvement" to be used by the native manufacturers, but the Indian craftsman did not always see it as such. The craft of snowshoe making persists in some localities as an Indian village enterprise,[14] and the minutiae of practices remain as of old, including dependence upon the primitive antler "needle." The iron specimen shown in figure 83d was obtained from a trader who had been active in the Sauk Rapids region, Minnesota, during the 1840's.

Spears, Harpoons, and Arrow Points

Among the specimens shown in figure 84 are a half-dozen lance heads favored by buffalo-hunting Indians, four barbed harpoons used by whites and Indians alike in spearing fish and muskrats, and a representative assortment of iron arrow points, large and small. The seven arrow points were recovered in northern and northeastern localities, but so far as their sizes and shapes are concerned, they might have been collected anywhere north of the Mexican boundary. The pattern exemplified by figures 84n, 84o, 84p, and 84s was the usual point produced in factories supplying the trade. Others, like figures 84q, 84r, 84t are representative products of backcountry forges where, on occasion, red men as well as whites operated smithies.

Figure 84a shows a Sioux lance point with its original shaft, which is now owned by the Missouri Historical Society. The specimen was presented to R. Faribault by Chief Red Leg of the Sioux, who described it as "a warrior's lance, very old. It was used by my people in fights with the Chippewa." The shaft is 3½ feet long.

Figure 84b illustrates an iron spear point or knife blade from the Yellowstone Valley. This specimen is No. 7266 in the Yellowstone National Park museums. See page 333 for the use of similar blades in "dags" of the north land. These artifacts turn up occasionally on northern Indian sites anywhere and everywhere from New York to the Pacific.

Figure 84c is an extra-large blade, which is now item No. 2064 in the State Historical Society, Pierre, South Dakota. The eccentric tang suggests that this specimen may have served as a machete-type knife blade, but it would do equally well as a spear point.

The country-made spear point shown in figure 84d, No. 116 in the Washington State Historical Society, Tacoma, is recorded as found in an Indian grave

---

[14] Adelaide Leitch: "Land of the Wendats," *The Berner* (Autumn 1963), pp. 14-19 [good photos].

in Wisconsin. Similar leaf-shaped iron points with short tang have been found throughout Iroquoia.

Figure 84e is a 10-inch iron spear point, cataloged as No. 117, Washington State Historical Society, Tacoma. W. P. Bonney of the society reported that this specimen was from Cairo, Illinois. Its unusual serrated base facilitated binding the head into the split end of a shaft.

Shown in figure 84f is a long-tang spear point in the Marvin Livingston Collection, Carlsbad, New Mexico. It was found in Dark Canyon in the northeast section of the Guadalupe Mountains. Note the smith's mark "A B 85." A point quite similar and of most excellent workmanship was found in a Caddo site, Arkansas, and is preserved in the Dorris Dickinson Collection, Magnolia, Arkansas.

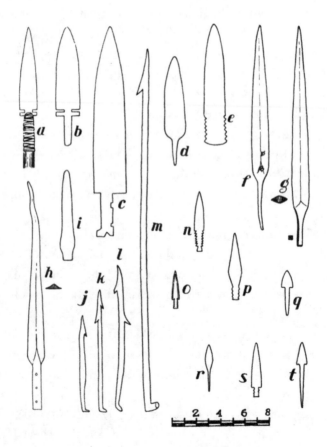

FIG. 84. *Iron Projectile Points.*

Figure 84g is a Hatchilla Mountains spear point, No. M-232 in the Laboratory of Anthropology, Santa Fe, New Mexico. Like figure 84f, the blade is a diamond shape in cross section, and the tang is square in cross section. Some anthropologists have regarded these slender points to be of Spanish derivation, and it is likely that these particular specimens are Spanish; however, entirely similar bayonet points were excavated at Fort Washington, 183rd Street and Pinehurst Avenue, New York City. These Revolutionary War relics of Anglo-American origin now at the New York Historical Society rather belie the idea that the model is characteristically Spanish.

> Arrowheads and spear points, both stone and metal, are present almost universally in collections of Indian artifacts. The iron points present a bewildering variety of sizes and forms. The Indian and probably the white trader were unaware of the fact, but not one of the styles of iron points in America was unique; each had had its counterpart during earlier periods in the Old World. Drawing by William Macy, Jefferson National Expansion Memorial, St. Louis.

Figure 84h shows a triple-edged lance head from Butte des Morts; it is catalogued as No. 396 by the Wisconsin Historical Society. This twisted specimen was once the personal property of Augustin Grignon, historical figure in the Wisconsin Indian trade and early affiliate of the American Fur Company. In 1835 the company ordered lances from Miles Standish, the celebrated manufacturer of beaver traps. These spear heads were requisitioned by Pierre Chouteau and Company, St. Louis, through Ramsay Crooks, American Fur Company, New York. Crooks wrote to Standish:

> 120 Assinboine lances as per sample. The tang to be 2 inches long and to have 3 holes in it for rivets at equal distance on the square part say 1 hole near the round, 1 hole near the extremity and the other hole half way between. The price to be $1.00, each. They are to be of your very best work, packed carefully and securely in good strong pine boxes—one or two boxes as you may deem best. Payment in six months after delivery to store No. 45 Liberty St., or in cash less 3½% discount at option of Co.

Marginal Marking 35
C & Co.
A.[15]

---

[15] American Fur Company Papers, Memos, 1834-40, Vol. 1 (microfilm reel 20).

On April 26, 1836, A. P. Chouteau, trader to the Western Creek Nation, Comanches, and Wichitas, on the Verdigris and at Camp Holmes near the Canadian River, ordered from the American Fur Company, New York: "One hundred Indian lances, 18 inches long, 1½ inches at the shank, and 100 iron rings ½ inch wide suitable for fastening the lance head in the shaft. Both these articles to be well finished."[16]

Figure 84i shows a Country-made spear point found in 1910 by W. C. Lawrence on the Sweetwater at Burnt Ranch, Wyoming. It is now part of the Lawrence Collection, Jackson, Wyoming.

Figure 84j is a fish (or muskrat) spear from the Fort Crawford site Villa Louis, Prairie du Chien, Wisconsin. As is typical, there is a "heel" at the end of this small harpoon that made it possible to achieve a secure mounting on a shaft of wood. Any spearing of muskrats with this short shank would have been done in the open or through thin transparent ice. Only a long shank could reach a muskrat through the walls of a muskrat house.

Figure 84k shows a double-barbed fish or muskrat spear from the vicinity of the Jacques Vieau trading post. The specimen is preserved as No. 28012 in the Milwaukee Public Museum. There were three modes of mounting these spearheads on handles: 1. The outer surface at the end of the shaft might be grooved longitudinally and a depression made for the "heel" of the iron spear. The spear point was laid into the groove, the heel driven home, and the iron held rigidly against the wood by a tight wrapping of wet rawhide or wire. Or 2. the heel might be made small enough to permit of inserting the iron into a hole drilled in the end of the wooden shaft. In this method an iron ring, band, or ferrule was driven down upon the end of the shaft to make the wood take a tight grip upon the iron. 3. Some eighteenth-century specimens were made with a socket into which the handle entered. In this form there was no heel.

Iron "harpoons" find a place in fur-trade documents as early as 1643, in which year it is recorded that the Montagnais used them in killing beaver.[17] Nicholas Denys's *Description* for the 1670's says of the Micmac: "They practice still all the old methods of hunting, with this difference, in place of arming their arrows and spears with the bones of animals, pointed and sharpened, they arm them today with iron, which is made expressly for sale to them. . . . With respect to hunting of the beaver in winter, they do the same as they did formerly, though

---

[16]   American Fur Company Papers, Orders Inward, Vol. 1, p. 251.
[17]   Thwaites, ed.: *Jesuit Relations*, V, 148, and VI, 309—11.

they have now a greater advantage with their arrows and harpoons armed with iron."[18] Wittry unearthed intact examples of the aboriginal bone harpoons in a Fox site of 1680-1730,[19] and recently Caywood recovered early iron specimens at Fort Meductic, New Brunswick.[20] The independent trader William Burnett at the St. Joseph River, Michigan, in 1799 ordered from his supplier in Montreal muskrat spears "made with a socket which the French call endouille."[21] In 1803 Meriwether Lewis procured forty of these single-pointed "giggs" with barbs at Harpers Ferry. They were made to his order and by him added to the stock of merchandise carried by the Lewis and Clark Expedition for presentation to Indians. A Memorandum Book (1808) of the U. S. Indian Office, George Town, D.C., lists iron spears for muskrats and fish; the American Fur Company Invoice Book, "Illinois 1821," lists "25 rat spears @ .62½¢ ... $15.62" in a shipment of trade goods sent from Michilimackinac; the Hudson's Bay Company's Chief Factor at Cumberland House, Saskatchewan River, in 1839 ordered from the York Factory: "60 long rat spears 3½ feet long ... the old short ones I have on hand shall be repaired, and they with the 60 now asked for will be enough for next winter;[22] and Francis X. Des Nover's Wisconsin Account Book of 1844 records the sale of two "rat" spears for $1.00.[23] Thus, we observe there is a two-hundred-year documented record for the fish-muskrat spear, most of it pertaining to the northern country.

Figure 84l shows a double-barbed harpoon for fish or muskrats from site of the Hudson's Bay Company post at Trout Lake, Wisconsin. It is preserved as specimen No. H-3814-19 in the Wisconsin Historical Society. Several of these were found at Trout Lake, and others have been collected at the Grignon-Parlier trading post site at Rush Lake; the Jacques Vieau post at Milwaukee; Green Bay; Prairie du Chien; Crawfish River, Fall River; and the Carcajou site at Lake Koshkonong—all in Wisconsin.

---

[18] W. F. Ganong, ed. and trans.: The Description and Natural History of the Coasts of North America by Nicholas Denys (Toronto): Champlain Society; 1908), pp. 442-3.

[19] Wittry "The Bell Site"p. 15, Fig. 7G.

[20] Personal letter, Louis R. Caywood to C. P. Russell, June 24, 1965.

[21] Burnett to Parker, Gerard and Ogilvy, Montreal, quoted in H. H. Hurlbut; Chicago Antiquities (Chicago; Eastman Bartlett; 1881), p. 68. Charles E. Brown: "Indian Trade Implements and Ornaments," Wisconsin Archeologist, XVII: 3 (1918), pp. 74-5, reports the recovery of a socketed fish-muskrat-beaver harpoon in Wisconsin: "Recovered from the Lake Mendota bottom near Fox Bluff at Madison. It is 18 inches long, square in section, with a conical socket in which is a rivet hole. The shaft where it joins the socket is about one inch square [and tapers]. The first of its two barbs is 4 inches below the tip."

[22] Chief Factor John Lee Lewis to James Hargrave, York Factory, February 5, 1839, quoted in Stanley P. Young: "The Evolution of the Steel Wolf Trap in North America," Western Sportsman (February 1941), p. 11.

[23] C. E. Brown: "Indian Trade Implements," pp. 74-5.

Shown in figure 84m is a single-barbed harpoon with long shank especially for muskrats. It is recorded as having been used by Winnebago Indians. The specimen is No. E-198-199, Wisconsin Historical Society. In the 1840's Henry Thacker, a member of the Oneida Community but then a resident of Chicago, wrote an account of firsthand experiences in muskrat spearing. He turned in his manuscript to the Community, and it appears in the Newhouse Trapper's Guide.[24] On a cold, snappy winter's day Mr. Thacker skated twelve miles up the North Fork of the Chicago River to marshes in the vicinity of present-day Skokie. There, among innumerable muskrat houses protruding above the ice of the marsh, he identified occupied houses by the deposit of white frost to be seen around the small air holes in the domes. Successively he approached occupied houses, drove his spear through the softest part of the walls as betrayed by the air hole, and impaled his victims on the long shank of his spear. Occasionally two rats were impaled by a single thrust. When a rat was hit, the spear was not withdrawn until a hole was chopped in the wall of the house, exposing the victim, which was then killed and removed, and the broken wall repaired. Mr. Thacker states that he took fifteen or twenty rats in a few hours, all that he could skin before the carcasses froze. He adds that a few rats were speared through 2 inches of clear ice as they swam under him. His spear was a rod ⅜ inch in diameter, 3 feet long, mounted in a ferruled wooden handle that also was 3 feet long.

W. Hamilton Gibson's Tricks of Trapping also describes the spearing of muskrats:

> Uncertain and unreliable, because the walls of the hut are often so firmly frozen as to defy the thrust. The spear is a single shaft of steel about eighteen inches in length and half an inch in diameter, barbed at the point and ferruled to a solid handle five feet long. In spearing through the hut the south side is generally selected as being more exposed to the heat of the sun. Great caution in approaching the house is necessary as the slightest noise will drive out the inmates. The spear should be thrust in a slanting direction a few inches above the ice. When it has penetrated it must be left until a hole is cut in the wall with a hatchet through which to remove the game.[25]

---

[24] *The Trapper's Guide* by S. Newhouse (Wallingford, Conn., 1867). An 1887 edition published in New York also contains the Thacker article, p. 146.

[25] W. Hamilton Gibson; Camp Life and the Tricks of Trapping (New York: Harper & Bros,; 1881), pp. 188-4.

Needless to say, the spearing of muskrats or beaver is passe as a mode of taking fur. This was true in the days of the author's boyhood, the early 1900's, but his Wisconsin homeland at that time still claimed numerous living citizens who had taken the bounty from the local fur fields, and their muskrat spears were to be found, with shafts intact, in granaries, tool sheds, and barns throughout the rural districts. The one in the author's tool shop did not get there because of any anthropological interests; it was a family property—a relic of practical "spearing" by a pre-Civil War generation that farmed the country around Lost Lake in Dodge County. These Yankee farmers were only a scant decade behind the Winnebago Indians and the French-Canadians who for two hundred years had harvested pelts on the same marshes.

Trade Iron into Arrow and Lance Points

Figure 84n shows a large "buffalo" arrowhead with a serrated tang. The specimen is No. 157 in the Missouri Historical Society, where it is recorded as being from the Sioux of South Dakota; it was collected in 1905. Stamped into the iron is ". . . J & Co.," which mark probably is the incomplete "P. C. J. & Co.," the trade mark of Pierre Chouteau, Jr. and Company, a big trading firm of the West operating out of St. Louis during the days of the mountain man. A number of identical points with the "P. C. J. & Co." intact are in existing collections.[26]

Figure 84o is an iron arrow point with a beveled edge. The specimen is preserved as No. H-391, Wisconsin Historical Society. The serrated tang was inserted into the split end of the arrow shaft, which was sufficiently slender to allow some of the iron teeth to project slightly beyond the rounded wood. A tight wrapping of fine sinew enclosed both teeth and wood. A thin glue prepared from hoofs was applied upon the wrapping. This hardened to make a firm and lasting binding.

Shown in figure 84p is a "buffalo" iron arrow point now in the State Historical Society, South Dakota. This specimen was taken from a bleached buffalo skeleton found years ago on the Dakota prairies. It was embedded in a vertebra. Long after the acceptance of the gun by the red man, he often clung to the bow and arrow as his best weapon in "running" buffalo. Osborne Russell, dependable observer and literate member of the trapper fraternity, provided an eyewitness account of buffalo slaughter with lance and bow and arrow. The place was Snake

---

[26] C. E. Brown: "Indian Trade Implements," p. 67.

River country some forty miles west of the present Yellowstone National Park; the Indians were friendly Bannocks, and the date, October 1835. Russell wrote:

> I arose at sunrise and looking southwestward I saw dust arising in a defile which led through mountains about five miles distant. Buffaloes were feeding all over the plain [before the defile]. I watched the motion of the dust for a few minutes, when I saw a body of men on horseback pouring out of the defile among the buffalo. The dust rose to the heavens. The whole mass of buffalo became agitated, producing a sound resembling distant thunder. At length an Indian pursued a cow close to me. Running along side of her he let slip an arrow and she fell. I immediately recognized him to be a Bannock with whom I was acquainted. He came to me and saluted in Snake, which I answered in the same tongue. . . . He said he had killed 3 fat cows and would kill one more and stop. So saying he wheeled his foaming charger and the next moment disappeared in the cloud of dust. In about half an hour he returned with a whole village and invited me to stop with him. While the squaws were putting up and stretching their lodges, I walked out with him to a small hillock to view the field of slaughter, the cloud of dust having passed away. The prairie was covered with slain. Upward of 1000 cows were killed without burning one single grain of powder.[27]

Figure 84q presents a small country-made iron arrow point. It is No. 1482 in the Bucks County Historical Society, Pennsylvania. This specimen was exposed by a woodcutter in 1882. It was embedded in a tree that had grown around it until it was enclosed within the center of the trunk. East and west, the tribesmen sought iron with which to tip their arrows. The Indian was adept at making his own iron points, using sheet iron, barrel hoops, and broken pieces of the white man's machinery. In some localities there were numerous Indian blacksmiths, but almost any Indian could fashion an iron arrow point without the benefit of a forge if he had access to a file, cold chisel, or hacksaw. Probably the most publicized instance of converting a machine to Indian armament was the demolition of the Lewis and Clark corn mill by the Mandans in 1805. The steel mill, which is accounted for in Captain Lewis's requisitions of 1803, was seen in action by the Mandans when a party visited Captain Clark on the expedition's keelboat on October 26, 1804. It was "the object which seemed to surprise them most. . . . It delighted them by the ease with which it reduced the grain to powder." On October 29, 1804, the explorers held a council with the Mandans. "A variety of presents were distributed, but none seemed to give them more satisfaction than

---

[27] Osborne Russell: Journal of a Trapper . . . (Boise, Idaho: Syms Fork Co.; 1921), pp. 40-1.

the iron corn mill which we gave to the Mandans."[28] Captain Clark's estimate of the Mandan "satisfaction" seems to have been mistakenly bestowed. In 1806 the Canadian Alexander Henry visited the Mandans and wrote:

> I saw the remains of an excellent large corn mill, which the foolish fellows had demolished on purpose to barb their arrows, and other similar uses, the largest piece of it which they could not break nor work up into any weapon, they have now fixed to a wooden handle and make use of it to pound marrow bones to make grease.[29]

Figure 84r shows a small Indian-made iron point. It is in the collection of The American Museum in New York City. The Indian was practical in making his arrow serviceable and proud in making its individual style or pattern conform to tribal tradition. However, the iron point, if made in the field, varied with the different circumstances under which the raw material and suitable tools became available to the tribesmen. Iron-tipped arrows were made in large numbers, because even under optimum conditions loss and breakage were to be expected. It was not unusual for big game animals to carry away the arrows that were supposed to kill them. One bit of testimony in this regard appears in a journal kept by a trooper of the Dodge Dragoon expedition in the territory of present-day Oklahoma:

FIG. 85.   *Bannock Buffalo Hunt, 1835.*

[28]   Allen, ed.; *History of the Expedition*, I, 117, 120.
[29]   Elliott Cones, ed.,: The Manuscript Journals of Alexander Henry and of *David Thompson* ... (3 vols.; New York: F, P. Harper; 1895), I, 329.

July 10, 1834. When we closed in upon this besieged buffalo as near as our horses would approach and at one well-aimed fire laid him prostrate, we immediately began butchering him. In his left shoulder, overgrown with flesh, we found the steel point of an Indian arrow which had no doubt been long there as the flesh around it had become completely calloused.[30]

Shown in figure 84s is a lethal point used by the Nebraska Sioux; it is now in the Union Pacific Historical Museum, Omaha. The tragic story of the murderous use of this specimen postdates the mountain man, but it is representative of many earlier attacks made upon trappers. This specimen was removed from the dead body of T. Tobin, foreman of a section gang at Overton, Nebraska.

Sioux Indians in an attack on May 12, 1867, killed Tobin and all but one of the men who were with him. Richard Costin is named as the individual who removed the arrow point and attended the remains of the victims. To view Sioux war arrows and bows one should visit the Custer Battlefield Museum. Photos and a brief account of these weapons appear in Harry B. Robinson's Guide to the Custer Battlefield Museum.

Figure 84t is an iron point with a long tang. No. E-194 in the Minnesota Historical Society, it is recorded as having been obtained from a North Dakota donor. Sixteenth-century records tell that some southeastern Indians make arrows having "nocks and feathers . . . whereby they shoot very stedy; the heads of some are vipers teeth, bones of fishes, flint stones, points of [iron] knives, which they having gotten from the Frenchmen, broke the same and put the points of them in their arrows heads."[31]

As early as 1671 the Hudson's Bay Company ordered two gross of factory-made iron arrowheads.[32] It seems quite obvious that the American aborigine generally craved and got by one means or another iron points almost immediately upon contact with the white man. Yet there was not always enough iron to meet the demand. A number of testimonials left by the mountain men show that more than a few Far Western Indians still depended upon flint and obsidian for arrowheads in the 1830's and 1840's.[33] This was seldom true, however, of the country from which the specimen shown in figure 84l came. From the days

---

[30] Company I Journal, Pawnee Piet Expedition, quoted by G. H. Shirk, ed.: "Peace on the Plains," The Chronicle of Oklahoma, XXVIII: 1 (1950), p. 16.

[31] John Spark, quoted In J. R. Swanton: The Indians of Southeastern United States, Bureau of American Ethnology, Bulletin 137 (1946), p. 572.

[32] Canadian Archives, Hudson's Bay Company Minute Book of 1671, p. 72, quoted in Innis: The Fur Trade, p. 27.

[33] Josiah Gregg; Commerce of the Prairies, ed. R. G. Thwaites (2 vols.; Cleveland, 1905), 11, 324.

of Lewis and Clark, the Plains tribes had been catered to by white traders and blacksmiths of both the United States and Canada. Even in the early decades of the nineteenth century, the several trading posts along the Missouri maintained smithies, and a few Indians themselves knew the rudiments of blacksmithing and engaged in the craft—after a fashion.

Figure 86a shows an American pike found at Fort Washington, 183rd Street and Pinehurst Avenue, New York City, and now owned by The New York Historical Society. The strap-socketed spearhead, such as this one, was one of several patterns adopted by Washington's troops in accordance with the general's orders issued at Valley Forge in 1777. Each officer serving on foot was directed to provide himself with a pole arm of this kind. Similar military specimens are owned by Fort Ticonderoga Museum. All appear to have been made by local blacksmiths. The strap socket makes for a strong and efficient mounting, but it is comparatively costly to manufacture. These military pieces may have inspired some Indian agents; at any rate, a few points of this design were procured for the tribesmen by the U. S. Indian Department early in the nineteenth century. No positive evidence has been found of the strap-socket pattern having been distributed to Indians by the trading companies.

This hollow-ground spear head (fig. 86) was obtained by Captain George E. Albee of the U. S. Army from the Lipan Apache, and is now No. E-85 in the Wisconsin Historical Society. In lieu of a metal ferrule, a wrapping of rawhide thongs, applied wet to the end of the shaft, gives firm mounting of the point. This type of spearhead was favored by the Navajo and the Comanche as well as the Apache. Its hollow-ground feature differs from the usual points distributed among most tribes. Presumably these hollow-ground points were of Mexican or Spanish origin and may date back to sixteenth- or seventeenth-century manufacture. Some, apparently, are made from Spanish swords, bear Toledo armorers' marks, and have engraved upon them maxims or salutations in Spanish script. One such, No. 111.333 in the Laboratory of Anthropology, Santa Fe, is classed as a "buffalo lance." Its blade, 14 inches with tang, is marked "Viva el Rey." It is still mounted on its 62-inch wooden shaft.

Figure 86c is a "buffalo lance" with its original shaft. It was collected in an unnamed Rio Grande pueblo and is now preserved in the American Museum, New York City. The slight curve in the 5-foot wooden handle is true to the style of many Indian lances in the Southwest. There is nothing distinctive about the ferrule-mounted tanged blade, which is of a style found almost everywhere among American Indians. Specimens nearly identical in pattern have been found at Eau Claire and Prairie du Chien, Wisconsin (Wisconsin Historical Society); in the Menomini country, Michigan (American Museum); Big Bend, Texas (Memorial Museum, Alpine); Shoshone country, Wyoming (Teton Hotel Collection, Riverton); Bannock country, Idaho (Idaho Historical Society); in Union County, Ohio (Barsotti Collection); and in California (Los Angeles Museum).

In California the spear of this type persisted in the hands of white men until the American period. In order that Mexican troops mustered for the repulse of invading United States forces in 1846 might be armed with lances, many "home-made" points were hammered out in numerous rancho and Mission blacksmith shops. Shafts were prepared from mountain ash or laurel, and often an impro-

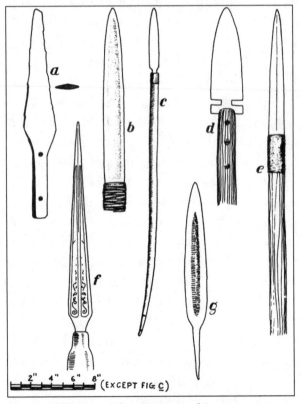

FIG. 86. *Pikes, Spears, and Lances.*

vised pennant was tied to them just below the spearhead. Micheltorena's troops were so armed. In the Los Angeles Museum are specimens of these lances from the battlefield of Paso de Bartolo, near Los Angeles. Official reports of Kearny's attack upon Pico at San Pasqual, a hand-to-hand fight, record that only two of the sixteen or eighteen Americans killed were felled by bullets; Mexican spears accounted for the others. In Mexico at this time, United States troops also encountered bodies of men who placed great reliance on the lance. Major H. K. Craig reported on May 24, 1846, that eighteen lances were captured from the Mexicans at Palo Alto and Resaca; at Monterey on September 24, 1846, 43 lances were taken.[34]

> The lance of the Spaniards became a mark of their American occupation and persisted as such through three centuries. Even in the Mexican War the Spanish-type lance found effective use against United States troops, Indians adopted the spears of any and all national patterns, and the Iron points became important articles of trade. William Macy drawing, Jefferson National Expansion Memorial, St, Louis.

Figure 86d is classed as an "American spontoon." The specimen was recovered at Fort Ticonderoga and is now exhibited there. In the terminology of the Quartermaster General of Revolutionary times, "Spontoon," "Pike," "Half Pike," and "Spear" were used synonymously. Such standardization as was attempted by the high command pertained to the length of staff, which for regular troops was specified as "six feet." The point figured here is much like the dag blades treated on page 320, and except for the greater length of tang, it closely resembles the blades used for spikes in war clubs described on page 175. As shown in figures 84a and 84b, this type of spear point was not limited to use by the military. Indian tribes of the Plains and the Rockies particularly are known to have used it. No clear evidence has been found showing an American source of supply; as in the case of the dag blades, an English source seems likely.

Figure 86e is a Navajo lance with its original shaft, which is preserved as specimen No. M-222, Laboratory of Anthropology, Santa Fe. It was obtained from the Navajos in Canyon de Chelly by Earl Morris in 1927. In lieu of a metal ferrule, a band of wet rawhide was sewed around the end of the shaft where the blade is mounted in the wood. Just as the specimen in figure 86c, the shaft, feet long, is slightly curved at the small end. An 1882 photograph in Morris's possession shows this long lance in the hands of a Navajo, together with a bear that had been killed with the weapon.

[34] S. V. Benet: A Collection of Annual Reports and Other Important Papers Relating to the Ordnance Department (Washington, D.C.: Gov't Printing Office; 1880), pp. 260—1.

Shown in figure 86f is a Spanish lance head marked (engraved on ferrule) "Santa Fe an. 1783." The specimen is preserved as No. B-96/55 in the Palace of the Governors, Santa Fe. The lance head is steel, ornamented with silver scrollwork. The metal ferrule, incomplete in the figure, extends 6 inches below the lance head. "Believed to have been carried by one of the soldiers stationed at the Palace of the Governors during the 18th Century." Both Coronado and Onate [35] brought the same type of spear into the American Southwest in the sixteenth century; the Indians of that section had, through three hundred years of contact, ample opportunity to become familiar with it. When the mountain man went among these peoples in the early decades of the nineteenth century, he found it to be the principal lance type used by the red warriors. The Indian pieces lacked the silver decorations.

Figure 86g shows a hollow-ground spear point found in Santa Fe Canyon. It is now in the Palace of the Governors, Santa Fe, New Mexico. Like the specimen shown in figure 86b, this point bears the marks of special crafting; it is not a run-of-the-mill trade piece. In the present survey of lance heads, pieces of this style were of Southwest provenance only.

Broadax, Adz, and Miscellaneous Tools

The tradesman's tools appear quite commonly among the artifacts dug from historic ground at trading posts and Indian sites. Iron chisels and hoes were valued among the red man's implements where they replaced earlier stone and bone tools; the recovered broadax and carpenter's hatchet may be less persuasive in the eyes of the investigator excavating an Indian site. Actually, both the white trapper and the Indian commonly put these tools to uses not planned by the toolmakers. The carpenter's hatchet especially was prized by the Indian because it functioned perfectly as a tomahawk, and the big broadax sometimes was chocked into a stump at the Indian camp and made to function as an improvised anvil. Upon the flat of its poll strips of brass plate or sheeting were cut with a cold chisel to make arrow points, or to fashion the bangles and "jinglers" needed for the dancers' garb.

Figure 87a shows a country-made broadax that is preserved as item No. 223 in the Holland Land Office Museum, Batavia, New York.[36] The light

---

[35] Harold L. Peterson: *Arms and Armor in Colonial America, 1526—1783* (Harrisburg, Pa.: Stackpole; 1956), pp. 318, 319.
        H. Charles McBarron's drawing of a Spanish lancer of the Onate Expedition armed with the long spear is on p. 130.
[36] I have the data on this broadax through the cooperation of Ralph Lewis, Lewis; 6-page MSS (February 6, 1988).

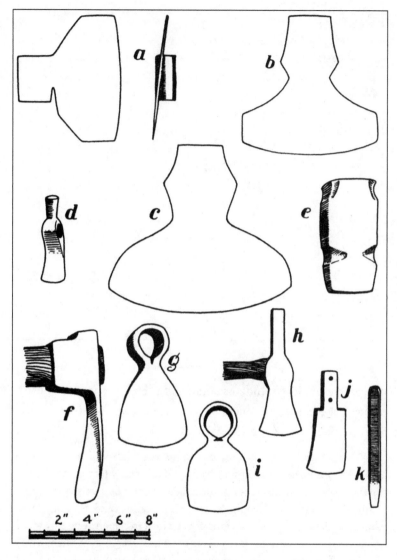

FIG. 87.   *Broadax, Adz, and Miscellaneous Tools.*

poll and the round eye place this specimen in the European class. Often the broadax has a chisel edge that permits of a perfectly flat face on one side of the blade. The flat face contributes to the shaping of flat, fairly smooth surfaces on logs or beams, because, like a chisel, this chisel-edged, flat-faced ax blade "hews to the line." To assure good control in hewing, the broadax maker always provides a short handle, and in order that the chopper's knuckles may clear the log or beam, the handle is bent, the eye of the ax is made off-center, or perhaps

285

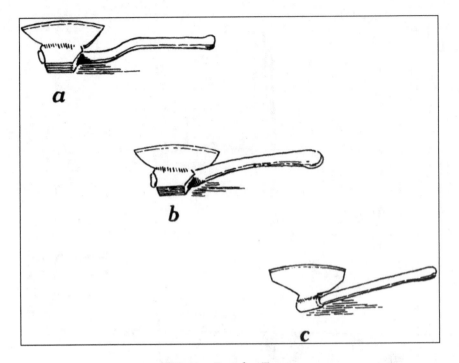

FIG. 88. *Broadax Types.*

both devices are employed. Indians obtained the broadax occasionally by theft. One of the first recorded instances of such stealing appears in Zebulon Pike's Arkansas Journal: Pawnees on the Arkansas stole a broadax in 1806.[37]

Trapper-trader parties often went into' the wilds well supplied with tools. Probably the most impressive evidence of this fact is the Astoria Inventory (see appendix), but additional authentic lists exist that reveal a surprising variety of equipment used in camps and trading posts. Understandably the larger inventories pertained to centers served by water transportation, as were the posts along the Missouri River. William Macy drawing, Jefferson National Expansion Memorial, St. Louis.

The broadax is designed to enable its user to do something that cannot be handily done with the felling ax—the forming of flat surfaces on sills, beams, floor puncheons, and similar timbers. Because the broadax is big and heavy, it is fitted with a short handle; a two-hand grip on this haft assures precise control. In order that the workman's knuckles may clear the wood as strokes are made, the eye of the axhead is often forged off-center, and further clearance is gained through the use of a bent handle. A variety of handle

[37] S. H. Hart and A. B, Hulbert, eds.: Zebulon Pike's Arkansas Journal (Denver: Denver Public Library; 1932), p. 123.

FIG. 89   *Port Union 1828—67.*

types exist. Three forms are shown here: a, the haft has been steamed and given a sharp offset close to the eye. This type has been termed the "swayed" handle, b, the haft has been steamed and bent, c, the haft is straight but it is fitted into a round eye that was forged off-center and canted obliquely away from the long axis of the blade (see fig. 87a).

A fur trader's broadax from the site of Fort Union, North Dakota, owned by the Montana Historical Society, Helena, is shown in figure 87b. This is one of two broadaxes found by M. B. Milligan in 1919 in the ruins of the blacksmith shop at this onetime largest and most important trading post in the western United States.

This emporium of the Western fur trade (near present-day Buford, North Dakota) occupied strategic place at the confluence of the Yellowstone and Missouri rivers. It was constructed under the supervision of the hard bitten Kenneth McKenzie, "King" of the Upper Missouri Outfit, American fur Company, who may be credited with the traders' most ambitious construction project on the Missouri. Into his employ came tradesmen or mountain men who functioned in the building arts—carpenters, stone-masons, blacksmiths, coopers, boat-builders, hamessmakers, saddlers, and, ultimately, wagonmakers. With the workmen came their tools. Since this post in the wilderness was well served from St. Louis by river transportation, it received tools in abundance, together with all manner of raw

FIG. 90. *Fort Hall on the Snake Interior View, 1834-55.*

materials and heavy equipment needed in the shops of the establishment. The state now owns the site. See Bay H. Mattison's "The Upper Missouri Fur Trade" for a concise history of Fort Union. Drawing by William Macy, Jefferson National Expansion Memorial, St. Louis.

Figure 87c is the second broadax recovered at the site of Fort Union in 1919 and now is preserved in the Montana Historical Society collections. Probably no other trading post displayed more examples of the house carpenter's craft or more evidences of the use of the broadax than did the elaborate Fort Union complex. Nevertheless, the smaller Western posts also developed and maintained numerous cabins, warehouses, shops, blockhouses, palisades, and other wooden structures, all requiring the attention of men equipped with the broadax.

The Bostonian Nathaniel J. Wyeth received shabby treatment at the hands of the Rocky Mountain Fur Company and declared to Fitzpatrick and William Sublette of that firm: "I shall roll a stone into your garden which you will never be able to remove." With his party of 41 men and 126 pack animals loaded with the rejected trade goods that he had brought from the East under contract with Milton Sublette, the outraged Wyeth left the Green River rendezvous and proceeded to the Snake River bottom. On July 16, 1834, he started the construction of a trading post at a site some miles north of present-day Pocatello, Idaho. Three weeks later the establishment, Fort Hall, was walled in with close-set cottonwood timbers which stood 15 feet high; bastions, a log storehouse, and cabins were under construction within the enclosure. John Townsend, the Philadelphia scientist and member of Wyeth's party, observed at this juncture that "the work is singularly good, considering the scarcity of proper building tools."

Fort Hall may be accepted as a fair example of the mountain man's small forts built in remote localities with a minimum of tools. Wyeth's equipment was assembled in the East ostensibly to transport a consignment of merchandise overland to a field party of the Rocky Mountain Fur Company. Building a fort did not figure in Wyeth's plan for this pack train, and construction tools were few or lacking in the packs. Even after three years of operation at Fort Hall, when Wyeth sold out to the Hudson's Bay Company, the carpenter tools and agricultural implements

FIG. 91. *Trapper's Winter Cabin in the Friendly Flathead Country, 1388-4.*

that changed hands were valued at no more than $45.00. It is of more than passing interest to note that under the aegis of the Hudson's Bay Company, agriculture became an important pursuit at Fort Hall. The British company continued to operate there for nine years after the settlement of boundary arguments in 1846. The agricultural produce grown at Fort Hall and the blacksmiths' service rendered there became of prime importance to emigrants making their way to Oregon; it is a foregone conclusion that the place was then fully equipped with appropriate tools.

A comprehensive account of Fort Hall history of Mat Wyeth's period, 1834-7, is available in Beidlemen's "Nathaniel Wyeth's Fort Hall." This paper contains an inventory of Wyeth's trade goods and other properties as of 1837. The illustration is based on a contemporary picture in 31st Cong., 2nd sess., Sen. Exec. Doc. No. 1. Drawing by William Maey, Jefferson National Expansion Memorial, St. Louis.

Customarily the mountain men "holed up" during the coldest winter months. Certain timbered localities sheltered from storm and removed from the established paths of the hostiles became traditional with the trappers as wintering grounds. Among these favorite places were the Thompson's River, Montana; the vicinity of present-day Ogden, Utah; the mouth of the Muscle Shell; Brown's Hole on the Green River; the Yellowstone, now Livingston, Montana; White River, Utah; Cache Valley, Utah; the Snake, near present-day Menan, Idaho; the Taos and San Luis valleys in New Mexico, and scores of similar places where feed for horses and meat for men could be depended upon. Usually the Indian's leather lodge constituted the trapper's "house" in winter, but some log cabins were also built. The cabin here pictured is described by its builder, W. A. Ferris, a literary mountain man who left a most revealing account of trapper-trader affairs of the 1830's. On January 1, 1834, he wrote: "Our house was now advanced to putting on the roof, for which we had cut a sufficient number of poles, intending when properly placed to cover them with grass, and finally with a coat of earth sufficient to exclude rain or melting snow in the spring." A few days later: "Moved into our house, which was rendered extremely warm and comfortable by having the seams filled with clay, a chimney [and fireplace] composed of sticks and mud, windows covered with thin, transparent, undressed skins which admitted sufficient light, and yet excluded the rain and snow, and a floor constructed of hewn slabs." (Ferris: "Life in the Rocky Mountains," Vol. Ill, pp. 156, 164.)

Ideally the cabin builder would have equipped himself with spade or shovel, sickle, saw, broadax, mortise ax, adz, chisels, gimlets, augers, hammer and nails, a calking tool, and a trowel. Lacking these, Mr. Ferris and his half-breed assistants may well have accomplished everything with a felling ax, hatchet, knives, and a punch. Wooden pins and rawhide thongs might serve in lieu of spikes and nails, and a wooden paddle could take the place of shovel or spade. Hardwood wedges, driven by a wooden maul or the ax did very well in splitting out puncheons needed for the floor.

Eric Sloane (in A Museum of Early American Tools, pp. 24-5) gives an illustrated resume of five systems of notching and fitting logs for cabin walls. William Macy drawing, Jefferson National Expansion Memorial, St. Louis.

Figure 87 d shows a small hammer-hatchet from the Cumberland Valley Forge Museum (now the Washington Memorial Museum). Probably this is an early lathing hatchet, a tool which because of its small size, light weight, and all-purpose features often was included in trapper-trader equipment, where it did not function in lathing.

FIG. 92. *The Hand Adz and the Dugout Canoe.*

Figure 87e is a heavy sledge hammer from the Hudson's Bay Company's Fort Nisqually, which was founded in 1833. It is preserved in the Washington State Historical Society, Tacoma. As early as 1619, the English colonists in Virginia imported this type of sledge,[38] and thereafter the big blacksmith's hammers went to those English settlements and posts, east and west, wherever smithies were established. They weigh from 6 to 16 pounds and are relatively imperishable, but, seemingly, few with known histories have been preserved in museums. This is probably due to the fact that sledges were seldom abandoned, broken, or lost; they were usually transferred from declining establishments to new scenes of action and there continued in use.

Figure 87f shows a carpenter's adz recorded as having been made by D. F. Barton, New York, in 1832. It is now in the Washington State Historical Society, Tacoma. This specimen was used in Indiana by D. J. Settle in 1834 and

The trapper's life in the American wilds Involved much activity In and on the inland waters. One of the great reliances of the beaver hunter was the log canoe; veritably it was in institution, east and west. Because cottonwood logs were to be had throughout much of the Western beaver country, many of the dugouts made by the mountain men were cotton-

---

[38]   J. Hudson: "Iron at Jamestown, Virginia," *The Iron Worker* XX: 3 (1956), p. 9.

wood. Pine trees served even better, and on the Pacific slope the acme of dugout perfection could be had in the Indian-made cedar canoes. If the adz appeared in backcountry trapper outfits, it was usually there because of its special usefulness in building dugouts. With felling ax and hand adz the selected tree could be cut, shaped, and hollowed with no great investment of time. Prior to his contact with the white man, the Indian combined fire and his stone or heavy shell scrapers in slowly hollowing out his log canoe. The hollow shell often was further shaped by filling it with water into which hot rocks were placed. The resulting hot water softened the wood, and it was possible then for the Indian to spread and shape the walls of the vessel by forcing transverse timbers between the gunwales. The white man dispensed with this shaping. Usually he attained a satisfactory result by chopping with the felling ax and broadax, when available, and with the steel adz. Thomas James tells of four men at the Three Forks of the Missouri, 1810, making two dugouts in three days. The westbound Lewis and Clark party on the Sweetwater in October 1805 made four large dugouts and one smaller one from pine trees in nine days. Existing specimens of the trapper-trader dugouts are quite numerous. In this illustration the outline drawings at left represent a 17-foot boat under the human figure was taken from the depths of mud at the bottom of the Natalbany River, Louisiana; it also is owned by the Cabildo. The lower sketch shows Jim Baker's 17-foot cottonwood dugout used by him on the Snake River during mountain-man days. It is owned by the Wyoming Historical Society, Cheyenne. William Macy drawing, Jefferson National Expansion Memorial, St. Louis.

was brought by him to Oregon in 1849. It is representative of the maul-head adzes or "foot adzes" which, beginning with Meriwether Lewis's requisitions of 1803, appear on the records of all Western expeditions and in many of the inventories of the fur companies. The Astorians were especially well supplied with adzes of the three forms designed for special uses (see pages 402-7). The smoothing and shaping of logs, and the facing of house timbers (framing, beams, floor puncheons, sills, doors, etc.) were done most handily with the adz, and the tool was especially necessary in making dugout canoes and in building skiffs and flatboats.

In the southwestern United States, a rather distinct form of adz is found occasionally on historic sites of Spanish provenance (fig. 95). The uses to which this type of adz was put were the same as previously described. The Indians of the northwest coast, always superior in their wood-carving techniques, met the shortage of conventional adzes by devising their own adz, as pictured in figure 96.

FIG. 93. *Making the Expendable Flatboat.*

Figure 87g is a heavy hoe of the early trade style. Now No. 28657 in the Milwaukee Public Museum, the specimen was recovered from a Menomini Indian site. Somewhat similar specimens, probably of French origin, were recovered by

Quimby[39] at the Fort St. Joseph site, Michigan, and at the Fatherland plantation near Natchez, Mississippi, both of which were occupied by Indians and whites, 1700-60. In the statement of expenses met by the French in waging war against the Fox Indians in 1716, hoes are listed at "10 livres and 10 sols, each"—approximately $2.60.[40] In 1808 the United States Office of Indian Affairs paid 70¢ each for the largest (9-inch) hoes, Philadelphia-made; the American Fur Company in 1821 paid $1.25 each for "Canadian hoes." It is interesting to note that the Collins Company[41] still produces for the Latin Americas "Hoes for Brush" that are heavy and of the same pattern as this Menomini piece.

At numerous establishments on the Missouri, the Platte, the Yellowstone, and some other important tributaries, the fur companies commonly built large scows, or flatboats, in each of which two or three tons of furs and skins could be floated to St. Louis. Packs of buffalo robes were particularly regarded to be appropriate cargo. Upon reaching its destination, the flatboat usually was dismantled, and its rough planks and timbers were sold for lumber. Since the making of flatboats was premeditated, the "boatyards" were always supplied with appropriate tools needed for the projects. Felling axes, broadaxes, adzes, chisels, sicks, augers, hammers, nails, spikes, bolts, angle irons, calking irons and, of special importance, pit saws, crosscut saws, and handsaws were used. On the Missouri drainage, the lumber for flatboats ordinarily came from cottonwoods and hardwoods. West of the Rockies, flatboats were made by the Hudson's Bay Company for freighting on the Columbia system. Here the lumber was cut from pine trees, and the boats moved upstream as well as down; there was no intentional demolition of flatboats on the upper reaches of the Columbia. Ferris (in "Life in the Rocky Mountains," pp. 156, 180) tells of the delivery in December 1833 of fresh vegetables from Fort Colville to the Hudson's Bay Company employees deep in the Flathead country, "7 or 8 days journey" from the Columbia. The two flatboats that brought the vegetables made the return trip laden with furs. In April 1834 Ferris left Flathead Post on Clark's Fork of the Columbia in a flatboat "loaded with about a ton of merchandise for the Horse Plain, and manned by four stout Canadians who propelled it with poles where the water was shallow, but when its depth would not admit of this, recourse was had to paddles." There is here implied the circumstance of ambitious navigation, a picture that helps one understand the accumulations of artifacts unearthed at such remote trading post sites as Walla Walla,

---

[39] G. I. Quimby; "Indian Trade Objects in Michigan and Louisiana," Michigan Academy of Science, Arts, and Letters *Papers,* Vol. XXVII {1941}, p. 548.

[40] Quoted by C. E. Brown: "Indian Trade Implements," pp. 73-4.

[41] Collins & Company: *Catalogo Illustrado* p. 69.

FIG. 94. *Making the Boat.*

Okanagan, Spokane, and Flathead. Drawing by William Macy, Jefferson
National Expansion Memorial, St. Louis.

Figure 37h is probably a shingling hatchet. It is preserved as Mo. B-130/51 in
the Wyoming Historical Society, Cheyenne. Perhaps the most notable existing
Western specimen of this class is the hatchet carried to the Columbia by Sergeant
Pat Gass, carpenter with the Lewis and Clark Expedition. The specimen
accompanied by documents is owned by members of the Gass family. Trappers'

shingling hatchets were not limited to use in shingling, of course. Most of the "permanent" Western trading posts did have shake roofs, and interior walls sometimes were finished with shakes; shingling hatchets thus found a limited conventional use, but their real purpose in the hands of the trapper was to function as extra-good tomahawks. Indians everywhere looked upon them as all-purpose tools and were happy to get them. A number of Indian burials, east and west, have yielded specimens now preserved in museums.

The documents and the printed literature of the fur trade are quite replete with accounts of the Mackinaw boat since it found wide use for one hundred years or more on the Great Lakes, the Ohio, and the Mississippi as well as on the Missouri system. It was pointed at both ends, keel-less and flat-bottomed, 10 or 12 feet in the beam, about 40 feet long, 3 or 4 feet deep (hold), and with a cargo of some twelve tons, drew 18 or 20 inches of water. Like the flatboat, it was made in the vicinity of numerous trading posts along tie Missouri; but unlike the flatboat, it sometimes made the tedious upstream journey back to the place of Its origin. On the Great Lakes it navigated anywhere and everywhere under the propulsion of oars and the wind, but on the Missouri it was valued primarily for its capacity to transport sizable cargoes downstream quite rapidly and safely. At Mackinac Island during the early decades of the 1800's, the American Fur Company imported numerous "Mackina" boats and their sails and other accouterments from Montreal. One hundred thirty dollars for one complete outfit was the maximum price paid. On the Missouri, the American Fur

FIG. 95. *Early Spanish Adz (Handle Supplied).*

Company, like all other interests there, made its own Mackinaw boats. An Interesting running account of the production of the boats in 1882 at Fort Pierre is found in the daily log of that post (Chittenden: The American Fur Trade [1954 edn.J 11, 975-83). The boat yard, named "Navy Yard" by the company, was the site of logging, sawing, and construction. The raw materials and the tools were the same as described for the flatboat shown in

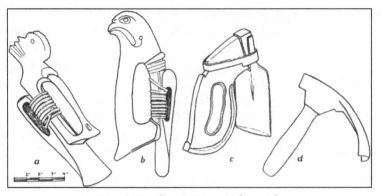

FIG. 96. *Northwest Coast Indian Adz.*

figure 93—with emphasis on the pit saws. William Macy drawing, Jefferson National Expansion Memorial, St. Louis.

Figure 87i shows an old-time hoe found at the Kiggs-Williamson Mission site, near Montevideo, Minnesota. No. 507. It is in the Minnesota Historical Society's collections. The Mission mentioned was active 1840-50, but the grounds thereabouts had been occupied earlier by a trading post. In the eighteenth century the shops at Fort Pitt were a source of supply for English-type hoes. In September 1761 the Huron Indians at Detroit asked Sir William Johnson to "procure us some hoes for our corn of which we stand in as much need as of anything else." Johnson instructed Croghan, his deputy: "I have promised

This adz was found In the ruins of the Spanish Mission buildings at Galesteo, New Mexico. No. 99, Colorado Historical Society, Denver. This poll-less, round-eye form dates back to the 1600's (Sloane: Early American Tools, p. 27). It is still made by the Collins Company, Connecticut, for the Latin American trade as the "Modelo Espano" (Collins Company: Catalogo Illustrado, pp. 25, 26, "Modelo No. 447" and "Modelo No. 520").

Pacific Coast Indian tribes produced some of the world's most interesting wood carvings, such as ornamentation of the plank walls of their houses, symbols on gravemarkers and "posts," and figurines and other decorations on their canoes. Even the canoes themselves are masterpieces of hand carving. These large carved objects find exquisite smaller counterparts in the form of bowls, platters, plates, tubs, buckets, spoons, and tool handles. Much of the finer carving was done with the crooked knife previously described (page 216), but the ax and the adz usually prepared the way. A small hand adz was particularly well suited for much of this work. In primitive times the coastal Indians mounted a Celt-like blade of chert or obsidian on a short wooden handle. After the white man brought the iron ax, these Indians did not long delay in adapting the trade-ax head to this special use. True to form, the Indian often made the wooden handle fancy as well as practical. This type of hand adz with removable iron blade may have been original with the Indians, but it was "nothing new under the sun." A similar tool (c) had long been in use by white men and is still to be had. Specimen a is from Nootka Sound; it is now in the Portland Art Museum. The adz shown in b was drawn after a photograph in Portland Art Museum. Specimen c is a hand adz made by the Collins Company. In d is a cooper's adz now in the Bucks County Historical Society, Doylestown, Pennsylvania.

the nations living in the neighborhood of Detroit a parcel of hoes for weeding their corn fields. You. will order a couple of hundred of the middling sort to be made immediately [at Fort Pitt] and sent by the first conveyance."[42] In the West, hoes in moderate numbers appear in the lists of merchandise procured by the Office of Indian Affairs and distributed as gifts to Indians.[43] Hoes in lesser quantity sometimes appear in the manifests of Western trading companies. These last, presumably, were consigned to traders for local use at trading posts—not for Indian trade. Even though the American Fur Company's purchases were comparatively small, some "shopping around" was done in obtaining the right hoes at the right price.[44]

Figure 87j is a tanged ice chisel now in the Allen County-Fort Wayne Historical Society. "Picks to break the ice in winter" were included in the French trade goods brought to Tadoussac in 1626. From that time and all through the eighteenth and nineteenth centuries, ice chisels figured prominently in the northern trade. Umfreville, in 1790, listed the ice chisel as third in importance among the items necessary to the sustenance of the Indian and his family.[45] An example of the use of the ice chisel is pictured in figure 16, "The Old-time Indians' Winter Hunt" (page 98). Beauchamp illustrates and describes a tanged specimen found in Fleming, New York, in 1887, which is like the Fort Wayne piece.[46] The Astorians, who took sixty of these to the Columbia, designated them "Broad Ice Chisels" to distinguish them from the twenty-five "Narrow Ice Chisels" also in their possession (page 404). Rectangular ice chisels of this

---

[42] Sir William Johnson: *The Papers of Sir William Johnson* (13 vols.; Albany, 1921-62), III, 501.

[43] An order for 1,000 hoes to be suppled by N. Lloyd, Philadelphia, 1808, Is detailed In "Letter Book, Pa., 198," U. S. Office of Indian Affairs, Philadelphia (MS), National Archives. See also invoice, merchandise received from Gen. William Clark for presents to Indians, 1823, in Forsyth Papers, Vol. 2, Item 2 (MSS), Wisconsin Historical Society.

[44] Edward H. Jacot, New York, was one of the jobbers who negotiated with Ramsay Crooks for a hoe contract. American Fur Company Papers, letter of December 21, 1841, Item no. 11915.

[45] *The* Present State of Hudson's Bay, quoted by Innis: The Fur *Trade*, p. 134.

[46] Beauchamp; *Metallic Implements*, p. 75, Fig. 76.

"broad" character are still on the market, but they are socketed.[47] During recent years a number of interesting slender, rodlike ice chisels, 10 to 16 inches long, have been recovered from riverbeds along the historic canoe routes between the Ottawa River and the Upper Great Lakes in the course of the "underwater search" conducted by the Minnesota Historical Society and the Province of Ontario.[48] Presumably these chisels were contained in kegs or bales of miscellaneous trade goods that were being transported into the interior of the country. The canoes in which they traveled were overturned or otherwise wrecked in rough water, and the merchandise has reposed in the depths for a couple of hundred years or more.

Figure 87k shows a cold chisel from the site of the 1832 trappers' rendezvous, Pierre's Hole, Idaho. The specimen is preserved in the National Park Service Fur Trade Museum, Grand Teton National Park. The chisel was found in 1900 by Judge S. W. Swanner while digging post holes along the banks of Leigh Creek, Tetonia, Idaho. The artifact was 18 inches below the surface of the ground in a locality known to have been occupied by some of the trapper camps in 1832. Cold chisels, albeit few in number, have never been absent, beginning with the Lewis and Clark requisitions, from the Western fur traders' inventories and invoices.

Fire Steels and Tinder Boxes

Inexpensive though it was, the fire-making flint and steel of the trader was of prime importance in his intercourse with the tribesmen. This was true in the earliest years of the trade and continued almost to its end. During the late eighteenth and early nineteenth centuries the popular lightweight steel retailed for a cent or two, and quite commonly it was presented without charge to the Indian whose good will was sought. The more sophisticated tinderboxes and strike-a-lights found only occasional use among Indians, but they were better known in the trading posts and in the wilderness camps of the white trappers. Probably the important thing to be said about any of these fire makers is that in their day they were almost indispensable, and even for the white man, they rested at the heart of his concept of and appreciation for fire. To the Indian, they became a part of the mysterious force that made fire sacred.

Figure 97a shows an oval fire steel from the site of Fort St. Joseph, Michigan; the specimen is now in the Fort St. Joseph Museum. This type appears

---

[47] Collins Company: *Catalogo Illustrado*, p. 58, No. 523.
[48] John Macfie in *Beaver* (Winter 1962), pp. 48-57; Sigurd F. Olson in *National Geographic* (September 1963), pp. 412-35; *Diving into the Past*, eds, Holmquist and Wheeler (1964), pp. 72-7.

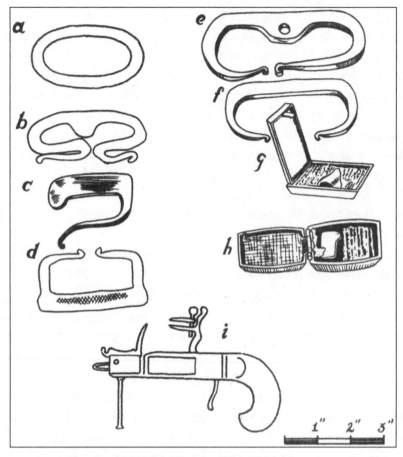

FIG. 97. *Fire Steels and Tinder boxes.*

among French artifacts of the late seventeenth and early eighteenth centuries, which have been recovered in a number of places in the Old Northwest,[49] and it continued to feature in the trade conducted by other nationals at least until the 1840's. In the underwater search conducted at Double Rapids on the French River out of Lake Nipissing in 1961, oval steels were found in their original packs with appropriate flints inserted in the space in the center of the steels.[50] In the journals of some North West Company agents are several bits of testimony which reveal that Canadian fire steels were sometimes presented to Indians. On the Red River in 1800 Alexander Henry gave a single fire steel to an Indian servant. In 1806, when he was with the Mandans on the Missouri,

---

49 Wittry: "The Bell Site"; Petersen: *Gentlemen on the Frontier* (Mackinac Island, Mich., 1984); Maxwell: *Excavations at Fort Michilimackinac;* and Brown: "Fire Steels," *The Wisconsin Archeologist* (January 1981).

50 John Made: "Short River Reveals Evidence of Long History," *Beaver* (Winter 1962), p. 52 (photo).

Henry presented his Mandan host "one steel and five flints."[51] In 1805, on the
Missouri above the Mandans, Francois Larocque gave to a party of Crow and

> White trapper and Indian alike made fire with flint and steel carried
> in the "possibles" bag, A slicing blow with the conveniently shaped steel
> struck against a small piece of flint caused sparks to fly. The downward
> directed shower of sparks was caught in a small bed of "punk" prepared for
> the purpose, and some of the fine fibers of inflammable tinier smoldered
> under the heat of the sparks. Dried, decayed maple wood was a favorite
> source of punk, but other decayed wood and also tow served. The tiny fire
> in the punk was coaxed into flame by the carefully controlled blowing
> of breath upon it. More substantial materials—dry wood shavings, fine
> splinters of wood, dry leaves and grass, and small sticks—were then used
> to kindle a bigger fire. The method was crude and troublesome, but it was
> an improvement upon the fire-plow and fire drill used by Indians through
> the millennia. James Mulcahy drawing, Jefferson National Expansion
> Memorial, St. Louis.

Shoshone Indians "8 fire steels and flints."[52] The requisition for "Presents to be
given to Indians" prepared by Meriwether Lewis in 1803 includes "288 steels for
striking fire." It was planned that these should be handed out freely all the way
across the country. Under "Camp Equipage" Lewis on the same occasion asked
for "30 steels for striking or making fire, and 100 flints to do so." These were
intended for the personal use of members of the Lewis and Clark Expedition.[53]
The U. S. Office of Indian Affairs, Philadelphia, on February 29, 1808, ordered
from William Gobright "6 gross fire steels to be imported by Teackle, and 2
dozen tin tinder boxes at 3.75 per dozen, complete with extinguisher, fire steel,
and 2 flints, each."[54] In 1805-6 John Johnston at the Fort Wayne Indian Factory
included in his account of disbursements "2 gross Fire Steels . . . $7.20."[55] One of
the more interesting Indian Office transactions was conducted by an unnamed
"Chiefs Lady" who at the Detroit Indian Factory in 1822 paid "16 prime beaver
pelts" (worth approximately $80.00) for an unspecified number of fire steels.
If the price charged for these steels were at all in line with the then-prevailing
Great Lakes value, the "Chiefs Lady" needed two pack horses just to transport
her steels.[56]

[51] Cones, ed.: *Manuscript Journals,* 1, 97, 330.
[52] L. J. Burpee, ed.: Journal of Larocque from the Assiniboine to the Yellowstone, 1805 (Ottawa: Publications Canadian Archives; 1910), p. 23.
[53] Jackson, ed.: *Letters,* pp. 72-3.
[54] Original order (MS copy) in National Archives, Washington, D.C.
[55] Griswold: *Fort Wayne,* p. 479.
[56] U. S. Indian Department, Day Book, April-August 1822 (MS in National Archives).

American Fur Company correspondence in 1838, 1839, and 1840 reveals that the oval steel commonly was sent into mountain-man country by Pierre Chouteau, Jr., and Company. These steels, "Warranted Bright Oval," were supplied by Hiram Cutler of Sheffield at 30¢ per dozen, and they came from the jobber put up in papers of one dozen to a package.[57] When Smith, Jackson and Sublette purchased the William Ashley merchandise in the field (Cache Valley, Utah) in 1826, fire steels were paid for at the rate of $2.00 per pound.[58] The oval steels are about 3 inches long, and the opening is big enough to allow the insertion of three fingers when the object is gripped for striking. The metal is flat and 3 3/16 inches thick; the weight, four or five steels to the pound.

Figure 97b shows a European fire steel a.d. 700-900; the specimen is preserved in the Naturhistorisches Museum, Vienna. It was found in a grave in southern Austria. The same form occurs in the graves of the Franks throughout much of modern France, and it persisted in most of south central Europe as long as fire steels were needed. For a specimen that came to America see figure 97e.

Shown in figure 97c is a more sophisticated fire steel used by a city dweller. It is part of the Morton Collection, Jefferson National Expansion Memorial, St. Louis.

Figure 97d is an Onondaga fire steel that was still in the hands of an Indian when collected in the late nineteenth century.[59] Brown describes and illustrates a similar piece found in a colonial tinder-box at Lexington, Massachusetts, which has the name "Harris" stamped on one face.[60] Approximately the same form is found at Fort St. Joseph, Michigan. These were individually forged—not mass-produced as were the "bright ovals" (fig. 97a).

Figure 97e shows a large example of the ancient Frankish form (fig. 97b) contained in a Menominee Indian medicine bag. The artifact is No. A-7051, Neville Public Museum, Green Bay, Wisconsin. During the very early years of contact with the whites, it was common practice among some tribes to make the town chief responsible for the care of the recognized sacred fire-making equipment used in starting annual ceremonial fires. In some tribes, the custom was retained until well into the twentieth century. Speck says of the Yuchi in

---

57 American fur Company Papers, items no. 5106, 5232, 7745 (microfilm reel 5); Orders Outward, I, 334, 383, in reel 12.
58 Dale L. Morgan, ed.: *The West of William H. Ashley* (Denver. Old West Publishing Company; 1964), pp. 158-9.
59 Beauchamp: *Metallic Implements*, p. 76.
60 Brown: "Fire Steels," *The Wisconsin Archeologist*, Jan., 1931, pp. 65-68.

Oklahoma, originally a southern tribe: "A fire steel is more often used as a sparker, as it is more effective [than are the two pieces of flint of the ancient ceremony].[61]

The fire steel shown in figure 97f is a style favored by whites and Indians alike. The specimen is catalogued as No. 1986 in the Chamberlain Memorial Museum, Three Oaks, Michigan. A "Hudson Bay" fire steel is like this but with the curved ends extended until they touch.[62]

Figure 97g shows a tinderbox with flint and linen tow that is now part of the Chamberlain Memorial Museum collection, Three Oaks, Michigan. This small brass box has a hinged steel cover with a latch. When the cover is open, as shown, the edge provides the steel against which the small flint can be struck. Resulting sparks fall upon the tinder in the box, causing a tiny smoldering fire that can be coaxed into flames when placed under appropriate kindling materials.

Shown in figure 97h is an all-steel tinderbox with tinder and flint. It is specimen No. 169 in the Neville Public Museum, Green Bay, Wisconsin. Fibers of unspun flax and scrapings from linen cloth often constituted tinder for fire makers in the "settlements." In the wilds, a fairly suitable punk could always be obtained from dead pine trees or from dry, decayed portions of hickory, maple, or oak trees. Swanton quotes from a dozen accounts of Indian fire making written by observers in the 17th and 18th centuries.[63] The principle of ignition through the striking of sparks from steel was always the same, but the efficiency in arrangements of paraphernalia improved through the years. Ultimately, slivers of sulfur-tipped wood made it easier for the fire makers to transfer a flame from the glowing coal in the punk to the kindling of the fire proper. Handy little pocket-sized tinderboxes of the kind illustrated in figures 97g and 97h must have been popular; specimens are to be seen in many collections. There are also numerous specimens of larger types for the home, in which the conventional steels, flints, and tinder are contained loosely in covered metal boxes—round, rectangular, and cylindrical.

Seldom did the trapper-trader write about his fire making, but George Ruxton, always to be depended upon for descriptions of the minutiae of the doings of the mountain men, has this to say about LeBonte's preparation for cooking the evening meal:

---

[61] Frank G. Speck; "Ethnology of Ac Yuchi Indians," *Anthropology Publications*, Univ. of Pennsylvania, 1:1 (1909), p. 42.

[62] Charles E. Hanson has one in his Fur Trade Museum, Loomis, Nebraska, which was obtained from the Northern Plains Indian Arts and Crafts Association.

[63] John R. Swanton: The Indians of the Southeastern United States, Bureau of American Ethnology, Bulletin 137 (1946), pp. 422-7.

Fire making is a simple process with the mountaineers. Their bullet pouches always contain a flint and steel, and sundry pieces of "punk"—a pithy substance found in dead pine trees—or tinder; and pulling a handful of dry grass, which they screw into a nest, they place the lighted punk in this, and, closing the grass over it, wave it in the air, when it soon ignites, and readily kindles the dry sticks forming the foundation of the fire.[64]

The occasion referred to was Ruxton's meeting with the trappers, LeBonte and Killbuck, in South Park, Colorado—Ute country—in the spring of 1847.

Figure 97i is a flintlock "strike-a-light" or fire lighter. The specimen is preserved as No. N-4937 in the Milwaukee Public Museum. Pistol-like strike-a-lights worked on the principle of the flint gun, but the pan ordinarily did not contain gunpowder. Tow, or "lint," was contained in the box under the frizzen. The cock, armed with a pistol flint, was pulled back and, when released by the trigger pull, descended upon the frizzen, which lifted under the impact, thus exposing the tinder to a shower of sparks. Under adverse conditions in wet or stormy weather, a few grains of gunpowder sometimes were added to the tinder, thus improving the chances of attaining a glowing coal in the box. Sometimes a rectangular, covered receptacle was built into the side of the strike-a-light as storage space for a reserve supply of tinder. The specimen illustrated has this receptacle. Strike-a-lights have been found in Iroquois graves that date back to the nineteenth century.[65] Evidence of their distribution in the early Far West has not come to the attention of the present writer, but, no doubt, they did find some use by Western Indians and by traders and trappers. The use of the flintlock pistol and long arm in starting fires must have been fairly common practice among the mountain men, as it was among earlier eastern frontiersmen.[66] To make a flintlock gun function as a strike-a-light, it was only necessary to put a temporary plug in the touchhole—if the piece were loaded—bring the cock to full cock, lift the frizzen and place tinder in the pan in lieu of gunpowder, return the frizzen to its closed position, then pull the trigger. Sparks showered into the pan ignited the tinder, thus producing the glowing coal needed to fire the awaiting kindling materials.

In sunny weather, the "burning glass" afforded means of starting fires. The glasses quite commonly appear in the fur-company invoices, and Captain Meriwether Lewis wrote "100 Burning Glasses" into his requisition of 1803.

[64] Ruxton, *Life in the Far West* (Hafen edition) (Norman, Okla.: Univ. of Oklahoma Press; 1951), p. 44.
[65] T. M. Hamilton, comp.; "Indian Trade Guns," *The Missouri Archeologist* (December 1960), pp. 100, 112.
[66] John Dillin: *The Kentucky Rifle* (Washington, D.C,; Natl Mile Ass'n; 1924), pp. 57-8.

Following through on the Lewis request, the supply officer, Israel Wheelen, ordered from C. and Th. Denkla of Philadelphia "8 [doz.] burning glasses 1½ Drs . . . $12.00." These lenses show up in the summary of Lewis and Clark purchases as weighing 11.25 pounds.[67] From the beginning of their westward trek, the explorers made it a point to present a "sunglass" or two to each group of Indians with whom they held council. The Journals record numerous instances of such giftmaking, and it appears that they still had some of the glasses on hand when they started the return journey in the spring of 1806. On April 2, 1806, Captain Lewis, then en route eastward on the Columbia, wrote: "Capt. Clark hired one of the Cashhooks [Indian] for a birning glass, to pilot him to the entrance of the Multnomah [Willamette] river and took him on board with him."[68] The United States Army at this time, and later, took cognizance of the usefulness of the burning glass as it offered instruction and guidance to troops: "If without other means of making fire, a spark may be obtained by taking out the object glass of a telescope, if there be one, and using it as a burning glass. The inside of a highly polished watch case also might answer."[69]

Summary

There are conclusions to be drawn from the evidences afforded by the foregoing accounts. One seems especially worthy of a final note. There can be no doubt that the westering American frequently entered the wilds well prepared to establish many of the symbols of his civilization. Almost at once his trading posts became small islands of a culture largely new to the aborigines. The savage welcomed the conveniences to be acquired in the form of certain tools and he grabbed at the better weapons, but generally he could not have cared less about the niceties in the white man's ways. His women bowed to the trappers' needs, however, and the trappers adopted some Indian traits. A new breed of half-Indian presently made it easier for the white man to hold place as "top dog" in the wild West, and there came about a remarkable blending of Iron and Stone Age practices. The artifacts resulting from this acculturation constitute some striking evidences of the fallacy of the notion that wilderness "conquers" the invader; the invader's iron brought about a conquest all its own. Here the invading white man "rolled with the punches." Some of the punishment taken

---

[67]   Jackson, ed.: *Letters*, pp. 72, 86, 93.

[68]   Bernard De Voto, ed,: *The Journals of Lewis and Clark* (Boston; Houghⁿton Mifflin; 1953), p. 339.

[69]   Edward S. Farrow: Mountain Scouting, A Hand-book for Officers and Soldiers on the Frontier (New York, 1881), p. 75.

by him was devastating locally and temporarily, but on the broad front he overcame both the forces of nature and the hostilities of man. Iron tools in the hands of the white man contributed to this triumph, directly and insidiously, in that it lessened the Indian's old-time self-sufficiency. In a surprisingly brief moment the Indian became a dependent; he looked upon the trader's merchandise as necessary and, to a degree, he modified his traditional techniques so as to take advantage of iron tools. He craved the help of white blacksmiths and ultimately he himself attempted rudimentary work in iron. A few of his kind became expert and, with the exception of the most isolated groups, practically all embraced iron as a boon. The Stone Age ended in the American West very soon indeed after tool shipments of the kind itemized on pages 402-7 reached the wilds.